THE ONLY THING
THAT MATTERS

THE ONLY THING
THAT MATTERS

BRINGING THE POWER OF THE CUSTOMER
INTO THE CENTER OF YOUR BUSINESS

KARL ALBRECHT

HarperBusiness
A Division of HarperCollinsPublishers

HarperBusiness books may be purchased for educational, business, or sales
promotional use. For information, please call or write: Special Markets
Department, HarperCollins Publishers, Inc., 10 East 53rd Street, New York,
NY 10022. Telephone: (212) 207-7528; Fax: (212) 207-7222.

FIRST EDITION

Library of Congress Cataloging-in-Publication Data

Albrecht, Karl.
    The only thing that matters: bringing the power of the customer
into the center of you business / by Karl Albrecht. -- 1st ed.
        p.   cm.
    Includes bibliographical references and index.
    ISBN 0-88730-541-5
    1. Customer service. 2. Customer relations.   I. Title.
HF5415.5.A425   1992
658.8'34--dc20   91-38324
                                                                 CIP

92 93 94 95 96 PS/HC 10 9 8 7 6 5 4 3 2 1

CONTENTS

CHAPTER **11**
**Your Change Management Strategy: Getting It Right
This Time**

RESOURCE SECTION:
Seven Tools for Customer-centered Process Improvement

PREFACE

The basic thinking process of Western management will change more in the coming decade than it has in the past 50 years.

The revolution is upon us and it isn't going to stop. Call it the customer revolution, the quality revolution, the service revolution, or whatever you like. All of the various energies and lines of action that businesses are putting forth now are beginning to converge to a single focus: winning and keeping the customer's business by doing the right things outstandingly well. That's simple to say, but actually doing it demands that we learn to manage in an entirely different way from the way we've been taught.

Many executives have become confused by the welter of books, models, methods, and consultants telling them they must do "quality." The so-called quality movement is one of the most confusing and frustrating panaceas ever to hit the business scene.

Other executives have fastened on the idea of "customer service" as the holy grail of business success. In its most simple-minded form, the customer service approach has become an undisciplined search for gimmicks to try to get the employees to "be nice" and the customers to "be happy."

Actually, neither "quality" nor "service" is the answer. There is no point in making "quality" a thing unto itself, like a strange bump attached to the organization. And there is no point in trying to love the customer to pieces if we don't make a profit or meet the related business objectives.

The quality issue and the service issue are no longer two separate issues—they are now one and the same issue. Once we leave behind the archaic distinction between "products" and "services," we begin to understand that the only thing that really matters in business is delivering *customer value*, which is always a combination of tangibles and intangibles.

Eight years and four books after I began working in the area called *service management*, I am now trying to shake off the image of "customer serviced guru." I don't want it. And I don't want to be a "quality guru," either. Quality is not the objective. Service is not the objective. *Customer value* is the objective.

Is McDonald's a product business or a service business? The answer is "yes." The Big Mac is inseparable from the context in which the customer experiences it. The customer buys a total experience of value, that is, a *customer value package*, not just a hamburger. Retailing is also a customer-value business. Banking is a customer-value business. Direct mail, air travel, hotels and hospitality, shipping and transportation, health care, construction, insurance, and all the rest—and yes, even government—are customer-value businesses.

We're witnessing the beginnings of a profound change in management thinking. It's a shift that will eventually change the entire landscape of business as we know it. The most fundamental of these changes in management thinking going on today is the shift from managing the boxes on the organization chart to managing customer outcomes.

This includes changing the definition or connotation of the term *service* to mean *serving* in the broadest possible sense. Not "service" in the old sense of somebody smiling at a customer over a counter, but *total service* in the sense that each person's work creates or adds value for the customer or for someone serving the customer. And the basic ideas of "quality" and "service" will fuse into a single idea, which I have tried to capture in the concept of *Total Quality Service*.

This book presents the results of eight years of investigating the best practices of outstanding organizations around the world, in an attempt to distill the best of the best. It reveals the five key secrets of the champions and shows how they conceive of, create, and deliver value to their customers. It shows how, time and again, the leaders of those companies think very differently from the leaders of their lesser competitors.

I believe that ten years from now, the major American business schools will be severely criticized for having conditioned several generations of executives and managers in the United States (and other countries) to a way of thinking that has cost America dearly in economic growth, international competitive position, and quality of life. The "B-schools" that today enjoy gold-plated reputations, supply corporations with graduate MBAs, and advise executives will eventually be seen as having contributed heavily to the stagnation of management thinking that has constrained America's ability to adapt.

The Japanese "quality miracle" has offered Western executives a lesson, but so far most have not learned it very well. While American management thinking after World War II got stuck in a focus on standardization, production efficiency, and cost control as driving values behind profit, Japanese thinking at that time turned toward *quality* as the driving value. While American thinking valued quarterly financial results, Japanese thinking valued market-share development and long-term relationships with customers. While American thinking valued the advertising and promotion of standard products, Japanese thinking valued constant incremental improvement in the appeal of the product. And while American management thinking was once considered the epitome of international business practice, American executives now have much to learn.

As the writers of business magazines lament the seeming inability of corporations to energize themselves and make a significant commitment to "quality," many Japanese firms have already moved beyond quality. They have committed themselves to *perpetually improving the customer's total experience*. And if you think the Japanese kicked our backsides in the areas of automobiles and consumer products, wait until you see what they do to us in the so-called "service" industries.

The Japanese are by no means the only ones we can learn from. My search for the best of the best has led me all over the United States, Canada, Australia, Hong Kong, England, Ireland, Norway, Sweden, Denmark, Finland, France, Italy, Belgium, and Switzerland. Leaders of business organizations in all of those countries have generously shared their views with me. In addition, my consulting colleagues in the TQS Group, Inc., have supported and contributed to my thinking processes and have offered valuable insights based on their daily work with many outstanding organizations around the world.

Companies all over the world are experiencing this fundamental *paradigm shift*—the shift to customer value. We're learning what it takes to manage *subjective outcomes*—something B-school management typically hasn't even thought about. We're learning to understand what goes on in the minds of our customers, and not to substitute our own arrogant hypotheses about what the customers presumably want. And we're learning that all quality improvement efforts in our organizations must be focused on adding value for customers, either external or internal. Just running around the organization measuring and counting things won't do it.

This book is an attempt to describe what we've learned so far about marketing, managing, and delivering in this new era of customer value. It also attempts to trace out the shape and trajectory of this new emerging paradigm and to show how it will cause us to think, act, and lead more intelligently. It presents these discoveries in the context of a universal change management model, Total Quality Service, or TQS, which is the way outstanding organizations align their strategy, systems, and people around the needs of their customers.

It's time for American organizations not only to join the Revolution, but to lead it. The stakes are too high not to.

THE ONLY THING
THAT MATTERS

1

Customer Centering: The New Quality Imperative

There is nothing so frightening as ignorance in action.

Johann Wolfgang von Goethe

Most of the service-quality programs now underway in organizations are doomed to fail.

This is, in a way, an optimistic viewpoint, not a pessimistic one. It doesn't suggest that the goal is impossible, only that most organizations are taking the wrong road in trying to get there. Sometimes a painful failure is a necessary prelude to success.

Over the past eight years, I have had the opportunity to work with and study hundreds of organizations embarked on the quest for "quality." These have been organizations from almost every conceivable industry, of all sizes, and with many differing styles of doing business. They have made many different kinds of attempts to find the holy grail of outstanding service quality.

I have seen more failure than success, more frustration than satisfaction, more agony than joy. The road to the promised land of superior service is strewn with the wreckage of ambitious programs with inspiring names and vaguely specified goals.

One organization after another has launched its authentic "this time it's for real," "this time we really mean it," "the customer is king," "service is our business" program, only to see it lurch along down the road for a few months or years and then the wheels come off. There is, unfortunately, more failure than success to report.

Most organizations are applying twentieth-century thinking and solutions to twenty-first-century problems. The difficulty is one of mindset, not method; the problem is cognitive, not cosmetic. When you start with wrong assumptions and apply crooked reasoning, it's hard to arrive at good conclusions.

The eighties was the decade of customer consciousness. It was the "wake-up call," letting businesses know they could no longer take customers for granted. Yet the thinking of the eighties brought little in the way of fundamentally new approaches or breakaway concepts for winning and keeping customers.

Books like *In Search of Excellence* and others following in its wake caused a deep stirring in the corporate psyche, but little significant rethinking of business precepts. Business books became fashionable, but it was basically business as usual. We were shown some admirable role models, but we were given precious little prescriptive guidance about how to do it.[1]

Service America!: Doing Business in the New Economy sounded the clarion call in 1985 for the American Service Revolution, and the book's wide international acceptance signaled a similar readiness in other countries for a new view of the business of service.[2]

Yet, for the most part, the eighties was the decade of talking and experimenting. It was a period of consciousness raising and brave declarations. Many organizations attacked what turned out to be a wholly unfamiliar problem by using reflexive solutions left over from a bygone era of manufacturing and industrialized thinking.

But it's now the decade of the nineties, and the twenty-first century is in sight. It is time to look back at the experience of the eighties and learn some hard lessons. We need to start with a clean canvas, paint a picture of the successful service/quality organization of the twenty-first century, and see how to use the best practices of today's outstanding service organizations around the world in creating the new reality.

There must be a fundamental revision in our way of thinking about customers, about service, about leadership and management, and about the culture of organizations if we are to build and maintain the kind of competitive customer-winning capability that will be able to survive and thrive into the twenty-first century. That change in thinking will take the form of a basic relearning of most of what we know about those subjects, and a reconceptualization of that knowledge. The following story gives an example of a situation where this new thinking was needed, yet wasn't available.

ANNE-MARIE GOES TO THE BANK: A QUALITY PARABLE

I have a friend, named Anne-Marie, who lives in Australia. She does business with one of Australia's biggest banks. Relating an experience she had best serves to summarize the convoluted thinking that has brought the banking industry to its present state of confusion and lack of direction. But in a much broader sense, it symbolizes some of the fundamental changes in management thinking that must take place in all industries.

Act One:

Anne-Marie got a letter from the bank telling her that her savings account was inactive, hadn't had any chargeable transactions in several months, and had too low a balance. If she didn't deposit more money, the letter said, the bank was going to deduct five dollars from her balance, which was about twenty dollars at the time.

She was a bit dismayed by this news, but decided to comply with the bank's demands. So she and her mother took her piggy bank (Anne-Marie was eight years old) and went off to the local branch of the bank to make a deposit.

They stood in line, waiting their turn, and finally presented their deposit to the teller. The exasperated teller didn't want to spend time counting the coins in the piggy bank, so they agreed to leave it there and pick it up later.

A few days later, Anne-Marie got another letter from the computer, announcing that it had just deducted five dollars from her account. Outraged, she and her mother paid another visit to the bank, only to learn that the clerk had misplaced the piggy bank and the deposit was never made. The bank had confiscated 25 percent of her net worth.

Act Two:

Anne-Marie's father, Dr. Kevin Austin, a consulting colleague of mine in Australia, returned from a working trip in Singapore to be greeted by a family on the verge of war. After about 30 seconds of hugs and welcomes, all six of them informed him of the atrocity perpetrated against one of their number by the bank. "We're moving all of our accounts out of that bank," they announced, "including yours." They had already been looking at newspaper and TV ads for banks, with the intention of selecting the new one.

Austin knew better than to oppose the wishes of six outraged customers, so he acquiesced in the decision. And the bank, in its efforts to get rid of an unproductive, unprofitable account, got rid of seven accounts without knowing it, including two very profitable ones.

It happened that Austin was working with me during my visit to Australia at exactly that time, and we both told that story to over 500 people during the course of a series of seminars and consultations that week. We mercifully omitted the name of the bank.

Now look at a story behind the story. Let's examine the apparently reasonable policy the bank used and the computer system that carried out the policy. Many banks and financial "service" businesses try to apply a practice called *customer base analysis*. The eighty-twenty reasoning says that accounts range from the very profitable to the very unprofitable. By analyzing the activity pattern of each account, the computer spots accounts that cost more to service than they earn in fees charged and interest generated.

Customer base analysis can be a gun that shoots in both directions, and handling it incompetently can be suicidal. Some executives even declare, with an air of clever smugness, "Let's get rid of these unprofitable customers and turn them over to our competitors—let them take the losses while we cherry-pick the market and focus only on profitable accounts."

That sounds like good macho business logic at first glance. But in the bank's case, it proved disastrous. Why? Because they hadn't given the computer the right information or the right reasoning process.

First, the computer didn't know that Anne-Marie was eight years old. If it had, it could have invoked a warning: not too many eight-year-olds live alone or support themselves, so Anne-Marie must be part of a larger market unit, that is, a family. It could then have asked itself, is this *family* profitable to us?

Unfortunately, it had no way to relate Anne-Marie to any other customers in its database. It was programmed to analyze *accounts*, not customers. So it obediently scanned all the accounts in its file, applied the activity algorithm given it by the programmers, who got the idea from their cost-obsessed operations executives, and did the same thing to all the other "unprofitable" accounts like Anne-Marie's.

A mistake was made long ago, a mistake we refer to in the TQS Group as a basic *construct failure*, i.e., an intellectual malfunction that leads to the wrong basic idea about what's going on. The construct failure was the notion of the computer's activity as managing *accounts*, not managing *relationships* with customers. It amounted to a decision to organize the computer's data structures in terms of accounts, not in terms of customers. Once the designers chose the account as the basic element of record keeping and analysis, they lost the opportunity to "customerize" or individualize their marketing.

The customer's name was merely an incidental item of data appended to the account identification. Since there was no tie-in based on customer identification, if Anne-Marie had had more than one account she would have appeared to the computer as several different customers. For the same reason, her family members existed as six unrelated accounts. The computer couldn't "perceive" the family.

So much for customer base analysis.

What's the point? The point is that there's no right way to do the wrong thing. If we're talking about a "service-driven," "customer-focused" organization, we've got to design the operation to work that way. It's more than just a slogan or a training message. It must involve the way we conceive of the total product, market it, design the delivery system, program the computer, communicate with the customer, train the employees, and all the rest. And when it comes to expensive computer systems, if you get it wrong, you *stay wrong* for a long time.

There is much to learn from the story of Anne-Marie. It illustrates, in many ways, the quintessence of the service-management problem. Banks whose leaders understand what business they're in—and it's *not* the business of warehousing money—develop holistic philosophies and cultures that support real value delivered to the customer. They win and keep the customer's business by meeting needs, solving problems, and adding value. Accounts are just artifacts of record keeping; they're not what banking should be all about.

Many banks seem to operate on the mentality of *extracting* value from their customers, not *delivering* value. They tend to view their customers as cows to be milked, missing no opportunity to levy penalties, extra fees, and special charges.

Interestingly, in Anne-Marie's case, as with many problems related to quality, the root causes of failure are not attributable to the people on the assembly lines or at service counters. Instead, they are "systems" problems created by the senior executives' way of thinking about their businesses and the issues confronting them.

If executives want to deal with their present situation effectively, they must be prepared for a revolution in thinking. That revolution must begin with how they think about customers, quality, and service.

CUSTOMER CENTERING: THE NEW THEOLOGY

The eighties was the decade of talking and writing about the customer. *In Search of Excellence* spurred the initial interest on the subject. *Service America!* intensified it. Feature articles in virtually every popular business and trade magazine built the issue to a crescendo. In spite of this attention however, few organizations today have been able to make the translation and transition to becoming truly "customer driven."

In fact, when it comes to their perspectives on customers, many companies are still trapped in the fifties. They still view customers as statistical units or sales targets. They define their primary purpose as selling more of whatever it is they make to selected consumers. They engage in "company-centered," or inside-out, thinking. "First, let's design our product or service. Then, let's decide how to package or present it most effectively to cause the consumer to want to buy it." This mindset—finding customers for products—is backwards.

- Organizations large and small can fall into the company-centered thinking trap. *Telephone service* is just one example of this kind of thinking. Over the past few years, AT&T and the regional telephone companies have developed a host of new technological marvels such as caller ID, call-back, distinctive ring, call trace, and call return.

  However, the communicating public doesn't seem all that thrilled with these "products." With a required break-even point of 25 percent utilization, less than 10 percent penetration has been achieved in pilot markets for most of these options. Indeed, today only about 30 percent of telephone owners subscribe to call waiting, ten years after the introduction of that innovative feature.

- *Insurance companies* have long suffered the consequences of product thinking at the expense of customer thinking. Many of them conceive of themselves as selling products, that is, literal documents that promise benefits to customers in the event of certain misfortunes. As a result, they know a lot about their products and almost nothing about their customers. *Customers are statistics to companies with this mindset, not people.*

○ *Banks* have also suffered from the same misplaced focus. Many banking executives speak of selling products, that is, different kinds of packages for delivering money and taking delivery of it. Like insurance companies, many banks—probably most—understand very little about their customers' lives, problems, and needs. They think in terms of accounts and products, not in terms of individual customers.

One of the most remarkable discoveries for me while working with organizations over the past eight years or so has been the great number of companies that have only vague notions of their customers on an individual basis, and how many of them focus their thinking and decision making almost exclusively on their products.

Company-centered thinking is not necessarily an affliction of size. *INC.* magazine recently reported on three small businesses that sank their own boats this way.

○ Texas-based Bounty of the Sea, Inc., introduced a tuna hot dog.

○ In California, businesswoman Lore Harp came up with a product named LeFunelle—a disposable sanitary funnel through which women could urinate while standing.

○ Thomas Crook, a Maryland Ph.D. in psychology, developed the concept for a nationwide chain of clinics that would test for memory and the onset of Alzheimer's disease.

These very different products shared a common failing and fate. They didn't arise in response to defined customer needs and as a result they failed.

Customer-centered companies present a strong contrast to these examples. They see the customer as the starting point, listening post, and ultimate arbiter for everything they do. They start with the customer's needs and expectations – the attributes that are desired. Then they develop and evolve products or services to satisfy them.

- *Marriott's Courtyard* is one of its best-performing hotel chains. The reason for their success is straightforward. As Marriott's advertisements for Courtyard state, the hotel chain was "designed by business travelers for business travelers." The Courtyard concept was developed based on extensive customer research. Marriott surveyed thousands of business people to find out how they felt about the experience of staying in a hotel. The surveys asked which trade-offs the business people would be willing to make among various items and the associated costs. Decisions such as whether to have a telephone on a desk as opposed to one next to the bed were driven by customer data, not by architects or interior designers.

- *Rubbermaid* is one of the most successful and admired American companies. Although its household products may be prosaic, Rubbermaid has succeeded very well in its market. Much of its genius lies in its ability to satisfy customer needs precisely and to make the small changes they demand.

  Rubbermaid does, of course, engage in the typical forms of market research, including demographic and life-style analyses. But the heart of its improvement process is the focus-group meeting with actual consumers. In these groups, no gripe is too small to be considered. For example, when focus-group participants complained about puddles under their dish-drying racks, Rubbermaid responded immediately with a sloping drain tray designed to allow water to flow into the sink more readily.

- *Australian Airlines* presents another interesting example of a company that set out to understand its customers better. Chief executive James Strong asked several hundred employees to meet with equal numbers of customers for luncheon discussions throughout Australia. The employees asked people to tell them about the experience of flying and to offer ideas for improving the company's service. They brought back mountains of useful information that led directly to improvements in the service offering. As a result, the company made a spectacular advance in its competitive position.

- *The London Metropolitan Police Force*, better known as Scotland Yard, has for a number of years conducted regular research on the attitudes of the general public toward the department and its services and the changing needs and problems of the communities. Under the leadership of Sir Peter Imbert, Scotland Yard has maintained a reputation as one of the most professional and service-oriented law enforcement agencies in any country.

○ *SAS International Hotels,* a part of the Scandinavian Airlines System, caters especially to the frequent business traveller. Several years ago, marketing Director Christian Sinding launched an intensive investigation into the attitudes and personalities of these people. Using a sophisticated computer technique, he was able to identify four distinct psychosocial styles among the customers, each with its own set of attitudes about physical quality and luxury, time and efficiency, personal attention and catering, and status and deference. All of the hotels in the chain are moving to implement this customer knowledge in their advertising, marketing, and on-site delivery of service.

○ *Paris-based Club Mediteranée* makes extensive studies of the attitudes and preferences of its customers, particularly of national and ethnic differences that may influence their perceptions of quality and personal interaction. Club Med's *chefs des villages,* or village managers, are expected to know the basic attitudes and preferences of different customer nationalities and to train staff to serve them in ways keyed to their needs. They also measure perceptions of the vacation experience according to these psychographic differences, with special reports on each nationality as part of their performance data.

Centering on the customer is easier said than done. In an organization, the language that people use when referring to customers, or when describing service-quality programs, signals very clearly how they view their customers and how they see themselves as relating to them. Many organizations have evolved a special terminology that enables them to *avoid* referring to people as customers.

○ To the insurance company you're not a customer; you're a "policyholder."

- To the gas and electric company you're not a customer; you're a "ratepayer."

- To the airline or the cruise ship company you're not a customer; you're a "passenger."

- To the doctor's office or the hospital you're not a customer; you're a "patient."

- To the taxi driver you're not a customer; you're a "fare."

These labels signal that the company sees the customer as a passive figure, an object to be acted upon, or something to be processed through a system. The choice of these words makes the customer into a thing rather than a person. The words make it easier to obscure the fact that customers are *people*, entitled to judge the quality of the delivered experience and who make the ultimate decision about doing business with the organization.

Apparently we don't like giving the customer that much power. We don't like the feeling of having to earn the customer's approval. We want to change customers into things we can manipulate, statistics we can analyze, or wild animals we have to capture to gain "market share."

> **The loss of this focus on the customer as a human being is probably the single most important fact about the state of service and service management in the Western world today.**

Companies at the forefront of the customer revolution realize that the way they talk about their customers and their programs sends a clear message. These companies center everything they do on their customers. They do not see the customer as an outsider. Rather, they see each customer as an individual and make every possible attempt to get inside his or her mind.

They think small to win big. The term of art today is "micro-marketing" and those companies on the cutting edge are making "one" the only number that matters. They see the customer as the individual person or company, the family unit, and the individual organizational customer. They "customerize" by committing themselves through their research, product design, and service delivery to win customers one by one. *In the age of twenty-first century thinking, the motto should not be "zero defects," but "zero defections."*

It's time to draw the organization chart in a new way, to include the customer relationship as a fundamental part of what goes on. Instead of using a "tree" diagram, or a hierarchy of boxes and sub-boxes, we should draw the operation as a cascade of concentric circles, each delivering value outward to its customers. It makes sense to represent the various customers (see Figure 1–1) as part of the immediate environment surrounding the organization—the outside circle. The first inner circle represents the *front line service* departments—the people who deal directly and continually with the customers. The second inner circle, inside the circle of frontline departments, represents the support departments, or the *internal service* departments. These are the people who help the others get their jobs done. They serve the frontline departments and one another.

In this approach, value flows outward. The internal service departments must deliver value to the frontline service departments. And the frontline departments must deliver value to the external customers.

At the very center of the system of circles is the executive management group—the people who provide the leadership for the organization. In addition to being formally in charge, they must serve those who serve. Their job is to enable and support the internal departments and the frontline departments in their efforts to deliver superior customer value.

The outstanding service organization is one in which all "servers" know clearly who their customers are; they know what constitutes value for them; and they work continually to deliver that value. Whether a particular department serves external customers or internal customers, or both, its mission is essentially the same: to deliver value to those customers.

TOTAL QUALITY: THE NEW MANDATE

Nearly every business organization today claims to believe in quality. Many advertise it to their customers. These claims range from the "Quality is Job One" advertisements for Ford, to the posters for Winston cigarettes on the side of a Chicago Transit Authority bus, to the message on the back of a package of Dolly Madison bakery goods. What many companies haven't figured out is that what they believe to be quality doesn't count.

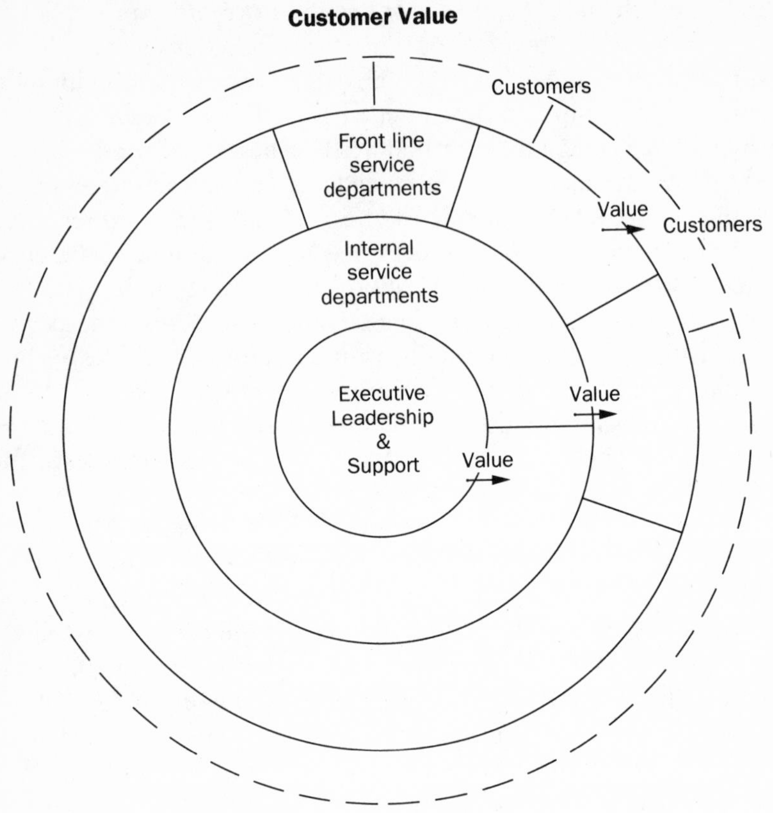

Customer Value

Figure 1–1   The organization must deliver value to all customers.
©1991 Karl Albrecht

> **When it comes to quality in the marketplace,**
> **the only thing that matters**
> **is the customer's experience.**

Quality is in the eye and mind of the beholder. And the factors your customers may take into account in evaluating quality are multiple and complex.

Until recently, the dominant view of quality, especially in manufacturing settings, was that something conform to physical requirements, meet standards, be error free, and have zero defects. This can be one element of quality. However, it is primarily a measure of physical characteristics and much too simplistic an orientation toward quality.

Many organizational quality programs get stuck in a quagmire of internally focused process measures that have no reference to the perceptions of the customers who are supposed to benefit from them. Many service-quality initiatives fall victim to the same misplaced obsession by using measurements that are *not* customer-relevant.

The first thing we need for a new twenty-first century view of service quality is a better way of defining service and a better way of defining quality. Here is a way to do that.

THE CUSTOMER VALUE PACKAGE: THE NEW COMPETITIVE WEAPON

Some organizations are working to improve "quality." Others are working to improve "service." Many of them don't realize they're both working on the exact same problem—or should be. The "quality" issue and the "service" issue are now becoming one and the same issue. The sooner we unite these two issues into one over-arching issue, *customer value*, the sooner we can make sense of the two. Then our conception of the problem becomes much simpler, and the approaches to solving it become easier to understand.

It's time to move beyond the old conception of service as a side-effect of selling merchandise, or as somebody being nice to customers, to a view of creating a holistic, total customer experience. It's time to move beyond the old conception of "quality" as measuring and counting physical things, to a new view of delivering customer value.

What we're delivering is a complete *Customer Value Package*—a combination of tangibles, intangibles, experiences, and outcomes designed to win the customer's approval and secure the right to survive and thrive in our marketplace.

We can think of the Customer Value Package, or CVP, as:

> *The Customer Value Package:*
>
> **A combination of things and experiences that creates a total customer perception of value received.**

The customer's entire experience determines his or her perception of quality. That perception is affected by the organization's "product," processes, and practices as they compare to the customer's expectations. *Quality* is the measure of the customer's satisfaction with the entire experience. The challenge to those organizations that seek to compete effectively in the business environment of today and tomorrow is to understand and manage that experience, making it a seamless and totally satisfying one. In order to accomplish that, the organization must be able to deliver a total experience of value.

Another way to think about making an organization customer-centered is to picture its relationship to its customers in terms of the *service triangle*, as shown in Figure 1–2. *Placing the customer at the center* of the organization draws attention to the overall sense of *alignment* that must exist between the strategy, the people, and the systems, in order for the organization to deliver outstanding value.

The *strategy* must help people make sense out of what they do. They must understand the concept of customer value and know how the organization is supposed to deliver it.

The *people* themselves need to have an individual and collective spirit of service, as well as the knowledge and skills necessary to create and deliver the total customer experience of value.

The Service Triangle

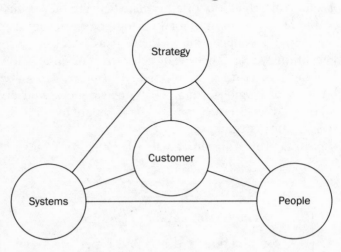

Figure 1–2   The Service Triangle.
©1984 Karl Albrecht

And the *systems* must support the employees in their efforts to create and deliver value. They must be customer-friendly, i.e., designed to support the delivery of customer value rather than designed to inflict discomfort or frustration on the customer.

The ultimate objective of any organizational customer-focus initiative should be to align all three of these components—the strategy, the people, and the systems—around the needs of the customers.

THE RHETORIC AND THE REALITY

Most students of service management date the beginnings of the American Service Revolution to 1985, with the publication of *Service America!: Doing Business in the New Economy*. Now published in Japanese, French, German, Spanish, and Portuguese, and going into other languages, *Service America!* is the acknowledged "bible" of service management. Since that time, there has been a virtual flood of books, articles, and video tapes about service quality and customer focus. Service is the hottest topic at association conferences, company management meetings, and seminars.

But here we are, well into the service revolution, and we must ask ourselves some serious questions:

- How widely accepted is this new view of the customer?

- How much have organizational leaders really learned about the management of customer experiences?

- What do they believe in, and to what extent are they prepared to act on this knowledge?

- How much progress have companies really made in becoming customer-driven?

- Is it reality or merely rhetoric?

Why is a total quality service approach critically important for businesses today? The most basic reason is that *it's becoming virtually impossible to create a sustainable competitive advantage through a tangible product alone*. Whether it's a computer, a new type of insurance, a new investment concept, or a new fast-food item, the time span from innovation to imitation by a competitor is becoming shorter and shorter. Tangibles alone can seldom contribute a permanent or even long-lasting competitive edge.

Therefore, the answer to business success lies in creating barriers to entry by bundling the "product" into a complete customer package comprised of process, practices, and various intangible features and benefits that take longer for a competitor to duplicate or surpass.

How important is service quality to business leaders? A landmark survey in 1988 of 3375 executives in Europe, North America, and Japan, conducted by Management Center Europe in conjunction with the American Management Association and the Japanese Management Association, concluded that service quality should be the highest organizational priority of all.

- More than 90 percent of the respondents saw service to the customer as being "more important" or "much more important" in the next five years.

- Almost 80 percent of the respondents rated improving quality and service to customers as the key to competitive success in their future.

- 92 percent believed that ensuring superior service is one of their key responsibilities regardless of organizational position.

However, when the pollsters asked the same executives about their perceptions of their companies' *current* practice and progress toward the goal of customer-focused operation, they got some disconcerting results. For example

- Only 56 percent felt that superior service to customers was an accepted corporate priority in their firms.

- Less than 50 percent reported that their companies regularly measure and report on customer satisfaction.

- Less than 40 percent of their companies train employees in service skills.

- Less than 25 percent regularly analyze competitors' services and products and compare them to their own.

Commenting on the results, noted British consultant John Humble, who led the research project, said:

> Managers *say* overwhelmingly that service is their top competitive priority. Why then do only half of them have regular feedback on measured customer satisfaction? Be sure that 100 percent of them

will have financial budgets with frequent comparisons and discussions on variances. Does customer satisfaction require any less rigorous management?[3]

Price Waterhouse saw similar results in a survey of financial officers at 50 of America's largest companies. These companies said that over the next several years they would rely on quality and customer service, as opposed to cost reduction, innovation, and advanced technology, in order to achieve and maintain a competitive position in the marketplace. Yet, if the Humble-AMA study is representative, there may be a big gap between the ambition and the execution.

The extent of that gap was also dramatized in a recent national survey of employees in American corporations completed for the American Society of Quality Control by The Gallup Organization. The study asked the employees to indicate the extent to which four quality policy objectives were important in their companies and to what extent their companies followed through on those objectives. The study discovered that:

- Nearly as many employees (25%) are dissatisfied with their companies' quality-improvement efforts as are satisfied (29%).

- More than one-third of employees (36%) in companies where quality-improvement activities are in place do not participate in those activities.

- True participative management is not widespread. Although two-thirds of employees (66%) say that they have been asked to be involved in decision-making (the illusion of participation), only 14%, say that they felt completely empowered to make decisions (the actuality of participation).

At this point in the progress of the service revolution, it seems fair to say that rhetoric and reality are running neck and neck, with rhetoric slightly out in front.

THE FIZZLE FACTOR: WHY MOST
QUALITY INITIATIVES WILL FAIL

- *Australia's Qantas Airways* launched a service program that crashed and burned before it got past the end of the runway. Called "The Spirit," it was an "all hands" training program intended to motivate employees toward the objective of excellent service. Patterned after Scandinavian Airlines' motivational sessions, it met with such cynicism and resistance from staff that it finally fizzled. The company never even succeeded in getting a majority of them to show up for the sessions.

○ *National Westminster Bank*, in England, started out with a standards-based quality program intended to improve service to its customers in the branch banks. One of the key measures, according to NatWest's Paul Goodstadt, director of service-quality programs, was a "courtesy standard" of having the employee say the customer's name at least twice during the transaction. According to Goodstadt:

> "It seemed like a good idea at the time. Shortly after introducing the standard, we measured a 26 percent compliance rate at branch level. After about a year of intensive efforts to raise that figure, with training, pep talks, reminders, and supervisors nearly threatening people with the sack, we managed to get it down to 20 percent. That's when we concluded we were on the wrong track. We discovered *Service America!* and realized that we had to re-launch the whole thing with a culture-based focus, not a measurement-based one."

○ *Chrysler Corporation* in Detroit launched an ambitious service program aimed at increasing dealer scores on the widely accepted J. D. Power customer satisfaction index, or CSI, a four-point rating scale that combines buying experience, after-sales support, and general customer treatment. Launched with a prize-point scheme for dealership employees, in which they could earn points and redeem them for prize merchandise if the dealership's CSI score improved from quarter to quarter, the program soon ran out of gas.

The passive resistance of over 4000 dealers and their historical commitment to abusive selling practices doomed the program to oblivion, despite the enormous company investment involved. Some of the dealer scores improved significantly; most did not. As of this writing, Chrysler's customer approval ratings across the board have improved very little if at all. It's still in the same boat with General Motors and Ford in terms of Americans' perceptions of car quality and total service experience compared to their Japanese competitors operating in the United States.

○ A *major American insurance carrier* attempted to launch a service-quality program that never got out of first gear. The most its executives could muster in terms of determination and commitment was to declare "customer service" one of five strategic priorities, in a group with efficiency, productivity, sales, and product development. A few executive retreats, presentations at annual sales meetings, and it was all over: back to business as usual.

○ A *major midwestern utility* tried to launch a customer-focus initiative by training all employees in service attitudes. After several months of running them through the "psychological car wash" of motivational "smile training," they finally gave up and dismissed the training consultant, a large firm that specialized in that kind of training.

○ A *New York brokerage firm* decided to launch a service-quality initiative, in hopes of defending its full-price position against the onslaughts of discount brokerages like Charles Schwab and others. After a series of customer research projects, investigations of branch-level activities, and a great deal of analysis, the program died in the midst of political infighting among key executives.

The list of failures goes on and on. In some cases, the companies have made renewed efforts; in some cases they have succeeded. NatWest Bank relaunched its program with noteworthy results. Many others have not been so successful.

After observing a wide variety of these service-quality initiatives, and—sadly—participating unsuccessfully in some of them, I have been forced to conclude that there is an inordinately high "fizzle factor." More of them fail than succeed.

Some fizzles have resulted from one of the failure modes, some from another, and some have resulted from a combination or even all of them. It has become clear that there are more ways to fail at service quality than ways to succeed. The successful programs and the operating styles of the highly effective service organizations show us the essential ingredients for success. Later chapters will explain the failure modes more extensively, offer ways to avoid them, and offer more reliable approaches based on twenty-first-century thinking about Total Quality Service.

THE BECOMING: A NEW ORGANIZATION, A NEW CUSTOMER-CENTERED CULTURE

It isn't hard to rank organizations in terms of the degree of customer focus they have attained and the extent to which they practice service quality as a way of life. Here is a way of evaluating your company and your competitors. It has five levels, or dimensions, based on the degree of commitment:

- Dimension 1—*Going out of business*. These are the organizations that have not solved the basic puzzle of income and expense in delivering a service experience that attracts enough customers and enough income to stay afloat.

- Dimension 2—*Dogged pursuit of mediocrity*. These are the companies that somehow manage to survive, almost in spite of themselves. There is no discernible quality ethic, no commitment to a quality customer experience, and no particular skill in delivering the product.

- Dimension 3—*Present and accounted for*. These organizations are doing OK, but operate with no particular inspiration or drive for excellence. They get their "natural market share," which is the portion of the business available by just showing up.

- Dimension 4—*Making a serious effort*. This is sometimes a transition stage and other times the high water mark beyond which some never progress. It is the stage of serious management commitment, investment of significant resources, and a shared determination to make things happen.

- Dimension 5—*Service as an art form*. The few organizations at this level dominate their industries and are recognized even by their competitors as being outstanding. They've got the right fix on their customers and the right definition of the customer value package, which they deliver with style and grace.

It is theoretically possible for all service organizations to become fifth-dimension organizations if they can survive and meet the basic requirements for staying in business. However, very few will attain that level.

But more organizations are now trying to lift their game. Still others are making serious efforts and are reaching the fourth dimension. Many others, of course, are groping around and unable to get beyond the third dimension, in the eyes of their customers.

Bear in mind that, according to this ranking, an organization must be at the fourth dimension at the very least, and preferably at the fifth dimension, for the customer-perceived quality of service to have a significant impact on market share, price freedom, or profit margin. "Present and accounted for" just won't do it.

It has also become obvious that fifth-dimension organizations are fundamentally different creatures from those lower on the ladder. The fifth-dimension organization is dedicated to, driven by, and operated on the premise of a superior customer experience. It operates as a service culture. The boldness of its vision, clarity of its mission, strength of its core values, and the steadfastness of its leadership make it a formidable contender.

Similarly, for an organization to move up from the third dimension or lower, through the fourth dimension and into the fifth, it must literally *become a new organization*. Its executives must embark on a fundamental learning process to understand who their customers are, what customer value package will win and keep their business, what business the company is really in, and what kind of leadership it must have to make the grade.

We have a fairly good idea of the general characteristics of the fifth-dimension organizations:

Characteristics of Fifth-Dimension Organizations:

- leadership that is mentally and behaviorally flexible

- special insights into the needs of their customers

- the ability to redefine the playing field and to deliver in ways that separate them from their competition

- a commitment to changing themselves in directions that are consistent with evolving customer needs and expectations

○ a recognition that human energy is the greatest untapped resource in an organization and a corresponding high value for "stakeholder" participation (customers, owners, and employees)

○ a culture that is caring and sharing

○ a drive to be the best and a commitment to continuous improvement in all aspects of their operations

From my point of view, *a service-quality program aimed at bringing an organization to the fifth dimension must be, in a very basic sense, a program that transforms the organization.* Cosmetic changes will not work. Smile training and motivational campaigns will not work. Numbers-driven neurosis will not work. Slogans and memos about quality will not work. What will work, if applied properly, with enormous energy and commitment, and with continuity and determination, is a journey of discovery—a revolution in thinking at all levels of the organization.

This is what a commitment to customer centering is all about. If the approach described in the following chapters turns out to be right, it may be one of the most fruitful journeys of our time.

2

Mindsets and Malfunctions: Manufacturing Thinking and Dinosaur Logic

The pursuit of mediocrity is always successful.

Anonymous

CROOKED THINKING ABOUT
BUSINESS, CUSTOMERS, AND QUALITY

Dr. W. Edwards Deming, one of the world-recognized leaders in quality thinking, contends that most of the quality problems in organizations today exist because of management—managers who do the wrong things or who do things wrong. Dr. Joseph M. Juran argues the same point. They both believe the whole thinking process behind manufacturing management is seriously flawed; it focuses on authority, legislation, and control, not on quality outcomes.

Most of their work has been devoted to getting managers in manufacturing organizations to change the focus of their thinking. More recently, both Deming and Juran have been pointing out similar malfunctions in the management of service businesses.

Most Western business leaders tend to behave from a governing mindset that emerged with manufacturing organizations, and that continues to dominate their thinking as they try to tackle service-quality issues. This framework has passed from person to person, professor to student, trainer to trainee, author to reader, and boss to subordinate boss for years. It has become The Way of management.

In the book *At America's Service*, I advocated revising the "General Motors" mindset of management to one that is more people-focused and more oriented toward outcomes that benefit the customer. Since that time, I've become even more convinced of the necessity and have added to the list of necessary changes in thinking.[1]

If we get our world view and our ideas straight, we can get our actions straight. For that reason it's worthwhile to pinpoint some of the kinds of *thinking traps* that can cause the leaders of service organizations, large and small, to give the wrong kind of vision and direction to the people who have to do the work.

FIVE THINKING TRAPS ON THE ROAD TO TOTAL QUALITY

There are five key thinking traps that business leaders can fall into by following traditional management mindsets. Each of these traps in some way results from the historically myopic "activity" view of management, which sees only the organization and its processes, not the ultimate aim of competitive customer value. Here are the most disabling of the activity-management thinking traps.

Thinking trap 1—Trying to disconnect "product" from "service." The total customer experience delivered by the organization includes both tangible and intangible components. Yet for many years managers have been taught to think and talk in terms of "the product," which usually refers to the physical merchandise—the toaster or the car or the bottle of shampoo or the personal computer or whatever "it" is that they make and sell. They have been taught to relegate the term "service" to the secondary "be nice to the customer" part of doing business. Service, in this mindset, is a miscellaneous element, something you have to worry about sometimes, not something that's integral to the delivery of value.

This unfortunate division of the customer's reality into two disconnected disparate parts almost guarantees that most organizations will be better at delivering "the product" than at delivering "the service." Why? Because the product is an *objective*, tangible outcome and the service is intangible—a *subjective* outcome.

> The traditional Western management approach is best suited to achieving objective outcomes; it is notoriously poor at managing subjective outcomes.

Many retail businesses over the years have installed "customer service departments," as if service were a separate, detachable, and optional aspect of the business. Most customer service departments have been little more than complaint departments. Most have virtually zero authority to do anything about customer complaints other than make refunds or exchanges.

Most hospitals have departments with names such as "patient relations department" who have the mission of trying to repair the situation after some other part of the organization has committed some atrocity against the customer.

Hence, the developing point of view now is:

> The whole organization
> should be one big customer service department.

Why should we further offend a dissatisfied customer by making him or her go through a tedious, time-consuming rigamarole to return a defective product? We were happy to sell it, and we should treat the refund as just one part of the process of delivering value or, at least as not subtracting value.

Thinking trap 2—Trying to make one size fit all. Another mental malfunction caused by the introverted activity focus of the traditional way of managing is *commodity thinking*—the utter failure even to try to differentiate the company's offering from that of its competitors. Certain industries in particular embrace this kind of primitive world view. The executives of these businesses consider their offering a "commodity," i.e., something that many competitors sell, and which is essentially standard in its characteristics.

Insurance executives, for example, often think and talk in terms of their "products," namely, various types of insurance policies and financial plans, as if they were tangible deliverables. The old mindset causes them to think in terms of documents as the end result of their efforts, not in terms of a customer experience and a subjective impression.

This is really quite an absurd view of things, especially when you consider how poorly an insurance policy qualifies as a deliverable item. As a form of communication, it's one of the most uninspiring, incomprehensible, intimidating, and off-putting documents you can imagine. The executives seem to think people sit up nights reading their insurance policies, savoring the good feelings they get from poring over rate tables and benefit statements.

Because very few people really understand insurance "products" and consequently have no clear idea of the differences between them, most insurance companies give up altogether on trying to differentiate themselves to their customers. As a result, they conceive of their industry as simply price-driven. And so it has become, because customers see no other elements of value on which to base their choices.

It becomes a vicious cycle: customers buy on price because they don't see any other differences among the choices, so the sellers try to compete on price because they think that price is all people care about. Insurance companies, banks, and others that see themselves as marketing financial documents, instead of customer value, take for granted that any new "product" they introduce will be met in very short order by similar offerings from their competitors. The prophecy fulfills itself.

Yet the signals from the new business environment tell us that people *want* differentiation—they *want* choices; they *want* to be treated as individuals. One size does *not* fit all, and those executives who believe it does have doomed their organizations to mediocrity in the eyes of their customers.

Thinking trap 3—Going out of business profitably. A few years ago I was working with a university extension in California, with the objective of increasing its revenues from courses and seminars on business subjects. Its customers were adult working people who wanted to take various business courses to improve their professional knowledge and gain career advancement.

This particular department had, for years, been the only one in the extension organization that earned a surplus from its revenues ("surplus" is a non-profit organization's code word for "profit.") The person who retired after managing the department for 15 years had a reputation as being a competent, hard-headed business person who ran a tight ship.

As part of the customer-research phase of the project, we mailed out survey questionnaires to over 600 people on record as registered in certificate programs, which were "packages" of 12 courses to be completed in order to earn a certificate of recognition in an area such as personnel, marketing, finance, or computers. We wanted to find out how many were still actively pursuing their original educational objectives and how they felt about various aspects of their certificate programs.

Our first finding came as a shock: over 400 of the surveys came back marked "undeliverable," "not at this address," or "forwarding notice expired." So it turned out that we had only about 200 customers, not 600. Further, a large number of respondents said they were no longer actively pursuing their programs. The reason most often given was, "You no longer offer the courses I need to complete my program." Many of them were stranded.

When I reviewed the history of the course offerings, I discovered why the retiring department manager always made a profit. Every time a course would fall below the break-even level in enrollments, she would drop it from the list and never offer it again. The department always showed a modest profit, but enrollments and revenues had been steadily falling. The department was going out of business profitably.

This is the legacy of the *cost-control mentality* that has dominated much of Western management thinking. It is the most sacred of all business reflexes: if profits are down, cut costs. *During recessions, many otherwise enlightened executives will completely abandon their business plans and go through a "slash and thrash" process of hacking away the competitive capability of their organizations to make the numbers come out right.* The profit performance of many large companies is no better than that which would be mathematically predictable based on just riding the economic cycle. How does that qualify as management, to say nothing of leadership?

When Scandinavian Airlines' chief executive Jan Carlzon launched that company's now legendary service-quality effort, the company was in red numbers along with almost all the other European airlines. Carlzon's strategy was counter-intuitive and certainly contradictory to conventional business-school teaching: he invested his way out of the problem.

"I knew," says Carlzon, "that all of our competitors would be cutting costs viciously, trying to restore profit. But we had already looked at that option and concluded that all we would do with a cost-cutting exercise would be to further reduce our competitive capability. I went to my board and presented a multi-million dollar plan to improve service quality, on the theory that the perceived difference between our competitors' declining service quality and our increasing service quality would steal market share. It worked."

Thinking trap 4—Trying to trade quality for cost. One of the first questions executives usually ask me during discussions of the strategy of service quality and its value for competitive advantage is, "What about the cost involved in improving quality?" "How can you be sure it's worth what you have to invest?"

Those questions telegraph one of the most deeply rooted convictions in the Western business mindset: one plus one equals two or conversely, two minus one leaves one. To get something you have to pay something. The analytical, left-brained habit of thought most senior executives have learned since their early school days simply has no room for the idea that you can improve quality, improve your competitive position by scoring better with the customer, and also save money in the bargain. Yet it's true.

Bruce Mackey, a senior executive with the State Bank of South Australia, tells a story that opens up a whole new realm of thought for Western business thinking.

"We attacked a specific quality problem in the area of customer communication. We weren't getting statements out on time for many of our customers and we were falling further and further behind on the problem.

The group responsible for the statements recommended spending $500,000 for a new high-speed laser printer to increase capacity. Instead of jumping into that investment right away, we formed a service-quality action team to look at the problem. In very short order, they identified ways to reduce the workload on the existing printer by some 18 percent. That was more than enough to accommodate the printing of the statements on time.

They continued to work on the problem, and within a few weeks had identified another 20 percent reduction in workload—things that simply weren't necessary. They solved the customer quality problem and did it with no investment at all."

Here's the punch line: according to Mackey, by getting rid of unnecessary printing jobs, the group also produced a huge saving in paper costs, which the company estimated at $300,000 Australian per year.

How's that for one plus one equals three?

That story is by no means unique. John Rampey, vice president of the Milliken Corporation, the textile firm that won the prestigious Malcolm Baldridge National Quality Award, says, "our direct savings the first year were more than enough to pay for the entire quality effort for the next three years. And we weren't seeking savings; we were seeking competitive levels of quality that would give us an advantage in a very tough market."

Thinking trap 5 — Trying to slam-dunk the customer. The "industrialization" of service operations resulting from the activity focus of the manufacturing era sometimes drives organizations to set up standard routine patterns for handling all customers and to try to force all customer needs and problems into these standard patterns. I call that trying to "slam-dunk" the customer rather than trying to solve his or her problem.

I recently had occasion to schedule a minor surgical procedure with my health plan. Because I travel extensively, I often have difficulty finding the right time for such things. This health plan is notorious for its customer-hostile scheduling system. When a young woman on the other end of the telephone line offered me an appointment about a month downstream, it wasn't one I could make. She said, "I'm sorry, that's the only date I have open."

When I asked about dates in the following month, she said, "We're not scheduling for that month yet. Call us back the beginning of that month and we'll see what we have." When I explained that I'd be out of town a great deal and that by the time I could call for another appointment my forward schedule would probably not allow me to meet any date within that month, she was stuck. She just kept repeating the instruction to call back later.

I said, "I'm sorry, but I need a better answer. Your system isn't solving my problem, and I think my request is a perfectly reasonable one." At that point she became angry and let me know in no uncertain terms that it was my problem, not hers.

In this particular case, I knew of a way to jockey their system. I called the "member relations" department and explained the problem.

An hour later, someone called me with a choice of several dates within the month that was supposedly unavailable for scheduling.

I have often encountered service operations that try to slam-dunk the customer into one of a minimal set of standard procedures rather than try to work with the customer to solve a problem. You have to learn to outwit their systems to get your needs met.

THREE WAYS TO DELIVER CUSTOMER VALUE

There are really only three basic ways to deliver customer value through service:

1. *Service at a distance*. The customer seldom or never deals with anyone from the organization on a face-to-face basis. The whole interaction takes place at long distance, i.e., over the telephone or by mail. In some cases it may even be done through an electronic system or a remote computer terminal such as an automated teller machine. This type of delivery format usually works for mail-order firms, credit card–processing companies, some kinds of banks, public utilities, and insurance companies. These are usually information-intensive kinds of interactions.

2. *Service at a facility*. The customer goes to some specific location such as a bank, retail shop, hair salon, restaurant, car dealership, or government agency office. The customer must be physically present at the organization's facility for things to happen. This "over the counter" transaction defines the service in the minds of the business operator and the customer.

3. *Service in a shared environment*. The customer necessarily "takes up residence" for a period of time in a special facility. The employees of the business and the customer are cohabitants for varying periods and they interact in the delivery of the service. This format is typical of hotels, resorts, hospitals, cruise ships, and airplanes. Of course, some businesses have parts or combinations of each format. We need to understand that the delivery format tends to dominate the thinking of both customer and service provider, sometimes to the detriment of a valid concept of value and managed experience.

There are outstanding organizations operating today with each of these three kinds of delivery formats, and there are many mediocre ones as well. The outstanding companies approach the service challenge from the point of view of managing the customer's experience, not from the point of view of *doing things*.

This "doing things" mindset seems to express an unconscious view of the customer as a nuisance. There is a powerful, unconscious tendency in most organizations to depersonalize and dehumanize the conception, discussion, and operation of the service delivery. *Things* are easier to deal with than *humans*, so we prefer to think of the people—both customers and employees—as just interchangeable elements of a big impersonal blueprint.

The customer-as-nuisance mindset and its consequent habit pattern of depersonalizing everything lead to several mental malfunctions that can doom an organization to mediocrity in the eyes of its customers. Each of the three service-delivery formats described above has its own special type of failure mindset. Let's look at them in turn.

THE "QUARTERMASTER": ISSUING MERCHANDISE

Anyone who has served in the military is familiar with the quartermaster experience: moving along obediently in line beside your fellow GI's and collecting various items of "standard issue" as they're thrown on top of you by surly supply clerks. I always get that mental picture when I think of retailers and others who use the delivery format of "service at a facility."

It reflects the previously described thinking trap of trying to separate "product" from "service"—and then forgetting about service. In the quartermaster model, the only thing that counts is moving merchandise. The attitude is "take this stuff and get out of here."

Case in point: my firm has invested heavily in personal computers and related high-tech products over the past ten years. On six or eight separate occasions we have purchased new equipment or upgraded our capability by replacing old units. Not once in all that time, to the best of my recollection, did any computer supplier ever deliver a system that was in complete working order. Missing components, improperly connected equipment, missing software, improperly installed software—you name it.

All of these companies saw themselves as selling "products," not delivering value. They didn't even try to sell *systems*—just individual boxes, cables, software, and miscellaneous parts. Rather than starting with a complete concept of customer-perceived value as their objective, they started with the objective of moving hardware out of inventory and into the customer's premises. Once the customer took custody of the hardware, the matter was finished.

Many retailers have traditionally regarded the post delivery part of the customer experience as a necessary evil, an unplanned problem, or a nuisance. The product-service schizophrenia leads them to think of the so-called service element in terms of extra costs they wish they didn't have to pay.

Have you ever noticed how salesclerks can change from sugary sweet when you walk out of the store with the shiny new VCR to sour and surly when you walk back in asking for a refund? You instantly change from a valued customer to a nuisance when the sales clerk's commission goes up in smoke.

In many ways, the super discount appliance store has fostered this kind of "move the product and damn the customer" thinking, although there are some stores that manage the complete experience effectively and still compete on price. Firms such as WalMart, K-mart, and others have done it well. Sears used to do it. The Price Club, a small regional chain, makes excellent profits by selling consumer goods in a giant warehouse facility, with virtually no customer-contact employees except cashiers. (But if you're going to play in that league, you have to be very price-aggressive.)

Much has been written about the famous Nordstrom department stores, which are legendary for *relationship selling*. Nordstrom salespeople have a mandate to treat the customer with the same warmth and respect when he or she comes back for a refund or adjustment as during the original sale. Retailing tradition says that an unsatisfied customer is an opportunity to make a sale, but many retailers haven't made this truism part of their way of operating. Nordstrom people have a clear idea that what they sell is the total customer experience, and the company's profit performance confirms that it works.

Unfortunately, the Nordstrom reputation has been tarnished a few times by incidents in which company employees claimed that their managers placed sales goals above the quality of work life. These individual incidents do not totally contradict the Nordstrom reputation, but they serve to illustrate how fragile a gold-plated image can be.

THE "CAR-WASH": PROCESSING THE CUSTOMER

Car-wash thinking is a particularly arrogant mindset that befalls people working in the "shared-environment" delivery mode. In hospitals, for example, workers "live" in the building and find themselves dealing with strangers, that is, patients, who invade their personal space one after another. In an unconscious effort to retain psychological ownership and control of the environment, many health-care workers have evolved customer-control strategies that depersonalize the interactions and keep customers feeling psychologically subordinated.

When this mindset operates at the extreme, the hospital tends to become a "human car wash"—a place that processes people through the facility rather than one that creates a total experience of value. The kinds of complaints people typically make about hospitals give the clearest indication that the car-wash mentality is operating all too often.

- "They treat you like you're a thing."

- "They have no respect for your privacy."

- "They talk down to you like you're four years old."

- "They order you around and put you through all sorts of procedures without even telling you what they're doing to you or why."

- "They don't care if you're upset, or scared, or in pain; they just do their thing and push you on to somebody else."

The people who work in *outstanding* hospitals and other medical facilities have a special understanding of the psychological needs of people undergoing medical treatment. They know that it is the total experience that counts, and they use their understanding and skills to add value to the psychological and interpersonal parts of the experience.

The car-wash phenomenon shows up in many other shared-environment service operations as well. Some airline companies and cabin crews give the distinct impression that they think of themselves as hauling live freight rather than delivering a complete travel experience to customers.

Too many hotel managers and employees see themselves as warehousing people for the night rather than delivering a total hospitality experience. Too many schools, school administrators, and school employees see themselves as "incarcerating" kids for the day rather than delivering a total educational experience.

The Queen's Medical Center in Honolulu, Hawaii, is an organization whose people have worked hard to rid the operation of carwash thinking. Queen's executives, managers, and staff, ranging from nurses to housekeepers, remind one another daily of their spirit of service and their tradition of Hawaiian values expressed in the concept of "aloha," which is a feeling of love, friendship, and concern for one another. It apparently works: in a highly competitive health-care market, Queen's typically operates at or near capacity.

THE "PAPER FACTORY": WORSHIPPING TRANSACTIONS

Probably the most extreme form of introversion on the part of a business that deals with its customers through a format of "service at a distance" is the paper-factory way of operating. It becomes a case of "out of sight, out of mind." When the customer is not physically present, he or she becomes psychologically absent as well, or almost non-existent in the minds of the people doing the work that is supposed to create value.

Insurance firms, for example, often fall into this mindset and its associated habit pattern: The day's work for the claims department becomes processing claims, not helping people get their lives, health, or property back to normal. Moving paper becomes the central reality and, eventually, the only reality.

The organization quickly becomes a bureaucracy, feeding on its own transaction processing. The peripheral "customer contact" portions of the operation begin to take on the same minimal, routinized, one-size-fits-all characteristics. Customers who call for help get processed just like the claims get processed. There's a standard solution for every need, whether it works or not. The idea is to get the customer off the phone and "get back to work."

The insurance agent trying to get a price quote for his or her customer may get the same brush-off or runaround that the policyholder gets. Insurance carriers all want agents to favor their "products" in building solutions for customers. Yet the number-one complaint of insurance agents and agency owners continues to be the impenetrable bureaucracies of the carriers' "customer service" organizations.

Similarly, credit card companies, banks, and mail-order firms often fall victim to the same "out of sight, out of mind" mechanization of daily work life. They become information factories instead of problem solvers. The implied value system is that "if the customers would only go away and leave us alone, we could get our work done."

Some of the highly respected service-at-a-distance firms, such as American Express and the legendary mail-order company L. L. Bean, have managed to retain a mindset of customer consciousness and customer value. Unfortunately, too many others want to be in the transaction business, not the customer-value business.

INTROVERTED ORGANIZATIONS: WORK-FOCUSED, NOT VALUE-FOCUSED

The hallmark of traditional, Western business thinking is its focus on *activities*. At the very roots of the "B-school" theory of business and organizations is the idea of designing an organization to perform certain functions, defining processes, jobs, and work standards, and then plugging people into the apparatus to do the work.

Skilled managers are supposedly those who can design and assign activities or at least make sure things get done. Even though work activities are the raw material of the organization's processes, they are not the proper starting point; they should *follow* from a clear idea of customer value.

Unfortunately, many organizations—probably most—are introverted in their thinking processes when they should be extroverted. In the introverted organization, people preoccupy themselves with activities, processes, procedures, rules, and routines, having lost sight of the ultimate objective of creating customer value. *In the extroverted organization, people understand the* why *that comes before the* what.

The traditional organization-as-machine world view tends to see the business enterprise as an economic apparatus, with nicely formed moving parts, fueled by capital. It develops all sorts of justifications for conceiving of people as simply elements of the apparatus, i.e., "cogs" in the great production machine. It has difficulty coming to terms with the personal, interpersonal, social, political, and psychological phenomena that animate the organization, make it real, and motivate the real goings-on on a day-to-day basis.

> This idea of the organization-as-machine, more
> than any other facet of the traditional, Western
> business mindset, is responsible for most of the
> misplaced focus and frustration of failed quality efforts.

It has a powerful tendency to transform people, both employees and customers, into things because it needs to deal with them as predictable, replaceable, and controllable elements of the big system. It has little patience with their quirks and peculiarities, their variability, and their personal needs for uniqueness. People are a nuisance for the traditional mindset, even though they are critical to the success of the enterprise, especially when customer interaction is involved.

A story about American president Harry S. Truman illustrates the ability of some executives to rise above that mindset. Truman had spent some time listening to one of the administrators of a certain cabinet department eloquently explaining his grand idea for improving the "machinery of government." He kept using that term repeatedly in his presentation. After he had completed his pitch and departed, Truman turned to his chief of staff and mused, "he really thinks it *is* machinery."

Time and again when we introduce the precepts of total quality service to business executives, I can almost see their mental "gears" turning as they try to fit the concepts into their long-cherished "apparatus" model of organizations. Their questions telegraph their need to mechanize, dehumanize, and depersonalize the theory.

They ask questions such as:

- "What does this do to the organizational structure?"

- "What's the effect on the bottom line?"

- "How does this affect the delivery systems?"

- "Will we have to rethink our products?"

- "What about standards?"

- "How do we measure results?"

It's not that these questions aren't relevant, it's just that they're usually the *only* ones asked. They are thing-management questions, not people-management questions. A broader view of the organization as a service culture might lead them to ask such questions as

- ○ "How can we learn more about our customers?"

- ○ "Will our customers really see the effects of an initiative like this?"

- ○ "How can we make sure the employees fully understand the importance of this?"

- ○ "Are our employees psychologically ready to accept this new approach?"

- ○ "What's in this for the employees?"

- ○ "How does this affect our leadership?"

There seem to be some national and cultural differences in managerial mindset as well. The Scandinavians often seem to start with people rather than things as they think about organizational change. Gören Carstedt, formerly the head of Volvo's car marketing and distribution in Sweden and now North American director of operations for the innovative Swedish furniture firm IKEA, believes the "people mindset" works better than the "thing mindset."

"In Volvo," according to Carstedt, "whenever we would launch any new initiative that would eventually affect the whole organization, we wouldn't plan it first and then talk about it to the people. We did it the other way around. We would raise the issue, get people talking about it and thinking about it throughout the organization, and we'd draw together the best ideas. Then we'd make the plan. In some cases, we went all through the organization doing focus-group discussions with employees, hearing what they had to say and making sure we understood how they felt. When we finally put together a solution and took it out through the organization, they already felt a part of it. We got almost no resistance at all. That's leadership, in my view, not management."

The conventional mindset of things and processes is one reason why executives in many organizations don't understand either their customers or their employees very well: *they aren't interested*. They don't believe there is anything significant they can learn by talking personally to their customers. And, so long as the employees aren't making trouble, there's no point in talking to them either. After all, they merely do the work.

Recently I spoke to a group of about 150 fitness instructors from workout centers all over the United States. When I asked for a show of hands indicating "how many of you work at centers that regularly survey your customers [i.e., members] to find out how they feel about the center and its services?" about three hands went up. So far as they knew, all the rest of the centers simply didn't ask.

When I asked a similar question about employee sensing while speaking to a group of about 100 personnel administrators, only about five or six of them said their organizations regularly conducted climate surveys to find out how people felt about working there. After so much talk and so many books over the years about quality of work life, morale, and employee involvement, you have to wonder how far we've really progressed.

SERVICE AS A TOTAL MANAGED EXPERIENCE

The Big Mac is inseparable from the context in which the customer experiences it. The stereo system is inseparable from the interaction between buyer and seller that puts it into the buyer's hands. The insurance policy is inseparable from the relationship between the company and the customer that validates the bond of trust between the two of them. There is no product devoid of an accompanying relationship between buyer and provider. In other words, service must be a total managed experience to be successful.

Dr. W. Edwards Deming has often observed that the prevalent focus on "customer satisfaction" is insufficient for business success. "It's not enough to 'satisfy' the customer," he says. "Not nearly enough. You've got to move beyond customer satisfaction to customer delight."

That concept is so obvious that it would hardly seem worth mentioning, except for the fact that it appears to have eluded many—if not most—executives over the years. The number of businesses that get it wrong far exceeds the number that get it right.

One business after another suffers and limits its potential because its leaders fail to understand the all-too-simple concept of managed experience. Computer stores insist on pushing people out the door with boxes of hardware and software they don't know how to hook up or operate. Insurance companies insist on foisting "products," i.e., policies, on people who haven't the faintest notion what value they're buying. Banks insist on trying to treat their customers as "accounts," not as unique individuals with individual needs.

The problem is epidemic, and it's a problem of mindset. For many reasons, it's easy for people running a business to fasten their attention on *what they do* rather than on *the customer who benefits* from what they do. It's easy to preoccupy yourself with the tangible logistics of the business activity rather than the customer outcomes that are the only valid evidence of quality performance.

IS YOUR MINDSET READY FOR A TRADE-IN?

The thing mindset is so firmly embedded in the brains of Western managers that even those who sense its influence have difficulty recognizing it or reaching beyond it. And the new, extroverted mindset of focusing on total value is not yet clearly understood. In order for more people to recognize the old, work-centered, industrial mindset and begin acting from the new, customer-value mindset, it is important to identify the differences explicitly.

Figure 2–1 presents an updated view of the paradigm shift that is moving us from the old, thing-centered, industrial orientation to the new customer-value orientation, in terms of ten key elements of thinking. These ten elements are briefly explained in the following paragraphs; they will be developed fully in later chapters.

1. *The business mission.* The industrial paradigm tends to see the business mission as selling merchandise. The objective is to make a good product and then go out and find buyers for it. The customer-value paradigm sees the mission as *winning and keeping the customer's business* by meeting needs, solving problems, or adding value for them in some way. The customer value package, in this point of view, must be something designed for the customer, not something we find customers for.

2. *The profit principle.* The dominant idea behind the industrial paradigm is basically the efficient use of capital and labor. In that view, careful control of costs in a context of parity with competitors with respect to product performance makes the company profitable. In contrast, the idea behind the customer-value paradigm is that *customer value* (i.e., the quality of the total experience as perceived by the customer), drives profit. In other words, if customer value is there, the profit will follow. We

The Changing Management Paradigm		
INDUSTRIAL PARADIGM	DIMENSION	CUSTOMER-VALUE PARADIGM
Pushing merchandise	BUSINESS MISSION	Delivering superior customer value
Efficient use of labor & capital drives profit	PROFIT PRINCIPLE	Customer response to value drives profit
Seen as expendable/ replaceable	CUSTOMERS	Seen as appreciating assets
Obedient doers: minimum discretion	EMPLOYEES	Highly empowered quality strategists: optimal discretion
Doing assigned tasks	WORK	Assuring quality outcomes
Evidence of task completion; outputs	MEASUREMENTS	Evidence of customer approval
Objective, material, rule-based; dispensing "jelly beans"	REWARDS	Psychological and personal as well as material
Taskmasters	SUPERVISORS	Leaders, enablers, and supporters
Structure and systems define work life	ORGANIZATION	Structure and systems serve people
Presiders	EXECUTIVES	Leaders, enablers, and supporters

Figure 2–1 The Fundamental Paradigm of Western Management Is Changing.

still must use resources effectively, but the accountants tell you where the ship has been; they don't decide where it should go.

3. *The customers.* The industrial paradigm sees customers as expendable or replaceable commodities. If one customer gets mad at us, there will always be another along to take his place. We don't have time to stop and coddle everyone who might be unhappy with us. The customer-value

paradigm sees the *customer as an appreciating asset*—a person who will continue to provide us with revenue if we do right by him or her and who can bring other customers to us.

4. *The employees.* The industrial paradigm sees the employees as obedient doers—operatives who carry out the tasks assigned by their supervisors. The customer-value paradigm sees them as *customer strategists and quality advocates* as well as task performers. The *internal-service* concept makes it clear that everybody has a customer: either the external paying customer or someone in the organization who needs support. For this reason, the customer focus becomes fully internalized in all dimensions.

5. *The work.* The industrial paradigm says the worker should keep his or her attention on the tasks assigned by the boss; performance of the tasks against preestablished work standards will lead to the ultimate organizational good. In the customer-value paradigm the employee must focus his or her attention on the *quality of the customer's experience* at each "moment of truth," whether the employee is directly involved with the customer or not. Each customer contact employee becomes the manager of his or her particular moments of truth.

6. *Measurement.* In the industrial paradigm, managers evaluate the employees' performance by measuring their output or seeing the evidence that they have accomplished their tasks. Note that managers typically do not measure themselves; usually, everyone in authority is exempt from the normative analysis of their daily work—only the frontline employees get measured. In the customer-value paradigm, *the primary focus of measurement is on outcomes*—on moments of truth and the efforts that make them happen. Service management recognizes that many things must happen for the moments of truth to come out well and that the role of an employee is only one component. By focusing attention on the delivery of value as perceived by the customers at the various moments of truth, service management considers the whole organization responsible for performance, not just the frontline worker.

7. *Rewards.* The industrial paradigm characterizes the employees as simply cogs in the production machine. Just as

machines will malfunction if you don't give them electrical power, oil, or other special substances they need for their processes, so too will employees malfunction, according to this view, if you don't give them money and working conditions. Terms like *compensation system*, *reward system*, and *recognition system* express a mindset keyed to inputs and outputs rather than to cultural values, appreciation of people as human beings, and the nurturing of a shared spirit of service among the members of the organization.

The customer-value paradigm explicitly recognizes the subjective, intangible, psychological side of doing business and treats it as a critical success element in and of itself. It recognizes that *people need payoffs in their lives*, not "inputs," and that a sense of pride in quality, ownership of results, and a sense of belonging are valuable payoffs just as money and material compensation are valuable.

8. *Supervising and managing.* The industrial paradigm sees the job of the middle manager or frontline supervisor as making sure the workers carry out preestablished tasks, in compliance with preestablished standards. Their policies, decisions, and interventions serve to shape employee behavior in the direction of task performance. The customer-value paradigm, in contrast, sees the manager's job, at any level, as being resourceful to the frontline employees who have to serve the customers. *The mission of managers is to enable* more than to direct or control, and their decisions and actions should help to make the employees more effective quality strategists.

9. *The organization.* In the industrial paradigm, the organization itself is the message, so to speak. The organizational structure, as a system for deploying resources, becomes the foremost intellectual reality. Structure, process, and legislative control become the primary motifs in the quest for effectiveness. In contrast, the customer-value paradigm sees organizational structure and apparatus as standing in *support of frontline workers*, not as exerting control over them. The function of the organization, in this view, is merely to help workers make the most valuable impact on their customers. It has no other reason for existing, and when it fails to serve that purpose, it needs changing.

10. *Executive roles.* In the industrial paradigm, the job of senior management is to preside over the organization and exert control through structure and process. The customer-value paradigm, in contrast, represents the primary role of senior executives as *creating and maintaining a service culture,* in which putting the customer first is the main preoccupation. The key leaders must exert the force of their authority and personalities to advance the primary values of a customer-driven organization.

It seems clear that outstanding service organizations in all countries operate on customer-value thinking, not industrial thinking. They have moved or are moving toward a radical new frame of reference for performance.

Most of the quality "fizzles" I and my associates have observed in a large number of organizations are caused, I believe, by executives and action people attacking the quality problem with the wrong mindset. Those who try to fight the battle with the wrong weapons are destined to lose. Some of their efforts never get off the ground. Some get part way down the track and grind to a halt. A few even turn into major organizational disasters. Most simply don't fulfill the aspirations of their architects.

I believe twenty-first-century service requires twenty-first-century thinking. The successful performers in the years to come will be those who break free from the old mindset and begin to see their businesses in a completely new way. They will be willing to go wherever the search takes them. They will be willing to develop their organizations into whatever they need to become to do the job. And they will be willing to allow organizational cultures to evolve that focus on quality and value, both for their customers and within their own operations.

Even with the new mindset, the road to quality won't be an easy one. But without it, the road is likely to be a dead end.

3

Paradigm Lost, Paradigm Found: New Thinking About Quality

If the only tool you have is a hammer, everything starts to look like a nail.

Abraham Maslow

A story surfaced just after the close of the Second World War in Europe about a Russian soldier who was part of the Soviet force that moved into Berlin to set up the occupation of the city. According to the story, the soldier entered a German house and saw an electric light for the first time in his life.

Fascinated by this magical gadget—this light bulb hanging from the ceiling at the end of an electrical cord—he decided he must have it. He drew his bayonet, cut the wire off at the ceiling, and tucked the device into his knapsack. Presumably, he intended to take it back to his native land, hang it from the ceiling, and enjoy its magical benefits.

Unfortunately, he knew nothing of the "theory" behind the existence of the light bulb. He didn't know about power plants, transmission lines, transformers, fuse boxes, wires running through the walls, or light switches. He just knew that this marvelous gadget produced light.

This story has come to mind many times over the past few years, as I've observed company executives, in their attempts to capture the magical essence of service quality by trying to imitate one or more of the legendary service companies. Lacking the frame of reference for thinking about service quality, they go around cutting down "light bulbs" and taking them home. The executives want to imitate Nordstrom, or Disney, or Marriott, or American Express. They don't understand that they must learn a whole new frame of reference in order to light their own corporate houses. Just like the soldier, they're having *paradigm* problems.

WHAT IS A PARADIGM, ANYWAY?

Many management thinkers are now saying that the old *paradigm* of Western management is failing, fading, or malfunctioning, and that it must give way to a new one. But what is a paradigm? What does it look like? How does it work? Can you paint it, or is it just a figment of the imagination? Let's talk paradigms for a moment.

To feel comfortable thinking and talking about the death or re-birth of a paradigm, it helps to have a simple definition of the word:

> *Paradigm:*
>
> **A paradigm is a mental frame of reference that dominates the way people think and act.**

It's a way of connecting ideas, prioritizing values, approaching issues, and ultimately forming habits of behavior with regard to a subject.

There are many paradigms in human thought—probably an un-countable number. There are paradigms for the institution of marriage, for example. They vary from culture to culture and even to some extent from person to person. A paradigm about marriage is a way of thinking about the elements of a man-woman relationship in terms of its longevity; its moral, legal, and social obligations; religious considerations; rights and privileges; and interpersonal roles.

Most paradigms, such as the marriage paradigm, tend to operate be-low the level of conscious thought. They tend to dominate a person's thinking without his or her direct awareness. They tend to make them-selves apparent only when something violates or contradicts them. For example, if two homosexual men seek to get married to each other, people who accept the "standard" paradigm of marriage as a legal and sexual union between a male and a female may not view their proposed merger as appropriate.

A paradigm is neither right nor wrong, but a person who adheres to it tends to believe it is right. In fact, it's fair to say that most people are so firmly committed to the paradigms governing their lives that they become disconcerted when others act or propose to act in contradiction to them. Many even become aggressive, hostile, or warlike when others threaten their paradigms.

Religious intolerance is a common example of behavior resulting from the stress of a perceived threat to a closely held paradigm. More human atrocities have probably been perpetrated under the name of religion than for any other cause. The concept of a "holy war" is hard to align with a religious paradigm that condemns killing, but it makes sense within a paradigm that considers the killing of nonbelievers a blessed act.

There are many, almost sacred paradigms in business. Most Western or Westernized organizations operate along similar lines in regard to hierarchy of authority, formal division of roles and responsibilities, rules for compensating people for their work, and so forth. This can seem like a bland observation until you consider the fact that you can walk into the offices of an insurance company in London, one in Madrid, in Athens, in Chicago, in Sydney, in Hong Kong, or in Tokyo and see just about the same structure and general method of operation.

Paradigms are communicated from person to person, company to company, country to country, and culture to culture by modeling and imitation. The management literature, trade publications, and steady migration of professional people from one organization to another cause a constant sharing and a resultant similarity of paradigms throughout the business world.

Some organizations gain an image in the eyes of others as being different from all the rest, of breaking the mold of the accepted paradigm to some extent. Sometimes this departure from the accepted way is disastrous, and sometimes it provides the spark of genius that brings success.

Apple Computer, for example, was a company that in its early days seemed to defy the standard business paradigm. Its "blue jeans" culture and its high-energy commitment to popularizing the personal computer made it a one-of-a-kind company in a new industry. As it grew, however, it began to look more and more like the other Fortune 500 companies whose ranks it joined as it became a billion-dollar company.

The famous Stew Leonard supermarket in Connecticut became known for its outrageous style of doing business and its energetic commitment to pleasing the customer. It virtually became a model in its own right, studied and marvelled at by others in that industry.

The Federal Express Corporation, brainchild of entrepreneur Fred Smith, broke lots of rules to create a package-delivery service that astonished those who thought overnight delivery was a pipe dream. To pull off that level of operational performance, and to guarantee it to its customers, "Fed Ex" had to do many things differently.

As you think more and more about paradigms and the way they govern our lives and dominate our thinking processes, you can sense their all-pervading influence. You can understand more easily why fundamental innovation is so difficult in business and why a truly new concept can shake people up so much. Many new business ideas and ways of doing things arise because someone throws off the tyranny of an existing paradigm and contradicts its basic precepts.

Government service is another interesting example of a powerful, controlling paradigm. Millions of government workers and managers have an idea of how public-sector agencies should operate. This is an area ripe for original thinking and a revolutionary dedication to quality service. But these changes won't come easily, because of the strength of the existing paradigm.

Returning to the opening statement of this chapter, we can get a better idea of what people mean when they say the Western management paradigm is failing, especially with respect to the issue of quality. It means that many of the ideas, values, priorities, precepts, rules, and behavior habits are making it difficult for organizations to evolve the kinds of cultures that can deliver superior value to the customer and make quality their competitive edge.

This is the rationale for a focus on twenty-first century thinking. Recognizing that the twenty-first century is now well in view and that changing organizational cultures is a long-term proposition, we are long overdue in getting to work on the formation of the new paradigm and putting its pieces into place.

PARADIGM PAIN

The need to change a paradigm becomes evident when it causes pain. In other words, we can no longer get what we want by following its rules for behavior. Its values and precepts constrain our actions and keep us doing the same old, wrong things. If we're going to behave in new ways, we first need to think in new ways.

In other words:

> **If you always do**
> **what you always did,**
> **you'll always get**
> **what you always got.**

A paradigm gets started in the first place as people tackle a new problem and develop successful patterns for dealing with it. These patterns tend to form around an underlying "theory" or a frame of reference that makes the approach consistent and communicable.

But a paradigm becomes outmoded, obsolete, dysfunctional, or antagonistic to progress when the original problem condition changes and the original paradigm fails to change with it. The current state of affairs in many Western countries reflects the failure of a number of dominant paradigms that worked well in the past but don't work well now.

Public education, especially in the United States, is in a disaster state because it is still built on the "little red schoolhouse" model appropriate to the turn of the last century, when the country was primarily rural and organized around small towns.

Much of the subject matter taught in most schools is now grotesquely out of touch with the life realities of the children attending them. The dominant educational paradigm is still "incarceration," not human growth and coping. Consultant Peter F. Drucker observes, "To most educators, the ass is the principal organ of learning."

Many churches and religious organizations have lost relevance to their "customers" because they have adhered to the original village-church model, appropriate to small towns. As the population has expanded, people have become much more urbanized and mobile, and they now have an enormous range of options for their leisure time. They no longer turn to the church as the center of social and community activity, and churches for the most part have not updated their "product" to follow the "market." The old paradigm of the community church doesn't work well now.

The recent "drug war" in the United States and other industrialized countries is another example of a failed paradigm. Conceived as a quasi-military undertaking, with the objective of preventing commerce in addictive mind-altering substances, the war on drugs is doomed to failure, and a very expensive failure at that. It is cast in a crime-stopping paradigm, while the underlying causes of drug addiction are the social conditions in which drug-takers exist.

A medical, educational, or social-service paradigm would seem to make more sense for the drug problem. Yet when a number of leading thinkers spoke out in favor of reconsidering the whole basis of the drug war and abandoning the criminalization paradigm, they were vehemently attacked by those deeply committed to the drug war. Mayor Kurt Schmoke of Baltimore, Maryland, one of those who called for a new debate on the issue, was branded virtually un-American and a traitor to the cause of "justice." William F. Buckley, Jr. became a target for accusations of soft-headedness, lack of courage and determination, and downright dangerous thinking.

Old paradigms die hard, even if they don't work.

Such is the case with respect to Western business practices and the current quest for "quality." The current quality paradigm, which evolved in the post–World War II period, has become progressively out of touch with the business imperative of the new age. Particularly with respect to what people have been calling "services," but also with respect to what they've been calling "product" quality, there is a need for a new conceptualization of doing things excellently and gaining a competitive advantage.

THE QUALITY PARADIGM AND HOW IT GREW

It's enlightening to trace the development of the quality paradigm during the past several decades, especially in the United States, which has had a big influence until recently on management thinking in many other countries.

One of the first obvious facts is that most business people have for years used a two-track terminology in thinking about quality. There is "product quality" and then there is "service quality."

In other words, there are two apparently separate dimensions of performance in the minds of many managers. It has been customary to say things such as "The product is fine but the service is poor." You can also hear people in manufacturing-oriented companies say, "We make good products, but we need to pay more attention to customer service."

The term "customer service" has for many years had a very narrow meaning: it's the way a certain group of people, called "the customer service people," interact with the customers. There are customer service departments in many organizations. This choice of terms reveals the structure of an important underlying paradigm. It implies that the real business of business is delivering *things*, and that sometimes that's not quite enough, so you also have to be nice.

If you follow this line of thinking over the past several decades, you can see that most of the "quality theory" that has governed Western business has its roots in physical-product thinking. There has been very little quality theory for the so-called service aspect of the business. The few cases of outstanding service businesses, the truly legendary examples, have been perceived largely as aberrations—almost accidents of nature.

For each of the past several decades, let's trace the primary driving forces behind the development of "products" and "services," identify commercial offerings that symbolized those decades, and identify the associated quality "theory" that arose to meet the needs of the times. (Figure 3–1 shows these relationships and trends graphically.) My description considers the developments from the perspective of the United States, which is probably the prototypical economy for Western commerce, but the same trends showed up in virtually all industrialized countries.

The fifties. In the decade of the fifties, there was virtually no quality theory. The driving force for the design of "products" and "services" was primarily the latent demand released after the war ended. People wanted to get back to home and hearth, back to the good life. Probably a good metaphor for the product axis in that decade was the *house* itself. In the service dimension, it was probably the *movie theater.* Business was all about a return to enjoying life. In the United States, the quality theory was simply "Good Old American Quality." America's products and American craftsmanship enjoyed the reputation of being among the best in the world. In other words, there was no quality problem and consequently no real need for a quality theory.

The sixties. Then came the sixties, the first decade of consumerism. The postwar expansion, the migration to cities, and the rapid industrialization happened in most Western countries, and

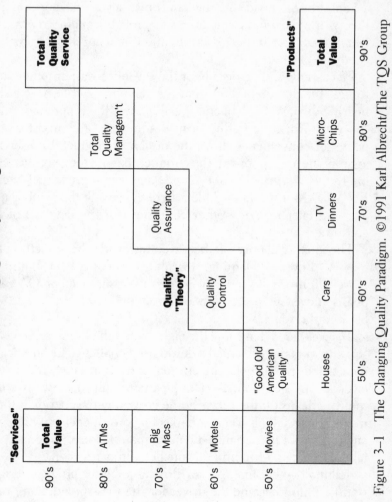

Figure 3–1   The Changing Quality Paradigm. ©1991 Karl Albrecht/The TQS Group

especially in America. The driving force for products and services became mass availability. On the product axis, the *automobile* probably represents the decade best of all; it made millions of people mobile, and its influence affected many other commercial and social trends. On the service axis, the *motel* might serve to symbolize the mass availability of service in the consumer age. The prevailing quality theory, if indeed there was one, was probably *quality control*, or QC, which meant we inspected things and threw out the ones that were no good.

The seventies. The decade of the seventies was, among many other things, the decade of "Life-style." Everybody had to have a life-style. Soaring divorce rates, liberal social values, the hippie movement, the "do your own thing" ethic, a new affluence, and an astonishing appetite for convenience drove the design of products and services. An appropriate metaphor for the product axis in the seventies is probably the *TV dinner.* For the service axis, appropriately, it became the *Big Mac.* McDonald's "golden arches" became the symbol in America, and later in many other countries, for the new age of life-style consumerism.

The quality theory of the seventies, with the impetus of people like W. Edwards Deming, Joseph Juran, and later Philip Crosby, moved from quality control to quality assurance, or QA. The emphasis moved to prevention of errors and problems. "Zero defects" became the watchword.

The eighties. Then came the eighties and the Japanese. The Japanese "quality miracle" presented a devastating challenge to American dominance of the product-manufacturing scene. It invaded virtually all Western consumer economies. The Japanese even successfully challenged the Americans on their own home ground with superior automobiles, in addition to taking over the market for consumer electronics, cameras, and a host of other quality-intensive manufactured products. Incidentally, Deming and Juran both predicted this invasion.

Technology became the key driving force for product designs. Curiously, it also became the driver for the mass production of services. The appropriate metaphor for the product axis in the eighties is probably the *microchip*, and its counterpart on the service axis is probably the *automatic teller machine*, or ATM.

Under intense competitive pressure from Japanese products, which had become legendary for their quality, the Western quality theory shifted to Total Quality Management (TQM), a highly structured set of methods which a number of American quality experts, notably Crosby, took back from the Japanese, who, after all, had learned them from the American theorist W. Edwards Deming. In fact, recently the emphasis in many Western countries, and particularly America, has been on applying TQM methods to improve manufacturing quality and even trying to use them to improve service quality.

The Deming Prize, awarded by the Japanese Union of Scientists and Engineers (JUSE) and won by even a few American companies, as well as the Malcolm Baldrige National Quality Award, have become monuments in recent years to the determination of more and more companies to transform their operations into quality-driven ones. Total Quality Management, the methodology of choice in many organizations, has had results ranging from the dismal to the remarkable. Some companies have applied it marvelously well, while others have struggled and failed. Probably the majority have seen moderate success.

This hypothetical journey brings us to the end of the eighties and the start of the nineties. The format of the preceding discussion suggests that we extend the quality trend forward and ask:

- What will be the business reality of the nineties?

- What will drive the design of choices presented to the customer?

- What will be the appropriate quality theory for the nineties and into the twenty-first century?

Will TQM, the much vaunted quality methodology of process control and conformance to standards, be an appropriate quality paradigm for the future? Or will it fall short of the needs of the new age? Is there paradigm pain now evident that suggests the need to rethink the quality paradigm, especially along the service axis of Figure 3–1?

Returning to that figure, you can make some important discoveries. Assuming for the moment that the underlying logic of the figure makes sense, look at the interplay between the product axis and the service axis. You can see that virtually the same thinking process has been driving developments along both axes. The ever-increasing emphasis on production efficiency, technological sophistication, standardization, and controllability of results has been driving the design of services just as much as products.

We have come to the age where everybody is expected to eat Big Macs, do business with ATMs, and pump their own gas. And yet there is a powerful demand among consumers for a return to the human element in service. High-touch service organizations are still alive and well. Big Mac consumers sometimes want a fine-dining experience; ATM users also want somebody to help them with their financial needs. And people who pump their own gas still want help when their cars need fixing.

As we move into the decade of the nineties and face the twenty-first century head-on, it becomes more and more apparent that the old distinction between "product" and "service" is obsolete. What exists is *total customer value—the combination of the tangible and the intangible experienced by the customer at the various "moments of truth" that become his or her perception of doing business with an organization.*

Now we somehow have to bend the two axes of Figure 3–1 toward the center so they meet and become one and the same axis. When we look at things this way we see that the "quality" issue and the "service" issue are not two separate issues. They are *incomplete fractions of the same issue.* Only when we combine them into a single, composite issue can we think sanely about quality as a competitive advantage and a way of operating a business.

It is increasingly obvious that customers do not care about the arbitrary distinction between the tangible and the intangible that business executives and quality experts have made. They want value for their money, and they consider that to be a total experience, in all its dimensions. Increasingly the term "service" means total customer value, embracing the tangibles and the intangibles, not just the smile-and-be-nice part of it.

And it becomes increasingly obvious that any workable quality paradigm must unify the approach to tangibles and intangibles into a single conception of the customer value package. *Quality in the twenty-first century must start with the customer, not with the tangible product sold or the work processes that create it.* This is a profound change in focus, from activities to outcomes. As later chapters will show, this new focus changes almost everything the organization does in the name of quality.

CHOOSE YOUR GURU

In recent years, the quality movement has gained momentum in Western industrialized countries as many manufacturing companies have tried to close the quality gap with Japanese products. Many companies have developed home-grown quality approaches, some have adapted ideas from various experts and contributors, and still others have followed very closely the exact principles enunciated by one or another of the "quality gurus."

Although there have been many contributors to quality theory, probably three men have had the greatest influence: W. Edwards Deming, Joseph M. Juran, and Philip B. Crosby. Each has his own concept of quality and each has his own followers. Unfortunately, some quality practitioners adhere to the teachings of one chosen guru, almost to the unreasonable exclusion of any ideas that might challenge or contradict them. Among the devotees, it's almost a game of "choose your guru," or "my guru can whip your guru." Probably none of the quality experts named above would condone such slavish adherence; each has his own distinct and valuable perspective on the problem.

To place the contributions of each in some sort of perspective, and to see how their ideas relate to the concept of centering on the customer, it is useful to recap their prescriptions for management action.

Whereas Deming, Juran, and Crosby all *now* speak emphatically of the role of the customer's interests in any quality initiative; in their original formulations, which have been very widely published and followed in Western countries, the customer focus is notably absent.

Here, for comparison, are Deming's 14 points, Juran's 10 points, and Crosby's 14 points.

Deming's 14 points. W. Edwards Deming, the most famous of Western quality experts, gives the following prescription:

1. Create constancy of purpose toward improvement of product and service.
2. Adopt the new philosophy. We can no longer live with commonly accepted levels of delays, mistakes, defective materials, and defective workmanship.
3. Cease dependence on mass inspection. Require instead statistical evidence that quality is built in.
4. End the practice of awarding business on the basis of price tag.
5. Find problems. It is management's job to work continually on the system.
6. Institute modern methods of training on the job.
7. Institute modern methods of supervision of production workers. The responsibility of foremen must be changed from numbers to quality.

8. Drive out fear, so that everyone may work effectively for the company.
9. Break down barriers between departments.
10. Eliminate numerical goals, posters, and slogans for the workforce, asking for new levels of productivity without providing methods.
11. Eliminate work standards that prescribe numerical quotas.
12. Remove barriers that stand between the hourly worker and his right to pride in workmanship.
13. Institute a vigorous program of education and retraining.
14. Create a structure in top management that will push every day on the above 13 points.

Juran's 10 points. Joseph M. Juran, a contemporary of Deming and a respected quality expert as well, advises the following steps:

1. Build awareness of the need and opportunity for improvement.
2. Set goals for improvement.
3. Organize to reach the goals (establish a quality council, identify problems, select projects, appoint teams, designate facilitators).
4. Provide training.
5. Carry out projects to solve problems.
6. Report progress.
7. Give recognition.
8. Communicate results.
9. Keep score.
10. Maintain momentum by making annual improvement part of the regular systems and processes of the company.

Crosby's 14 points. Philip B. Crosby, best known as the popularizer of the quality movement in the United States and other countries, advises the following steps:

1. Make it clear that management is committed to quality.
2. Form quality improvement teams with representatives from each department.
3. Determine where current and potential quality problems lie.

4. Evaluate the quality awareness and personal concern of all employees.
5. Raise the quality awareness and personal concern of all employees.
6. Take actions to correct problems identified through previous steps.
7. Establish a committee for the zero defects program.
8. Train supervisors to actively carry out their part of the quality improvement program.
9. Hold a "zero defects day" to let all employees realize that there has been a change.
10. Encourage individuals to establish improvement goals for themselves and their groups.
11. Encourage employees to communicate to management the obstacles they face in attaining their improvement goals.
12. Recognize and appreciate those who participate.
13. Establish quality councils to communicate on a regular basis.
14. Do it all over again to emphasize that the quality improvement program never ends.

As a mental exercise, you might want to glance again at the three lists of action points above and count the number of times you see the word customer. In a total of the 38 original points among the three quality gurus, *customer* does not appear—even once.

This fact telegraphs better than any other the origin of the thinking process underlying all 38 points—improving physical manufacturing processes.

As Figure 3–1 suggests, the same thinking process that has been driving the design and creation of manufactured products over the decades has been influencing attitudes about services. And the people who have been working to improve the quality of manufactured products are now trying to use the same techniques to try to improve service quality, with varying success.

Now it's time to stop playing "choose your guru." It's time to get back to the fundamental ideas each of the quality theorists have been advocating. It's time to start choosing concepts, models, methods, and mindsets that work. To quote Aldous Huxley, "It's not *who* is right that matters; it's *what* is right." *And what is right, for the 21st century, is a view of quality that starts with the customer, anchors all definitions of quality criteria to the customer-value model, and rewards people for creating value, not just for following procedures.*

THE NUMBERS APPROACH DOESN'T ALWAYS WORK

An Australian banking firm ran into trouble when its preoccupation with numerical quality indicators caused negative side effects. According to Jim Cummane, senior consultant with The TQS Group, Inc., "I was sitting with a telephone service employee at her workplace, gathering data about the kinds of quality issues the customers brought up. I noticed that, when she was occupied with a call and the other line would ring, she just picked up the other handset and hung it up again.

"When she was free to talk, I asked her why she hung up on the second customer. She told me the company had a very strict numerical standard that required her to answer every call within three rings. But when I protested that the second customer might perceive the disconnect as worse than having to wait a few rings longer, she had a very simple answer.

"'Oh, that's not a problem,' she said, 'the telephone company's service is so bad, the customers usually think it was them. In any case, that's what we say if they complain.'"

According to Cummane, "I was astounded. Here was a case where a numerical standard, applied in a simple-minded way, actually created worse service quality, not better."

Much has been written in the past decade about Total Quality Management, or TQM. A number of management writers, consultants, quality practitioners, and corporate executives have contributed to the development of the general approach that goes by that label. Most of them trace the roots of their theories to the *statistical process control* (SPC) methods introduced by Dr. W. Edwards Deming, and to a great extent also to the teachings of Dr. Joseph M. Juran.

What has evolved over those years is a general philosophy and a set of analytical methods for a full-scale, organization-wide attack on the problem of product quality. Particularly in the United States, companies have responded to the Japanese "quality miracle" by getting serious about the quality of their products.

Several large manufacturing organizations have made huge commitments to TQM or SPC programs and have realized excellent results—in some cases, phenomenal results. Among the most noted of these, although by no means the only ones, are Xerox, Milliken Corporation, Corning Glass, General Motors' Cadillac Division, Motorola, and Florida Power & Light Company. Some of these companies have become renowned in their industries for their quality efforts. A number of other companies have made significant efforts and have achieved correspondingly significant improvements in product quality.

Unfortunately, a much larger number of organizations attacking the quality problem using the TQM/SPC approach have not fared quite so well, especially in service organizations. Total quality has been a very difficult undertaking for many, and an unattainable goal for some. Even the executives of the most quality-committed organizations readily concede that it's an extremely challenging venture, requiring the most strenuous and persistent effort imaginable.

Major General Michael J. Butchko, commander of the U.S. Air Force's huge Development and Test Center at Eglin Air Force Base in Florida, talks about what he calls *The Rule of Three:* "It takes three times as long, costs three times as much, and is three times as difficult as you ever imagine it will be." Most quality advocates would probably agree with him.

Although the SPC methods have had mixed results in manufacturing organizations and in the "physical plant" areas of others, they have been considerably less effective outside those areas. As I mentioned before, attempts to apply the TQM model to service operations, that is, departments that deal directly with customers, internal service departments, and work processes dealing with intangibles that are difficult to measure and count, have often been met with frustration.

Paul Goodstadt, Director of Quality Improvement at the highly respected National Westminster Bank in the United Kingdom, says

> We first attacked the service-quality problem from the numbers angle. We set service standards for all areas and went about trying to get people to meet them. But we soon found it a frustrating experience. It had no life to it; it didn't turn anybody on.
>
> So we eventually relaunched the effort, after studying the service management approach described in *Service America!*. We decided we needed a culture-based approach, not a standards-based one. We were much more excited about our progress after we abandoned the numbers game and began getting the customer-value message to the people.

The question of how to measure the *subjective aspects of quality* has plagued many organizations. Many executives and quality practitioners are learning to approach it more thoughtfully.

General Hansford T. Johnson, commander of the U.S. Air Force's Military Airlift Command, the 90,000-person organization responsible for moving American forces and military equipment all over the globe, took a careful approach when he began a worldwide quality initiative in the command. According to General Johnson:

> It became clear to us that it would be easy to bureaucratize the quality process with a lot of specifications, measurements, and standards. We wanted headquarters to be in the helping mode, not the measuring mode. I wanted to make sure we didn't measure destructively and make a rat race out of it.

The Military Airlift Command has parted company with the strict SPC approach and has even redefined one of the most traditional military functions: the Inspector General, or "IG." All military services have an IG function in one form or another, which is a headquarters group that goes around to various military units and inspects their operations to judge how well they're performing. MAC's leaders decided to change their IG function from a "gotcha" role to a quality-support role. They are reorienting the function, giving it the mission of helping the various units define their own service-quality approaches for themselves and launch their own initiatives to improve it.

Other organizations are coming to the same realization about measurement-oriented approaches to service quality. Indeed, even the staunchest advocates of TQM have begun to question how well the SPC approach applies to the nonmanufacturing areas of organizations. According to a publication of Arthur D. Little, Inc., one of the most prestigious American consulting firms,[1]

> ... the crucial importance of quality—in products, in services, and in the systems and structures organized to create them. Yet, for many firms, *the goal of total quality management (TQM) remains elusive.* (italics supplied)
>
> Many companies are now struggling to extend the application of TQM tools to areas outside manufacturing. They are discovering that *the key principles of quality improvement are often difficult to implement in the non-manufacturing world.* (italics supplied)

When the U.S. government created its Federal Quality Institute in Washington, D.C. in 1988, with the mission of spreading the quality commitment throughout the federal establishment, TQM seemed to be the method of choice. But when the Institute's quality consultants began visiting various agency executives and presenting introductory TQM seminars, the message they got back was loud and clear.[2]

"You're bringing us a manufacturing model," the federal executives said, "but we're in the service business. We need something for the environment we work in, especially the nonprofit environment. We don't think TQM fits our needs very well."

Since that time, quoting the Institute's first director, the late John Franke,

> We've found that most agencies, and certainly our own consultants, have moved further and further away from the original statistical measurement methods, and have evolved their own homegrown approaches to their needs. They want something that's *much more customer-focused*, so they can get people in their organizations switched on.
>
> The numbers game is just too bureaucratic for the federal establishment, which is already extremely bureaucratic to begin with. A few agencies still adhere strictly to the statistical process control approach, but most have moved on to more of a customer focus.

A number of U.S. Navy organizations have been developing their own special approach, which they refer to as TQL, or total quality leadership. This name follows from the emerging point of view that the term management connotes an obsolete, bureaucratic, administrative, organizational mindset. They prefer a focus on leadership, to emphasize the human and personal nature of the quality revolution.

THE NEW EMERGING QUALITY PARADIGM

Many organizational leaders and quality advocates find themselves now in a state of confusion regarding quality methods. They've heard too many horror stories and too few success stories. Many of them have tried one or more quality theories and found them complex and intimidating.

None of the foregoing commentary should be construed as criticizing or minimizing the contributions of quality thinkers such as

Deming, Juran, and Crosby. It's simply that the times have changed and the quality problem has changed. Deming, Juran, and Crosby originally formulated quality approaches geared to the needs of physical manufacturing. In the early days of the quality revolution when companies were fighting for survival against increasingly formidable competition, the game was making and selling products. That was the problem we were trying to solve. The shift in Western economies, especially the American economy, from a manufacturing structure to a service structure went largely unnoticed until the advent of the book *Service America!: Doing Business in the New Economy*, in 1985.

Until the eighties, executives, academics, management writers, and quality experts gave little thought to the problem of creating quality in nonmaterial form, that is, in the *subjective experience* of a customer. For that reason, Deming, Juran, Crosby, and their counterparts simply did not have any compelling reason at the time to attack the service-quality problem—they had other problems on their hands.

Now we are coming to realize that the quality paradigm must embrace both tangibles and intangibles, both objective value for the customer and subjective value. The service revolution and the quality revolution will merge to become a single revolution, of crucial significance to all business organizations. And the various contributions of all serious thinkers on the subject will eventually be unified into a single thought process appropriate to the challenges of the twenty-first-century way of doing business.

4

Creating
Customer Value:
How The Best Do It

Change your thoughts and you change your world.

Norman Vincent Peale

We have focused attention so far largely on failures, malfunctions, and mistaken ideas. This is not because pessimism is justified, but because the truth is important. It is our opportunity to learn. And now it's time to focus on success. What can we discover about making quality initiatives succeed?

LEARNING FROM THE BEST

Much of my time and energy over the past eight years has gone into the investigation of *best practices* in various industries and organizations. Best practices are those ideas, philosophies, attitudes, approaches, operational methods, systems, and techniques that have put the top players at the head of the pack. They are the "signature" elements that are the hallmarks of effectiveness. They are the inventions or discoveries the quality champions have put to use to lift their organizations above the expectations of their competitors and their customers.

Learning from the best seems like such an obviously valuable approach to organizational performance, or to anything else, that one would expect it to be much more common in business than it is.

If you would like to be an outstanding guitar player, cabaret singer, tennis player, sculptor, novelist, surgeon, stand-up comedian, interior designer, or anything else, it makes sense to study the best in your chosen field. How do they do what they do? What are their critical skills? How do they approach the challenge of excellence? How do they think? What are their success attitudes? How did they get to be the best?

Studying the best gives focus and direction to one's efforts to join their ranks. It isn't necessary or even possible to imitate them exactly. An aspiring actor or actress can learn a great deal by watching Sir Laurence Olivier and Katharine Hepburn at work without trying to be just like them.

Similarly, it makes good sense for the leaders of any business organization to study the best practices of the champions in their own field. The goal is not to try to make an organization a carbon copy of any other, but to discern the truth of their success and implement that truth in their own unique way.

If the critical key to business success in the nineties will be customer value, then it makes sense to learn from the champions of customer value. Who are they and what have they learned that we must also learn?

This search for the critical truths of competitive advantage based on superior customer value has led me to organizations all over the world since 1983. The search has not been as methodical or as thorough as I would like it to have been, nor has it considered all—or even most—of the truly outstanding customer-centered organizations in the world. But it has turned up some very interesting and compelling "trade secrets" of customer value.

I have had a great deal of advice and assistance during this continuing search. A number of company executives have graciously invited me to visit their organizations to see how they think and how they operate. Executives of my own client organizations have been most candid about what works and what doesn't. And a number of my counterparts—authors, consultants, and academics in the United States and abroad—have given me valuable ideas and insights too numerous to catalog here. There are many bright people working on this problem around the world, and their contributions are giving shape to the rapidly developing view of what quality will mean in the twenty-first century.

In addition, I've learned a great deal during company visits as part of a number of executive study tours devoted to the subject of customer focus and service quality. In cooperation with Management Frontiers, a Sydney-based firm specializing in such things, I have accompanied executive groups to Europe, Asia, and Scandinavia. The leaders of the companies we visited have been remarkably willing to share their time, views, knowledge, and even their basic business strategies.

Companies in the United States, Canada, Australia, Norway, Sweden, Denmark, Finland, England, Ireland, France, Germany, Italy, Belgium, Switzerland, Hong Kong, Singapore, and Japan have contributed to this accumulation of wisdom about what wins and keeps the customer's business and what makes an organization capable of delivering outstanding value.

The task I set for myself was to sort through this wealth of information and try to discern the truth about success in creating and delivering superior customer value. I have also devoted a great deal of effort over the past seven or eight years to sorting through the various management theories, quality models, and change-management approaches.

It eventually seemed that no one management theory or approach was the best one. No one company's business approach was the correct one. No one company seemed to have solved all the problems. None seemed to have a foolproof model. None seemed to have the best answers or the best methods in all areas. Some organizations were outstanding in some areas and wanting in others. Each, however, had something special to offer in one or more critical dimensions of quality or customer focus.

It seemed clear that the only valid model would be a synthesis of the best approaches used by the best organizations. It seemed that by putting together the best of the best and arranging those elements into a coherent model, it might be possible to have the best of all worlds. This is the search, and the thinking process, that has led to the creation of the conceptual model that I have come to call *Total Quality Service*, or *TQS*.

This name, Total Quality Service, originally focused on the needs of organizations in so-called "service" industries. But it soon became compellingly clear that *all* organizations are in the service business, and it is only the relative proportion of tangibles and intangibles involved in the customer's experience of value that makes one different from another.

In broadening the scope of the TQS concept to include the entire "quality" issue, it became very important to combine and unify the two previously separate thought processes of "quality" and "service." For this reason, the term *Total Quality Service* seemed to be the best available synthesis of the critical factors involved.

In addition, I felt strongly at the time the TQS model was coming together that many service organizations were blindly adopting the manufacturing-oriented TQM, or "total quality management" approach, with its fixation on numbers and work processes and its scant treatment of customer value. I felt strongly that we needed to shift the emphasis from "management" to "service," which is the ultimate purpose of the whole preoccupation with quality. This point of view argues that a focus on "management" is inappropriately near-sighted, and that the appropriate focus is to take the long view and focus on the reason for the organization's existence, which is to serve.

This chapter describes the thinking behind the development of the TQS model, shows how it works, and shares some experiences from companies that are employing it in their quality efforts.

THE FIVE KEY SECRETS OF THE QUALITY CHAMPIONS

The outstanding organizations have mastered five critical processes that lead to superior customer value. The basic TQS model, in its overall conceptual form, is simply the unification of these five action elements discerned by observing these outstanding organizations. Each of the five areas has its own specific methods and practices. Each deserves a great deal of attention and study because it offers a wealth of possibilities for making a quality initiative successful. All are explored in some depth in five succeeding chapters.

I would like to emphasize the point that the TQS model is more of a discovery than an invention. It is a perception that emerged from the study of the philosophies, leadership approaches, and business practices of a large number of outstanding customer-committed organizations. They all seemed to have these five basic things in common, and these common elements seemed to form the basis for a new world view about business, customers, and quality.

For the current discussion, we can summarize the five basic action elements as follows.

Market and Customer Research

The outstanding service organizations understand the very basic needs, instincts, life situations, problems, and buying motivations of their customers. They see their customers as unique people, not as market units. They know what critical elements of value will win and keep their business.

It takes two kinds of research to understand your customers: research on the market and research on the customers themselves. *Market research*, in this connotation, is the investigation of the structure and dynamics of the marketplace you propose to serve. This includes identifying market segments, analyzing demographics, targeting critical market niches, and analyzing competitive forces.

Customer perception research goes at least one step further than conventional market research. It attempts to understand the expectations, thoughts, and feelings of the individual customer toward the service product and service provider. It hopes to discern one or more critical factors in the customer's perception of the total experience. This enables you to come up with a *customer value model*, which is a set of criteria that drive the customer's choices between you and your competitors.

Many large organizations do excellent market research. Many, however, do little or no customer perception research, or do it ineffectively. Many middle-sized or small organizations do virtually no research at all. Probably a majority of business organizations do not have an adequate understanding of the critical personal factors that influence their customers' perceptions of value.

Strategy Formulation

Outstanding organizations have cast their lot with the principle of customer value. They have developed, evolved, or designed business approaches that win and keep customers by offering value. They know clearly what business they are in, what their missions are, what their core values and beliefs are, and what strategic approaches they must take to succeed through customer value. They understand how to subordinate technology, operations, methods, and organizational structures to the overarching demands of a customer-value business strategy.

Frequently, becoming fully customer-centered or improving service quality demands repositioning the organization itself. This requires its leaders to review various aspects of the competitive strategy and possibly even to rethink the vision, mission, core values, and basic direction for the company. They must reexamine the *customer value package* they bring to the market, down to its very fundamentals. They may, in this process, either confirm their current concept of their customer relationship, adjust it slightly, or even completely revolutionize it.

Education, Training, and Communication

The top performers are skilled at communicating the customer-value message to everyone in the organization. They understand and accept the magnitude of the investment required to develop and maintain the collective human knowledge, capability, and commitment necessary to deliver outstanding customer value. They know how to create and maintain healthy information cultures, i.e., the collective know-how that comes through shared values, shared beliefs, shared facts, and shared performance. They have learned how to win and sustain employee commitment to the spirit of service and the values that make it real.

I know of no outstanding service organization that does not use an intensive, continuous, dedicated process of educating its people about their customers, about quality, and about their roles in delivering superior service. The methods of education, training, and communication play a central part in helping everyone understand the customer's needs and expectations, the vision, mission, and values of the organization, and the strategies for winning and keeping the customer's business. This is a critical process in getting the organization moving along the total quality service track, and it remains critical in sustaining its commitment.

Process Improvement

The outstanding organizations are good at changing themselves and becoming the kinds of organizations they need to be to meet their business missions. They will not tolerate the kinds of bureaucracy and organizational craziness that cripple so many of their competitors. They have a commitment at all levels of leadership to *continuous quality improvement*, and they actively seek ways to make their organizations work better on behalf of the employees as well as the customers. The effort to make the organization's systems more "customer friendly" must be perpetual.

It is essential to continually examine, question, and revise if necessary every process, procedure, policy, rule, or work method. In an effective service-committed organization, all systems owe their existence to the ultimate objective of delivering customer value, either to the external paying customers or to the internal customers who contribute their part to the ultimate objective. All systems are on probation all the time. All are eligible for revision if they do not add value.

Assessment, Measurement, and Feedback

The excellent service performers understand that information empowers people, and they go to great lengths to help people know what their customers want and need, and how they are doing in meeting those wants and needs. They are continually assessing themselves from all angles. They also make sure people get feedback, recognition, and appreciation for the contributions they make to customer value. They have aligned their internal reward processes with the business purpose, to make sure that people do indeed receive personal value when they commit their energies to delivering customer value.

The only way to guide the efforts of the people in any organization toward total quality service is to give them feedback about their progress. Every organization needs a carefully thought-out approach to measuring customer value and the critical organizational processes that create it, a way to share this information with the people, and a way to react constructively to its meaning. This has been one of the most confusing aspects of quality improvement for many people. Making all standards and measurements customer-focused helps a great deal to clear up the measurement issue.

Figure 4-1 shows these five action areas united into a wheel model, with the goal condition of total quality service at the center.

Taken individually, each of these five areas has its own appeal. Each could be an appropriate starting point for an organizational quality initiative. But the secret to superior quality is in combining these action elements into a working, unified approach. This is what makes TQS a change management model; it is a prescription for becoming the kind of organization that can achieve and sustain the dynamic state of affairs characterized by total quality service.

To put all five of the action elements of the TQS model together into a perspective, we might invoke a nautical metaphor. If total quality service is the ideal, ultimate, never-to-be-arrived-at destination, then the TQS approach is the journey. Customer research serves as the compass, strategy formulation provides the navigational chart, education and communication put the wind into the sails, process improvement provides the rudder that keeps the ship on course, and measurement and feedback tell the captain and crew when and how to change course. It is the effective interplay of all five factors that keeps the ship sailing properly.

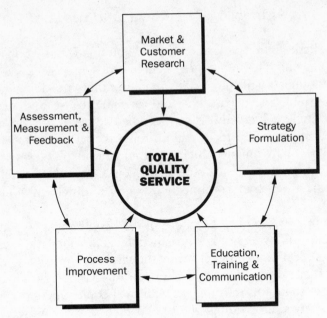

Figure 4-1   The Total Quality Service (TQS) Model.
©1988 Karl Albrecht

A NEW LANGUAGE FOR THINKING ABOUT QUALITY

This new way of thinking requires a new way of talking. As we enter the twenty-first century and we see the human values of service and concern for people begin to prevail ever more strongly in business organizations, we need a vocabulary for a customer-centered, service-oriented way of doing things.

At the risk of appearing to insult the intelligence of those who read this, I'll offer some definitions of some very basic terms. These particular definitions, however, signal a critical shift in our thinking about service, quality, and value.

> *Service:*
>
> work done by one person
> for the benefit of another.

From the standpoint of business, *to work is to serve,* no matter what the work involves. All work is service work. From the most microscopic level of one person's job, all the way to the macro level of the organization's delivery of value to its customers, service is what is happening.

It no longer makes any sense to talk about "product" businesses or "service" businesses. The act of assembling a personal computer, sewing a garment, or molding a chocolate bar is a way of serving others, just as much as is the act of selling it to a customer or advising the customer how to use it.

We need to get comfortable with the broadest possible connotation of the term *service*; it means *serving.* It encompasses all of the work going on, everywhere, in business organizations.

Next, we need a working definition of quality.

> *Quality:*
>
> **a measure of the extent
> to which a thing or experience
> meets a need, solves a problem,
> or adds value for someone.**

Note the key word *measure* in this definition. Quality is a measure. It's not merely a feeling, a belief, a value, or a commitment. It's not just an ethereal concept, or a philosophy, although those are all parts of the way we must think about quality. It is a measure that reflects an ultimate judgement of value received. And it necessarily includes both subjective and objective criteria.

Nothing in the definition of quality offered above confines it to any physical characteristics. It incorporates both tangible and intangible measures. Therefore there is no point in trying to talk about "quality" and "service" as if they were two separate concepts. Service—total service—is everything we do in any organization, regardless of how tangible or intangible the outcomes are. So quality, by this definition, is the measure of value for total service.

With this wide-angle view established, let's focus on a definition of Total Quality Service, or TQS, and see how it transcends the old distinctions between "product" and "service."

> *Total Quality Service:*
>
> a state of affairs
> in which an organization
> delivers superior value to its stakeholders:
> its customers, its owners, and its employees.

This implies a business philosophy, a form of leadership, a collective spirit of service, and a way of operating that embraces quality and customer value as its guiding principles.

If you examine this particular choice of words, you can see that it implies a goal condition to be sought, not any particular method of operating. Methods arise to help achieve the goal, not as ends in themselves.

It uses the customer's response to value delivered as the basic litmus test of its success. It forces us to pose the question, "Have we created and delivered real customer value, as evidenced by the customer's reaction to what we've done?" It proceeds from the view that customers who receive superior value will reward the organization with their continued patronage.

And it recognizes the needs of the organization as well as the needs of the customer. Total quality service requires that all stakeholders get their needs met. You can deliver great customer value but go out of business because you're not operating cost-effectively. And if the employees aren't receiving value as members of the organization, you can't sustain their commitment.

Any state of affairs can change. As J. Willard Marriott, Sr., founder of the Marriott Corporation, said many years ago, "Success is never final." There is nothing anyone can ever do to guarantee that an organization will maintain a state of total quality service forever. Marriott believed it was harder to stay an outstanding service company than it was to get there in the first place.

THE PHILOSOPHY OF TQS

The TQS approach, as observed in complete form or partial form in the outstanding service organizations, has a very clear and strong philosophy behind it. It implies certain attitudes, points of view, and beliefs about doing business that have caused these organizations to thrive and prosper. Just as the thinking traps identified in Chapter 2 keep people from delivering value to their customers, so this new mindset, philosophy, and paradigm give them more successful ways of winning and keeping customers.

Let's explore some of the special features of this way of thinking about customers, quality, and service.

One of the keystones of the TQS philosophy is the belief that all quality standards and measures used in the organization should be customer-referenced. That is, they should relate directly or indirectly to a model of customer value. They should help people guide their efforts in such a way that the whole organization delivers outstanding value to its customers. Quality standards and metrics should be the means to that end, not ends in themselves.

Secondly, this customer-value focus should apply *internally* as well as *externally*. In the service culture, everybody has a customer. All departments, including those who have no contact with the external paying customer, have customers. Internal service departments must understand the needs and problems of their organizational customers, and they must work to deliver a defined value to those customers, just as the departments do that serve the external customers. They need to operate according to valid customer value models of their own, and they need to assess their performance against these value models.

Another critical difference between TQS and the more traditional numbers-based approaches to quality is that TQS explicitly recognizes the importance of *subjectively perceived quality* as well as the more familiar forms of *objectively perceived quality*. Numbers-based quality approaches tend to deal only with those concrete aspects of the operation that can be conveniently measured and counted, bypassing many of the critical elements of customer perception. TQS, on the other hand, recognizes the need to see subjective measures as just as important as objective measures.

How the customer feels about the experience of buying and owning the automobile, or the suit of clothes, or the VCR, or the personal computer is every bit as critical to the business success of the seller as assuring that the technical characteristics of the product conform to a standard. And in business areas where the customer receives little or nothing in the way of tangible deliverables, his or her subjective evaluation is all there is by which to define quality.

Furthermore, while numbers-based quality approaches typically focus on the *reduction of variability* in all processes, i.e., on doing things exactly to a prescribed standard, *TQS makes choices about variability*, depending on whether the quality objective is a tangible deliverable item or a subjective element of customer experience.

For example, when a nurse gives an intravenous medication or feeding to a patient, there are aspects of quality involved in which variability is unacceptable and aspects where variability is desired. There should be little or no variability in the composition of the IV admixture, or the sterility of the equipment, or the proper placement of the IV line in the patient's vein. But the way the nurse deals with the subjective aspects of the patient's experience, such as making the patient comfortable, explaining the procedure, and calming the patient's fears, should be largely at the discretion of the nurse. Our quality model must incorporate both of these.

Whereas the numbers approach deals only with the objective elements of quality, TQS deals with both *objective* and *subjective* elements. A critical limitation of the doctrinaire numbers approach to quality is that it cannot distinguish between high-discretion work and low-discretion work. In some cases there must be a very stringent control of outcomes, minimal discretion, and close observation of performance. In others there must be an element of style and flair. The employee must have reasonable freedom to use his or her best judgment and skills to deliver a customer experience. And the measurement of results in such instances must come from the customer's perceptions, not from mindless compliance with some arbitrary set of actions.

Chapter 10 deals with this issue of subjective and objective outcomes in some depth and shows how the issues of quality measurement, control, and employee empowerment come together in the concept of quality strategy.

Another important departure taken by the TQS philosophy is the focus on customer experience in deciding what to change or improve, as opposed to a focus on work activities and outputs.

For example, advocates of the traditional numbers approach would go into a purchasing department and begin counting the number of purchase orders issued per day, the number of errors of various types on the purchase orders, the number of backordered items, and so forth. They would then try to reduce the incidence of errors and increase compliance with standards and procedures for processing purchase orders and related documents. The TQS approach, however, would begin very differently.

The TQS approach would start by identifying the customer value model held by the internal customers of the purchasing department. Using this customer value model, it would measure customer perceptions to see how well the purchasing department was currently scoring on the critical value elements on this "report card." It would then pinpoint the critical areas for quality improvement as the customers saw them and set priorities for intervention. It would develop certain quality objectives that the customers could recognize as valid in improving performance against their expectations.

The TQS approach would then work backward from these quality objectives to identify the types of malfunctions that needed to be measured and corrected, and the systems improvements needed to meet the quality objectives. The intervention would certainly target subjective factors as well as objective factors.

For example, if the customers gave the department low scores on cooperation and "can do" attitude, a critical quality objective might be to earn higher scores. This would mean diagnosing the reasons for the low scores by finding out what specific experiences or procedures the customers are reacting to. The quality improvement effort would then focus, at least in part, on those experiences and procedures.

In other words, the TQS approach measures processes and activities *after* it establishes the quality objectives, not before. Its first measures are the measures of customer approval at the level of the customer value model. Process measures follow from those.

In keeping with this "outside-in" philosophy instead of the traditional "inside-out" approach, the TQS approach leads to broader approaches to quality improvement. For example, once you have a valid *customer value model*, you can then develop an organizational vision and mission to meet the demands of that model. Then you design, redesign, or realign the basic *customer value package*, which is the total offering your organization provides in response to that model. And then you begin a process of perpetual improvement in the organization's ability to deliver that value.

It is in the process improvement phase where objective measures of quality (accuracy levels, error rates, failure costs, and so on) come into play. At that point we are prepared to measure and track numerical performance on processes that really count.

Another key part of the TQS philosophy is the view that the quality improvement process should be inseparable from the overall strategic business approach. Each, in a sense, defines the other. For example, the element of Market and Customer Research that helps you understand what will win and keep the customer's business is the same element that helps you set the strategic direction for the organization and decide how to position it against its competitors.

The Strategy Formulation component that helps you define your concept of delivered value and your customer value package also includes the same thinking process for defining your organizational vision, mission, core values, and strategic key result areas. And the other three components of the TQS model—Education, Training, and Communication; Process Improvement; and Assessment, Measurement, and Feedback—help you implement your quality approach, which should be fundamentally the same thing as implementing your strategic business plan.

So the TQS process and the planning process are not two separate processes or two separate streams of thought. They should be one and the same process. If an organization has not done an effective job of strategic planning, the TQS process will likely enable—or force—its leaders to do it. If they haven't figured out what business they're in, they'll know by the time they work through the TQS process if they do it effectively.

Later chapters on customer research and strategy formulation explain more fully how the TQS process dovetails with, becomes part of, and even sometimes incorporates the process of setting the direction of the business.

The TQS concept departs from traditional thinking in a number of other ways, which are easier to understand in relation to its five action components. Each of the five chapters, devoted to the five respective action components, develops this sense of uniqueness further.

TQS IN THE REAL WORLD

Taken together, the five action components of TQS have one overriding purpose: to align the organization's strategy, people, and systems around the needs of its customers, as illustrated in the Service Triangle figure shown in Chapter 1.

Since the introduction of the TQS model in 1988, a number of organizations in various countries have adopted it as their foundation concept for change management. Many others have begun using it as a common language for quality and customer value. Others have adopted various elements of it as parts of their existing "home-grown" approaches.

For example, the Natural Gas Company of Sydney, Australia (formerly known as the Australian Gas Light Company) used TQS to launch a company-wide quality initiative that involved all 2500 of its employees. CEO Len Bleasel says, "We had a clear idea of our business direction and our market strategy, and we needed to take that message throughout the organization. We used TQS as a way to introduce everyone to the strategy and to help them understand the changes we had to make to get there."

According to Bleasel, "we found it extremely important to have a clear, simple concept and a common language to talk to people about quality service. The buy-in at all levels was tremendous, and the managers could get a clear idea what they had to do to make it happen."

The state of Hawaii applied the TQS model to the issue of reforming its civil service system. Director of Personnel Services Sharon Miyashiro says, "our civil service system hadn't been updated in almost 50 years, and we felt a need to rethink it from the standpoint of value delivered to our various 'customers,' or stakeholders. We used the TQS approach to define the customers more clearly, identify the value models they brought to the experience of dealing with the system, and rethink the entire design of the system from the point of view of delivering that value."

The Queen's Medical Center, also located in Hawaii, uses the TQS approach to improve its internal service processes. According to Angie Twarynski, the hospital's Director of Organization Development, "our middle managers were looking for a way to focus employee attention on quality and service to their internal customers. We selected TQS as our model for change management because it incorporated all of the key elements—customer value, strategy, education and training, process improvement, and measurement."

Several commands within the United States Air Force have adopted the TQS model, especially for managing internal service, that is, service provided to other Air Force commands. One in particular, the USAF Morale, Welfare, and Recreation Command, has redefined its philosophy and operating emphasis using TQS thinking. According to MWR Center commander Colonel Roy Sheetz, "we're going to incorporate Total Quality Service into all of our training courses. Marketing is not going to be called marketing—it's going to be called customer needs assessment. And we are going to go for continuous improvement. We're not going to be satisfied with the status quo. Modeled after the customer-driven programs of Karl Albrecht's *Service America!* and *Service Within*, Air Force MWR lives by its slogan: Doing Good Things for People. We've provided copies of Albrecht's books for every library in the Air Force as well as copies for every MWR chief."

Bausch & Lomb's International Division used the TQS model to improve its competitive position worldwide, implementing it throughout its operations in 23 countries. According to CEO Ron Zarella, "we operate in very competitive vision and healthcare markets. We wanted to strengthen our position by keying in more closely on our customers' sense of value, and by mobilizing the whole organization to deliver that value more effectively."

The Division implemented the TQS approach in each of its subsidiaries, starting with a clearer customer focus, a tighter strategy for customer value, and a program of communicating the quality message to all employees. According to Zarella, "we were extremely pleased with our accomplishments. We found extraordinarily high employee acceptance of the service quality concept, and virtually all of our subsidiaries showed substantial improvement in customer perceptions, much of it translatable to bottom-line results."

THE TQS ACTION MENU

Each organization's journey of total quality service must be unique to its own needs. There is no one-size-fits-all, paint-by-number program that works for everyone. Organizations are so different that it is essential that each one chart its own course. Still, there are certain actions and approaches that make sense in just about any quality initiative. There are certain bases you need to cover in getting the organization started on the journey and supporting its learning process as it goes.

Again, drawing from the best practices of outstanding organizations, I have tried to identify some of the key *points of intervention* most worth considering. In this process I have discovered some 17 "things to do" that can have the most powerful effects in shifting an organization's culture toward a customer-centered way of life. These interventions are basically organization development actions that can cause people to start thinking about their work in a different way.

Few of the outstanding organizations do all of these things, but most of them do most of these things. Each one does some of them better than others. It is the attitude and mindset that these kinds of actions convey more than the particular actions themselves that we should study.

I prefer to think of these 17 points as an *action menu* for achieving total quality service. How an organization applies this menu will be unique to its own situation and needs, but it does give the broad outlines for a structured approach with a well-considered implementation strategy.

It is very important to keep in mind that there is nothing sacred about the sequence of these actions as given here. It can vary considerably according to each organization's unique implementation strategy. Many of these actions can overlap or go on simultaneously. Some may have already been accomplished. Others may be unnecessary for a certain organization. And each deserves an appropriate degree of emphasis, again based on the needs of the organization. But it is certainly appropriate to at least consider all of them in approaching any quality initiative.

Here are the basic elements of such an action menu and some of the possible ways of getting them done.

Educate and Commit Senior Executives

Make sure the leaders of the organization have a reasonably deep knowledge of the concepts, issues, models, methods, and tools of customer centering and continuous quality improvement. This may include executive seminars, top-level meetings about customer focus, required reading of current books and publications on the subject, invited speakers, and having executives attend conferences or participate in study tours devoted to service and quality.

Educate and Commit Managers at All Levels

Seminars for mid-level executives, middle managers, and supervisors; special emphasis given to customer centering during existing supervisory courses; meetings and strategy sessions with executives and their subordinate managers; managers develop departmental plans for continuous quality improvement.

Create a Focus for Change: Quality Task Force

Recruit a small group of the most quality-committed and forward-thinking action people to spearhead the effort; give them special training and a variety of developmental experiences to make them experts in TQS and change management.

Implement "Early Wins"—Quick Improvements

Take decisive action to improve some of the most obvious quality problems and make some of the most noticeable changes in the delivery of the customer experience; draw attention to the quality focus by giving people some concrete examples.

Identify the Customer Value Model(s)

Conduct customer perception research using various methods like focus-group interviews, preference analysis, analysis of customer needs and priorities, and creative analysis of customer feedback to discern the key elements of customer value; do this for each of the major categories of paying customer; internal service departments do it for their various organizational customers; develop a specific set of customer value factors for each type of customer and formulate them into a published customer value model.

Define the Organizational Vision, Mission, and Values

Set the direction for a quality-focused approach to doing business; executives use strategy meetings or retreats to formulate a vision, mission statement, and statement of core values that will drive the organization's cultural transformation; develop and refine these statements until they can stand as significant, meaningful, believable, and actionable guides for everyone in the organization.

Set Critical Quality Improvement Goals

Select one or two critical areas of significant customer impact as a focus for change; executives should designate these as top priority key result areas and get people all over the organization working to improve them.

Profile the Culture: Organizational Audit

Understand the current state of the organizational psyche, that is, the attitudes, beliefs, and expectations of employees at all levels toward the issue of customer focus and the effort to enhance it; find out how employees feel about the executive commitment to service, the degree to which the organizational culture seems to value quality of service, and the quality of their own work life as they see it.

Empower Middle Managers: Departmental Missions

Middle managers apply the TQS model to their own departments, whether they are serving internal or external customers; they conduct their own customer research if appropriate, formulate customer value models for their operations, and develop quality improvement plans for their areas.

Educate Employees About Quality and Customer Value

Use training and communication activities to give every single employee an understanding of what the customers want, how the organization is supposed to do business, and what customer centering means to each of them in their jobs and their work lives.

Target Quality-Critical Processes for Improvement

Zero in on the organizational systems, processes, policies, rules, or procedures that have the greatest impact on customer-perceived quality; select the critical ones and subject them to careful and critical analysis to see how they can be made more customer-friendly and more cost-effective.

Activate Quality Service Action Teams

Train and prepare employees to attack quality problems using group meetings, a disciplined step-by-step process, and a set of simple process improvement tools with which they can identify problems, analyze them, develop solutions, and present their solutions to management for implementation.

Set Customer-Focused Quality Criteria

Choose a few critical aspects of the customer experience that can benefit from formal performance targets; set targets that are simply expressed, observable, and under the influence of the employees charged with meeting them; choose them based on their value in shaping the customer's perception of value received in one or more critical areas of the customer value model.

Create Customer Feedback Systems

Set up a system to sample customer perceptions of the organization's performance on each of the elements of the customer value model; use questionnaires, interviews, focus groups, and other means for continuously gathering data on customer perceptions; create ways to encourage customers to give feedback and contribute ideas about how to enhance the value they receive.

Develop a Recognition and Appreciation Process

Work with leaders at all levels to help them increase the level of recognition and appreciation they give to employees who contribute to quality and customer value; avoid bureaucratic "reward systems" but develop a process that is spontaneous, creative, and led by managers, that identifies outstanding performers and shows them the organization's leaders appreciate their contributions; make managers responsible for recognition and appreciation, and use organizational processes only to support them, not take over their roles in this critical area.

Develop Managers into Customer-Focused Leaders

Change the emphasis in the organization from *managing* to *leading*; train managers at all levels in the basic thinking of customer value; help them view their employees as customers and accept their roles as leaders who empower people, not bureaucrats who "administrate"; set up systems or processes that have employees evaluate their bosses on their leadership behavior; give this feedback to the managers and help them react to it positively and use it for their own professional and personal growth.

Realign all Support Systems

Eventually get around to evaluating every single support system in the organization in terms of its contribution to ultimate customer value; this includes systems like recruiting and hiring, placement, training, performance appraisal, management development, planning, budgeting, resource allocation, computer software systems, physical technology, facilities design, and many more.

Figure 4-2 provides a quick-reference list of these 17 points.

YOUR PROGRAM IMPLEMENTATION STRATEGY: FIGHTING THE FIZZLE FACTOR

When the executives of Telecom Australia's Corporate Customer Division announced their intention to launch a quality initiative, the managers and employees of that telecommunications giant gave us one reaction over and over in the field interviews we conducted as part of the early research: "What makes you think it'll work this time?"

They had been through one headquarters-imposed program after another. They saw no reason to believe this one would be anything besides one more "flavor of the month." The fizzle factor mentioned in Chapter 1 was alive and well, as it is in so many service organizations.

The TQS Action Menu

1. Educate and commit senior executives.
2. Educate and commit managers at all levels.
3. Create a focus for change: quality task force.
4. Implement "early wins"—quick improvements.
5. Identify the customer value model(s).
6. Define the organizational vision, mission, and values.
7. Set critical quality improvement goals.
8. Profile the culture: organizational audit.
9. Empower middle managers: departmental missions.
10. Educate employees about quality and customer value.
11. Target quality-critical processes for improvement.
12. Activate quality service action teams.
13. Set customer-focused quality criteria.
14. Create customer feedback systems.
15. Develop a recognition and appreciation process.
16. Develop managers into customer-focused leaders.
17. Realign all support systems.

Figure 4–2. The 17-point TQS Action Menu.

Many quality drives begin with the best of intentions. The executives really are fired up; they really want to make it work. But something seems to happen along the way. Over a period of two or three years, and sometimes only two or three months, they see the dream begin to fade and finally die. All that remains is a wisp of the original idea, and sometimes bad feelings after some unpleasant experiences. The workers have seen it all before.

The employees of one American company, which shall remain nameless, even developed their own acronym for these types of programs. They called it "B.O.H.I.C.A.," which stood for "Bend Over, Here It Comes Again." They had seen one too many glitzy headquarters programs come along; none of them ever lasted long enough to make a difference in anything.

The issue of *implementation strategy* is probably the most crucial key to the success of a quality initiative in any organization. There are more ways to mess it up than there are ways to do it well. The leaders of any change initiative proceed at their peril if they do not give careful thought to the culture of the organization and its reflex responses to change. They must fit the implementation strategy to the realities of the situation facing them.

Simply defined, a program implementation strategy is:

> ***Program Implementation Strategy:***
>
> **a well-conceived approach**
> **that guides the choice of actions,**
> **the timetable of events,**
> **and the roles of the people**
> **involved in a quality improvement program.**

This element of implementation strategy is so crucial to the success of any quality effort that it merits a separate chapter at the end of the book. At this point, however, we can summarize the hallmarks of a well-conceived strategy.

An effective program strategy is an approach that:

- Maintains a customer-focused view of change

- Starts where the organization is, in terms of culture, climate, leadership capability, and image in the eyes of the customers

- Has a strong human element, i.e., a genuine appeal to the heart and a sense of meaning and satisfaction for people

- Proceeds from a sense of great and worthy purpose, not from a bureaucratic tradition of measurement and administration

- Employs all five TQS action elements effectively

- Engages frontline employees early and makes sense to them

- Works with, through, and on behalf of the middle managers, not around them

- Achieves some respectable early successes

- Follows a sequence of events that builds momentum as it goes along

- Works from realistic expectations about how much can be accomplished based on the organization's state of readiness

- Has a strong focus of action, taking on one or just a few big quality opportunities, rather than attempting a wall-to-wall attack on everything at once

- Proceeds from facts, measurements, and evidence, not just "gut feel"; measures key vital signs and reorients itself based on how things are going

- Uses measurements, indicators, and quality assessments constructively to help people see their progress in concrete terms

These last two points, about proceeding from evidence, are especially critical. Many organizations, perhaps most, tend to use what I call "ballistic" program strategies. In other words, they launch the program with great energy and aim it where they think it should go, just as a ballistic missile lifts off its pad, headed toward a fixed target.

However, if the target moves, the ballistic missile has no way to adapt. So it is with many quality programs—they have no built-in means for changing course because they have no way to know whether they are on the course. Without reading the various vital signs to sense the organization's reactions to the effort, they are basically flying blind. Every program strategy needs to have this built-in course correction capability to help it stay on track and adapt to the unforeseen.

This introduction to the philosophy and basic methods of Total Quality Service has been deliberately brief. It is intended as a starting point for thinking about service and quality in the twenty-first century, not as the final word. There is much more to say and there will be much more to learn. Each of the succeeding chapters deals with one of the five action components of the TQS model, as well as with the critically important concept of the spirit of service.

Let's proceed to explore the implications of the TQS way of looking at the world, and see what actions and strategies make sense in each of the five action areas. By the time we complete this once-around excursion, the critical questions should be answered.

Please bear in mind, however, that there is still much to learn about achieving the fifth-dimension level of service quality. As time goes on, we will learn more and more. We will revise some of our views and possibly abandon others altogether. Let's consider Total Quality Service, not as a finished product, but as a prototype for what management thinking will probably become over the next decade or two as we move into the twenty-first century. If it turns out to be mostly correct, it can serve our purposes well.

5

The Spirit of Service: The Source of "The Force"

No ray of sunlight is ever lost, but the green which it awakes into existence needs time to grow; and it is not always granted to the sower to see the harvest. All work that is worth anything is done in faith.

Albert Schweitzer

Many organizations will fail in their quest for total quality service, not because their leaders don't understand the conceptual or technical requirements for achieving it, but because they don't realize that *the heart of the service journey is spiritual rather than mechanical.* They will bureaucratize the whole thing and make it look like every other "program."

Too many quality initiatives are sterile, intellectual, and administrative from start to finish; they don't appeal to the human heart. They're based on a view of the organization as an apparatus rather than a society. They don't start with human energy as the focus of change.

Spirit is the invisible force that moves organizations and people. Spirit in an organization reflects the core values, attitudes and beliefs that shape the way people see themselves, their customers, and the business world, and cause them to behave the way they do.

Mired in their history and habits, many organizations do not have a spirit of service. They have instead a rational spirit, a technological spirit, a financial spirit, a manufacturing spirit, or some other dominant orientation that creates and defines the company's culture—those things deemed to be important and "the way we do things around here."

The journey to total quality service is as much an individual and personal one as an organizational one. If the people don't want to go there, the organization won't go there; ultimately, they *are* the organization. The spirit of service must come alive, stay alive, grow, and flourish if the organization is to leap beyond the bounds of mediocrity.

WHAT IS THE SPIRIT OF SERVICE?

> *The Spirit of Service:*
>
> **An attitude**
> **based on certain values and beliefs**
> **about people, life, and work,**
> **that leads a person to willingly serve others**
> **and take pride in his or her work.**

As customers, we've all seen this spirit of service at times, even if only too rarely. It's an element of giving—a spirit of generosity that makes people give something of themselves in addition to just doing the job. It's going beyond the bare minimum or the standard actions. It's being attentive to the *person* behind the need, and responding to the *person* more than just responding to the need. It's being there psychologically and emotionally as well as being there physically.

It's the automobile mechanic who gives you tips on how to make your tires last longer. It's the waitress who gently steers you away from the chili and suggests something she knows the cook can make edible. It's the nurse who pops in the door just to check on you one more time before you go to sleep. It's the department manager in the store who detours on the way to the office to show you where to find the shoe department. It's the police officer who stops you to let you know your passenger door isn't completely shut, so your kids won't fall out.

It's the travel agent who's been to the place you want to go and gives you some tips for saving money and having a good time there. It's the postal clerk who volunteers a way to get you the lowest rate for sending your package overseas. It's the captain of the cruise ship who stops to flirt with the elderly ladies on the way through the cocktail lounge. And it's lots of little things and big things like that.

It's also the person who works unseen, operating a machine, or analyzing figures, or writing a computer program, or cleaning the building at night—doing his or her job with a sense of commitment and contribution.

The spirit of service lives in almost all human beings to some extent, but it's a highly variable level of energy. People are malleable creatures, and highly reactive to the environments they operate in. Some people can easily find the kind, generous, caring part of themselves all or most of the time, and work steadily with a spirit of service. Others may be less mature, less emotionally resilient, or less self-loving and self-caring. They have a harder time giving of themselves.

The spirit of service comes from very basic personal feelings about self, work, and other people. If you have a high regard for yourself as a human being, and your values include a high regard for other people and their needs and a desire to make your own work meaningful, you probably find it fairly easy to reach out to others and help them with their needs.

But if you have low self-esteem and self-respect, have low maturity, and feel resentful toward other people and the world in general, it's going to be very hard for you to deal with others in a generous, caring way.

WHEN THE FLAME GOES OUT

We all agree that the spirit of service is a wonderful thing. We love being treated by people who genuinely show it. And we dislike being treated by people who seem to have lost it. It's such a powerful force that it can affect people's feelings toward service organizations for a lifetime. Some companies have built reputations for spirit that make them legendary in their industries.

Yet if we all agree the spirit of service is so great, why do so few organizations really have it? If it exists at least latently in all people, why doesn't it come out more fully? What happens to it? Why do so many service people act apathetically or indifferently toward their customers? Why do people in organizations treat their coworkers badly? Why do departments that should be depending on one another for success spend so much of their time feuding and backstabbing?

The answer is that the spirit of service gets killed, or at least severely injured, in most organizations. It gets killed by stress, by pressure, by conflicting priorities, by boredom and repetition, and by simple neglect. People turn inward, away from their customers as human beings, and start dealing with their jobs only from their own self-centered interests.

A young person comes to work willing and able to do a good job and make a contribution. But after a few months of familiarization, the job gets dull, repetitive, boring, and unchallenging. The customers all start to look alike. "Nobody around here seems to care very much," the new worker thinks, "so why should I? I'll just put in my time and collect my pay." So one more person joins the ranks of the vast uncommitted; becomes a nobody, a drone, a person filling a space instead of making a contribution.

A highly committed nurse begins to feel the stress of overwork in an understaffed department, along with pressure and criticism from a toxic supervisor, low pay and poor working conditions, and complaints from patients who are disgruntled with the breakdowns in the quality of care they are experiencing. She becomes fatigued, jaded, angry, and resentful. Every patient now becomes a nuisance, a problem, or another source of harassment rather than a person needing help. She heads for burnout, and her spirit of service heads south.

The new food and beverage manager in the hotel takes her job seriously and wants to deliver a high-quality service experience to the customers. But the new hotel manager is a numbers man who begins driving everybody to get their costs down. He gets pressure from the regional manager to make the numbers look right on the profit and loss statement.

So the food and beverage manager soon forgets about service and becomes a cost manager. Everyone working for her soon detects the same priority, and it shows up in all aspects of the operation. The customers sense a stinginess, a rigidity, a sense of minimalism about the service. There's nothing extra, nothing special, nothing beyond what's on the menu. The hostess is cold and officious. The servers are apathetic and unhelpful. Even the busboys don't seem to care about anything except their paychecks. The flame has gone out.

The term *burnout* has become a standard part of the lexicon of business over the last two decades, but there is only scant evidence that most executives know how to prevent it or even want to. It seems to be one of those "well, that's the way things are" phenomena. Yet employee burnout can have devastating effects on the collective spirit of an organization and on the quality of the service its customers experience.

NatWest Bank's Paul Goodstadt, director of service quality says, "Disgruntled employees are terrorists. They're out there sabotaging the customer's experience by their alienation, anger, and resentment. We must get to them and turn them around. We must get them on our side, and (more importantly) on the side of the customer."

Burnout is clearly a consequence of people working under psychologically intolerable circumstances. In some cases, they burn out because they don't have the emotional maturity or coping skills to handle the normal levels of stress associated with making a living. But more often they burn out because they have to operate in a work environment that takes more *from* them than it gives back.

Many service jobs involve some degree of "emotional labor," that is, the kind of work in which a person's feelings unavoidably get involved. Jobs like emergency room worker, firefighter, police officer, and social worker tend to involve people in situations that tax their emotions. Others may not involve danger or emergency, but may still involve emotional labor.

For example, the person who stands behind the lost-luggage counter at the airport typically doesn't get a lot of good news or praise. Not many customers drop by to tell the person how much they appreciate having their luggage arrive on the same flight they did; they only pay a visit when it doesn't arrive or when it arrives damaged. People who deal with disgruntled or distressed customers almost all the time find it difficult not to take on some of the overt negative emotions directed at them.

Not only do people in those jobs have a higher risk of psychological burnout, but their careers and personal lives begin to suffer unless they get help with their stress load.

Police officers are especially susceptible to job and career burnout and a complete loss of commitment to a spirit of service, especially in crime-prone countries like the United States. Many American cops see so much of the negative side of human behavior and deal with such a disproportionately large sample of the mean and the maladjusted that all human beings start to look like crooks to them. They find it hard to deal with the "ordinary citizen" from a service point of view.

Couple this with rising crime rates, an out-of-control drug problem, the aggressive disdain that many teenagers and inner-city young people often show toward police, and the legal bureaucracy that puts the arrested person back on the street before the officer has completed his or her paperwork on the arrest, and you have a recipe for cynicism and disillusionment.

According to Norman Stamper, executive assistant chief of police for the San Diego Police Department, "Cops typically go through a period of disillusionment somewhere between five and ten years on the job. This period can last quite a long time for some, and less for others. They struggle with the question of whether it's all worth it and whether they believe in what they're doing any more. Those who go through this phase generally go one of two ways. Some of them burn out completely and join the ranks of what I call the 'delinquent subculture,' who continue in psychological pain and experience a sense of isolation or anomie. Others turn back to their profession and recommit. They tend to 're-up.'"

According to Stamper, those few police who burn out completely and become disaffected from their profession and the values behind police work can become potential "bad apples." They carry around a low-grade feeling of frustration and hostility they can't discharge. This can come out in the form of unnecessary force used during arrests or field interviews with suspects, brutality in some cases, and even shootings or crimes committed against innocent citizens. It wrecks their homes and marriages and causes side effects in their work relationships with other officers.

Most police departments provide far too little psychological support even to those patrol officers who are coping adequately. They do little to detect and deal with dangerous levels of burnout on the part of the growing number who have difficulty coping with the negatives of a highly stressful job.

Even employees who don't have high job stress still tend to lose the spirit of service unless something or someone helps them sustain and develop their commitment. They don't burn out; they just fizzle out. But the result is pretty much the same. They sign off psychologically and just become part of the furniture.

CULTURE, CLIMATE, AND EMPLOYEE EMPOWERMENT

What can stop this terrible waste of human energy and potential? What can keep the spirit of service alive? What can kindle, reinforce, and amplify the spirit until it becomes a force for excellence?

There can be only one answer to the question: *leadership*. People who lead with a spirit of service in their own hearts and minds will ultimately have workers who work with that same spirit. People who "manage," or "administrate," or preside, or dominate, or rule will have workers who are self-centered rather than service-centered. Those workers will be too busy looking after their own psychological needs, fighting with one another for status and turf, and trying to guess what the boss wants, to commit their energies to quality.

And the customers will certainly feel the effects of the leadership provided. Customers usually pick up a feeling, an impression of one kind or another, from the employees they contact in doing business with the organization. A spirit of introversion, anger, and resentment will translate to apathy or even hostility toward the customers. A spirit of collective teamwork, caring about one another, and pride in their contribution will translate into genuine interest in and concern for the needs of the customers.

> *Feelings are contagious:*
>
> **The way your employees feel
> is ultimately the way
> your customers will feel.**

Most executives these days recognize the element of "culture" in the management equation, and many strive to understand the cultures of their organizations. Many work hard to build the kind of employee commitment to service that is needed to compete effectively. But many others, frankly, haven't got a clue. They're so preoccupied with time and money and resources that they simply have no time and no place in their hearts for the human element.

I've seen some amazing approaches to motivation taken by organizations in almost 20 years of working with them. I can still be amazed, but I don't think I can be horrified any more. One of the amazing things to see in change efforts is how naive, narrow-minded, or myopic some very senior executives can be about getting people in organizations to go down new roads.

Some of them seem to think that all they have to do is send out a directive: "Ve vill haf kvality around here now!" and everything will change. Some simply decree that all departmental plans will have quality objectives in them—*that* should do the trick. Some simply appoint a "quality executive" and then turn their minds to other things.

Some executives even try to "dictate" a quality commitment by blaming the employees and subordinate managers for the organization's problems. The chief executive of one large organization I worked with—briefly, I'm relieved to say—decided his employees were basically lazy and uncommitted, unlike the good people in their sister division. He decided that all employees should have "passion."

He devised a "passion index" and decreed that all managers and employees should be evaluated on their passion levels, with improvement goals for everyone. I had been asked to work with the organization to help the executives and middle managers figure out their approach to quality. When they told me about the passion index, I didn't know whether to laugh or cry.

It isn't quite that simple. He thought you could use a military approach and "issue" the spirit of service to all employees. He wanted to make people committed and passionate by his edict, not by their acceptance of a meaningful reason to be committed. If he could have had them all inoculated with some magic passion serum, he would have.

But it *is* simple, in another way. Passion and commitment and spirit are simple things. They exist if there is a reason for them to exist. They exist if the work environment expresses the values of quality, service, and concern for the individual. They exist if the vision of the organization calls them forth.

Dr. Charles Garfield, noted speaker and author of *Peak Performance*, concludes that passion arises largely from meaning—meaning in one's work and meaning in one's life. He recounts his experiences as a scientist working for NASA during the early days of the Apollo space program.[1]

> I've never, in my whole career, seen such a group of people so turned on and so committed as the people I worked with during those days. We were all galvanized by the mission: we were going to put a man on the moon.
>
> People worked incredible hours, made remarkable personal sacrifices, and gave the best they had in them. Many of them had an almost glassy-eyed intensity about the way they went about it. I felt an energy, a passion, that I've seldom sensed among working people anywhere before or since.

Garfield believed that the clarity and perceived value of the mission presented to them was the primary factor that called forth the tremendous amount of energy and commitment they gave. He later developed this notion as a key idea behind what he called *peak performance*, the state of affairs in which a person gives his or her total energies to something and reaches remarkable levels of achievement by the sheer focus of energy and belief. Peak performance, Garfield believes, is possible when you know your mission.

I've come to refer to this phenomenon as the "Apollo effect," because of everything the Apollo project seemed to mean to Americans. It meant a great and worthwhile challenge, something so new and so spectacular as to dazzle the imagination, and it was something to be proud of. Unfortunately, in the two decades following the Apollo landing, American pride took some hard hits. The Viet Nam war, the Iranian hostage crisis, the decline of American dominance in world markets, and the loss of quality leadership to the Japanese, all caused great consternation. Americans began to doubt their own ideas of their legendary role as the thinkers, leaders, and doers of the world.

Now and then another Apollo comes along, and with it can come the possibilities for people to feel committed again, to feel good about being involved in something, and to feel worthwhile.

Carole Presley, Senior Vice President for Marketing at Federal Express Corporation, refers to this extra energy and commitment as "discretionary effort." According to Presley,

> Each employee obligates himself or herself to a certain level of mandatory effort as part of accepting the job. That's what the employer can expect in return for the wages paid. But if the employee is involved—turned on, committed, and feeling part of something important, then he or she adds a certain amount of discretionary effort to the job. This is the something extra that comes from belonging and believing.
>
> There is no way management can demand, extract, or coerce this discretionary effort. It is the employee's to give. One of the competitive edge factors for our organization, I believe, is this margin of extra energy FedEx people give. We in management work hard to earn and sustain that extra contribution and to make people feel they get something back for it.

The chief executive who invented the passion index didn't understand that passion comes from meaning. Sheer undirected energy, even if you can generate it, has little value. As the early twentieth-century satirist Ambrose Bierce observed, "a fanatic is someone who redoubles his effort when he has lost sight of his aim."

There is a great deal of talk these days among management experts about *employee empowerment*. This promises to be yet another slogan in the long parade of good ideas that few people take the trouble to understand. Many executives have very ambivalent feelings about empowering frontline employees. "It's great in theory," they seem to be saying, "but you have to be careful. You can't let people run around loose, or they might mess things up."

The passion issue is inseparably welded to the empowerment issue. It's hard for people to work with commitment, passion, and a spirit of service in their hearts when their leaders don't trust them and overcontrol them. Many executives seem to think that empowering people just means turning the control knob to give them a tiny bit more freedom of action in certain well-defined situations.

We know for certain that most workers can handle much more authority than they typically have, if they possess the information, knowledge, and training to deal with it. Of course it's foolish to give a person wide discretion on pricing if that person knows nothing about costs, competitors' prices, or customer expectations. But armed with that knowledge, that person may be able to do the job as well as or better than a manager who has the same information.

Many a nurse has "saved the bacon" for a doctor who made a mistake on a patient's prescription or treatment protocol because she knew almost as much about the situation as the doctor. The doctor may have had the in-depth theoretical knowledge, but the nurse knew quite enough to catch the error or misjudgment.

It's interesting to wonder how many frontline workers know just about as much as their supervisors about the key elements of the group's work. How many of them could actually make their own decisions, with just about the same success rate as their supervisors?

Getting people "turned on" isn't difficult at all. All you need is a clear and meaningful vision of what the organization must accomplish, a strategy for the quality journey, a clear set of values to guide the way, and a form of leadership that trusts people enough to give them the power to work passionately. On the other hand, maybe it's not so easy, in view of the fact that many executives seem to have trouble with one or more of those elements.

Robert Galvin, ex-CEO of Motorola, and the man responsible for that organization's highly regarded achievements in manufacturing quality, believes workers are largely victimized by expectation levels that are lower than they really could be. He feels that they themselves and their managers have learned to accept levels of quality and performance that are not worthy of their talents.

"Expectation levels in the United States are almost universally insufficient by an order of magnitude," according to Galvin. "People have yet to realize that they can run the three-minute mile, rather than the four-minute mile, in virtually everything they do. At Motorola we have come to the realization that if it's imaginable, it's do-able. Furthermore, unless we aspire to the accomplishment of the imaginable, we won't accomplish it."[2]

Learned expectations play a crucial role in the levels of performance and commitment of which people are capable. One of the reasons most third-world countries are stuck where they are is that their leaders and people suffer from diminished expectations. In my travels through countries like China, Mexico, India, Turkey, and Argentina, it has been apparent that they have little or no awareness of the kinds of hard work, individual enterprise, and quality of outcomes that people in the developed countries consider normal.

People in iron-curtain countries typically have no idea how hard their counterparts work in the industrialized countries. Their expectations for a material standard of living are many levels lower than their counterparts take for granted. They have no outside reference for quality. They've only seen the shoes and clothes and houses and health care and education available in their own countries. They don't even know what's possible.

The same holds true to a great extent in all organizations, including those in the developed world. As Galvin points out, most leaders and workers in a given organization haven't really looked outward to see what's possible elsewhere. As a result, they take whatever level of quality they currently experience as the norm.

The syndrome of limited expectations is reminiscent of the way animal trainers tame young elephants. When the elephant is very young, they fasten a chain around its leg and tether it to a strong stake driven firmly in the ground. After a period of pulling and fighting against the chain, the elephant eventually gives up and accepts that it is a prisoner. As the animal grows older, the trainers can substitute a lightweight rope tied to any convenient stake in the ground; the elephant never again tries to break away.

As organizational creatures, we human beings are sometimes like that elephant. Once we accept a view of what can and can't be done, we work within the bounds of those expectations. Organizational life seems defined more in terms of what can't be done than in terms of what can. It is a critical role of leadership to help people *see* their real possibilities and raise their expectations of themselves, both individually and collectively.

EXECUTIVE EMPOWERMENT: THE WILL TO LEAD

Much is being written today about the need to empower frontline employees, but empowerment is not just an issue at the bottom of the organization. When it comes to making the total commitment required for customer centering and breakaway service, *some of the least empowered people may be the ones in charge*.

Many executives are not nearly as powerful and free to act as those watching them believe. Just as an elected political leader makes a lot of compromises along the way to the position, so a corporate executive comes to accept certain organizational realities and constraints. The typical organizational process for socializing executives and the standard role expectations created for them can be highly confining.

By the time many managers become executives they have turned into automatons, trapped in corporate straightjackets—conditioned to behave and view the world in certain ways and to function within narrowly defined parameters and prescribed roles. It is a rare individual who can truly transcend the traditions, roles, and rules of executive life and assert an original view of the way things should be.

This is one reason so many members of the general public tend to view executives as overpaid empty suits, filled by interchangeable old men who really have nothing original to offer. In too many cases, they are right. Many large organizations virtually run themselves; it is questionable how much added value their executives contribute. Nicholas II, czar of Russia, is said to have commented on his deathbed, "You know, I never really ran Russia. It was 10,000 clerks who ran Russia."

Whereas some executives are truly free people, unfettered by the roles and expectations placed on them by others, probably most are highly conditioned to some extent to be "standard executives." A fully conditioned, typically male executive, at least in Western organizations, has some, most, or all of the following tendencies:

- to maximize productivity and profitability on a quarterly basis.
- to be served rather than to be of service.
- to play by the rules.
- to not voice ideas that challenge traditional ways.
- to not make any significant waves or back any losers; to trust himself more than others.
- to use staff to ward off contact with "undesirables," i.e., employees and customers.
- to rely on his own expertise.
- to hoard information and knowledge.
- to build departmental empires.
- to give feedback, not to receive it.
- to emphasize strengths and not admit weaknesses.
- to believe information rather than intuition.
- to maintain the company's rituals.
- to appreciate the trappings of power and status.
- to believe that the majority of the knowledge and competence of the organization resides at the top.
- to assume his expertise gives him some divine right to govern.
- to give orders rather than to listen.
- to protect the status quo.

Executives like these are defined more by the job than by themselves and what they bring to it. For executives who have made it to the top of the mountain, it's tough to see down to the bottom, to where the employees and customers are. It's even more difficult to hear the customers' or employees' voices accurately because there are so many intermediaries who screen and filter information and distort the executive's construction of reality.

Edwin Crego, managing director of the TQS Group, Inc., believes that executives who want to be service leaders have to throw off the bonds of their own roles and conditioning. According to Crego,

> To liberate those in the middle and at the bottom of the organization to make the transformation to become customer-centered, the executive must first liberate himself. He must become a pathfinder—a true believer. If he is to champion the cause of the customer, he must find it within himself to accept the undertaking as an article of faith.

During an interview with the chief executive of a major corporation, we asked what his priorities for the business were. He named market share, profitability, cost containment, technical leadership, and (oh, yes) customer service. He mentioned customer service proudly, probably because he perceived us as the "customer guys." He thought he was following the recipe exactly—providing top management involvement, commitment, leadership, and elevating customer service to a major priority.

However, we knew then that this particular quality-improvement effort was in troubled waters. Why? Because service quality cannot survive as just one priority among others. It then becomes a competing priority and will be set aside when push comes to shove and there's a downturn in the organization's economic fortunes or results are not achieved immediately.

For service quality or quality in general to make a difference, it must be viewed as the driving force—the enabling factor for achieving the top priorities of the company. The best-run companies have made this commitment. They have strategically decided to live (or die) by quality. They know that quality is what drives everything. It defines the culture—what is important and how things are done.

The conflicting priorities issue is so pervasive that some companies never get around to service-quality improvement. Many top managers have two lists in their heads, a "hard" list and a "soft" list. Issues on the hard list are items like profit, productivity, costs, market share, shareholder value, and financial ratios. Subjects such as service quality, human resource development, and customer research are on the soft list.

Many managers take pride in keeping their eye on the ball and doing the things on the hard list. Soft-list items can either be delegated or, occasionally, temporarily elevated into a priority status. Executives of some companies are psychologically incapable of getting around to the soft lists. They are the prisoners of their past.

People who work with quality programs say repeatedly that executive commitment is essential to success, or at least that the organization can achieve much more with their commitment than without it. Some executives understand that and some don't. Some are sensitive to the issue but haven't a clue what they should be doing about it. And a few others personally take up the gauntlet and make quality their own mission as well as the mission of the organization. They decide not just to allow the quality revolution to go on, but to lead it.

INTERNAL SERVICE: THE KEY TO HIDDEN PROFIT

Everything you can say about the spirit of service toward the organization's ultimate customer you can also say about service to the internal customers—service within. The most often-quoted statement from *Service America!* is:

> *Internal Service:*
>
> **If you're not serving the customer,
> your job is to serve someone who is.**

We should have the same spirit of service toward each other as coworker customers that we have toward the "real" customers. Those who serve others within the organization need the same clarity of purpose, sense of contribution, and willingness to serve that the so-called customer-contact people have.

At a time when organizations need to work harder than ever to compete and succeed, wasting internal resources is becoming increasingly intolerable. It's no longer enough to do the basic work of delivering customer value in an excellent way. The next important gains in organizational effectiveness will be on the internal-service scene. The lost energy, wasted resources, and failure of new ideas that most organizations have come to accept as "normal" will no longer be acceptable. Quality of internal service is emerging as just as important as quality in the value package delivered to the ultimate customer.

When the spirit of service fades and dies out in an organization, internal service also suffers. As customers of one another, we get the service we demand. If we tolerate poor service from other departments, and they tolerate it from us, we end up with a collusion of mediocrity. It becomes a round-robin of:

The Cycle of Mediocrity:

I can't,
because he didn't,
because she doesn't,
because he won't,
because they never...

and on and on it goes.

We all need to learn to be better internal customers as well as better internal servers. We need to speak up for our needs, demand the service we're entitled to, not accept brush-offs or excuses, and ask our internal suppliers why they can't do what we need done.

Sometimes internal service departments complain that their customers refuse to follow their procedures. "They're always trying to beat the system" is the accusation. In many cases, beating the system may represent healthy, goal-striving behavior in the face of a system that doesn't deliver value. Ideally, the system should be designed so that it becomes the most effective option available to the customer department for getting its needs met.

SERVICE LEADERSHIP AT ALL LEVELS

There is no escaping the fact that the spirit of service in an organization flourishes or dies depending on the actions of its leaders. If they can't provide the vision and the values, the impulse for change, the guidance and emphasis, and the chance for people to surpass themselves, then the organization is doomed to mediocrity. It is doomed to a spirit of "doing the day's work," not a spirit of service.

But if they can indeed provide the leadership—never mind about "management"—then ordinary people can do extraordinary things.

Theories about leadership have appeared and disappeared for many years, but few of them have focused on service as a guiding principle.

It's time we looked at *service leadership*, that is, leadership with a service focus:

Service Leadership:

Service to the customers,
Service to the employees,
Service to the organization.

Service leadership will have to be different from the old-style, militaristic, "kick-in-the-ass" leadership, the kind that got things done and prided itself in "not winning any popularity contests." Service leaders will *have to be popular*, because they must call forth the most perishable of human emotions: enthusiasm, the desire to make things better, and pride in one's work.

One of the few things we know for sure about leadership is that you can't legislate, direct, or coerce human feeling and human commitment. Just as the executive's passion index was a doomed idea from the start, so is any notion that people will be committed just because an executive or manager says they should. This is what training expert Robert Mager calls the "you really oughta wanna" syndrome. Those who don't know how to reach the human heart with vision and meaning just end up haranguing the employees and trying to make them feel guilty about not having passion.

Recently, IBM chief executive John Akers made a series of statements in the press that telegraphed a profound sense of frustration on his part and signaled what may be the start of a crisis in leadership that will take that company years to resolve. Exasperated with IBM's financial performance and the steady decline in its market share and customer acceptance of its products, Akers lashed out at his managers in an internal memorandum. He berated them for lacking the leadership, commitment to hard work, and willingness to manage aggressively. His comments went into the company's worldwide electronic mail system and showed up on the monitor of every middle manager's computer in the company. It also found its way into the hands of the press, who had a field day with it.

Not satisfied with berating his managers, Akers heaved another brickbat, this one aimed at IBM employees and this one expressed directly to the press. He rebuked the employees for not working hard enough. He told them in no uncertain terms that IBM's number one priority was generating the proper return on equity for its shareholders and if they knew what was good for them they'd get busy.

This series of messages astounded many IBM watchers: "What happened to the old idea that IBM means service?" "What about the concept of quality?" "What about the focus on customer value as the key to our success?" Tom Watson, Sr., may have made a revolution or two in his grave at about that time. It's hard to escape the nagging feeling that Akers was indicting himself and the company's top leadership as he accused the managers and employees of causing the company's failure.

Did he send out "E-mail" messages and press releases during the growth years, talking about how the managers and employees did such a good job? Or was the assumption that the company's success resulted from wise and forward-looking management?

Here is the chief executive of one of the oldest and proudest American corporations, known for its values and commitment to its customers, seemingly in a state of frustration bordering on despair. It's hard to conceive of the possibility that "Big Blue" could be falling prey to the dinosaur syndrome that befell Sears, General Motors, Ford, Chrysler, and other legendary giants of the American business scene, but it's possible.

More and more organizations are feeling the need for a new leadership. One reason a number of Western corporations were caught off guard by the Japanese quality assault, particularly American firms, was that Western management approaches stagnated for several decades, while Japanese approaches evolved to meet the needs of the times.

It's not that American management declined or got worse, it's just that it failed to get better. It got stuck at the level of the sixties, when the Harvard financial management gospel came fully into its own. Newly minted MBAs came out in droves with degrees in finance and calculators in their pockets. While American executives and their European counterparts were pursuing production efficiency and quarterly earnings growth, Japanese firms were thinking in terms of annual financial performance and five- and ten-year plans based on market penetration and market share.

Now Western business organizations desperately need a new dynamism, a new thrust, a new ethic of *service leadership* to displace the old ethic of financial management. (A later chapter explores the components needed for this new model of leadership.)

One of the Latin names used to refer to the Pope is *servus servorum*, or "the servant of servants." Many famous leaders in history have taken this service attitude in influencing others. People like Winston Churchill, Mohandas Gandhi, Albert Schweitzer, John Kennedy, and Martin Luther King have won the admiration of people because they gave of themselves. They led with a spirit of service, not a spirit of control or domination.

More recently Mother Teresa, the Sisters-of-Mercy nun who has worked in countries like India, serving the poorest of the poor, has been recognized as a service leader. With little authority except that of moral conviction, she has had a huge impact on the lives of many poor people and on the thinking of many others. She expresses the essence of the ancient Greek concept of *agape*, which means a spirit of unconditional love and concern for others. Her vision and values have inspired many, as has her willingness to engage in hard physical labor even at an advanced age.

This is the kind of leadership needed for the twenty-first century. It is the kind of leadership that organizations need at all levels, from the boardroom to the front counter. It may sound too saintly to be possible, but there are more and more examples of executives and managers willing and able to provide it. And it emerges even from people who have no formal entitlement to lead. They lead because they believe in what they are doing and they influence others to embrace those beliefs as well.

6

The Psyche of Your Customer: Finding the "Invisible Truth"

> *It is a capital mistake*
> *to theorise in advance of the facts.*
>
> Sherlock Holmes

Do you remember the eye test you took years ago—the one with the card the optometrist showed you with a big circle crammed full of colored dots of different sizes? All of the dots were one main color, but set into the middle was an arrangement of dots of a slightly different color that formed a large number or other recognizable pattern. You had to see the big number 8, or whatever it was, to pass the eye test.

Knowing your customer is like passing that eye test. Customer perception is the big circle and the little dots represent the various features of the total experience you or your competitors provide. The trick is to see the figure hidden among the dots—the subtle but powerful organizing idea that captures the essence of value for the customer. This is the "invisible truth." It is the unexpressed message that explains what they really want to buy and why they would want to do business with your organization.

The Market & Customer Research component of the TQS model is the crucial key to learning what customer value is and how the customer expects to receive it. *It is the key to the invisible truth.*

Discovering this invisible truth is no simple process. It requires the right approach. It requires asking the right questions in the right way.

And it requires a seasoned insight that enables you to see the number hidden among the dots. You have to understand the difference between data and answers.

And, most importantly, you have to understand the distinction between features and benefits, which is the same as the distinction between the objective product characteristics of what you offer to the customer and the subjective value he or she derives from experiencing it.

Case in point: several hundred thousand people each year buy quarter-inch drills from hardware stores. Very few of them want quarter-inch drills: they want quarter-inch *holes*.

Millions of people pay to have gas and electricity delivered to their homes. They don't want gas or electricity. They want what the gas or electricity does for them. The reason one person buys a small Honda and another person buys a Mercedes lies not in the products themselves but in the *meanings* those products have in the lives of the respective buyers. It is those meanings we have to discover—the hidden truth behind the objective characteristics.

Charles Revson, chief executive of the multibillion-dollar Revlon cosmetics firm, summed up the idea of *subjective value* best in explaining his firm's products. "When it leaves the factory, it's lipstick," he said. "But when it crosses the counter in the department store, it's hope."

Many people look at customer research data and see only dots. Those with the ability to exercise creative perception and examine the data from the point of view of customer value will be able to unscramble the customer's code. They will see the big number 8—the invisible truth staring right at them. This unique insight will enable them to define a *customer value model* that is valid and distinctive. That model will provide the basis for formulating a breakaway strategy for winning and keeping the customer's business.

MARKET MYOPIA: HOW LITTLE WE KNOW ABOUT OUR CUSTOMERS

> *Learning:*
>
> **The biggest obstacle to learning anything is believing you already know it.**

The longer people work in a certain industry or area of competition, the greater the likelihood they don't really understand their customers—although they certainly believe they do. The state of practice in customer research, especially in so-called service industries, is fairly dismal.

Although a few outstanding firms devote intensive efforts to discovering and understanding customer needs, most do relatively little. Many do nothing at all to get inside their customers' minds and find out what they're thinking and feeling.

Many organizations will never see the invisible truth because they fail to interpret the subtle signals their customers are giving them. They are victimized by a kind of customer myopia with regard to customer contact. They can't see beyond the ordinary, repetitive sales transactions with their customers to sense the subjective factors that lead people to choose in the ways they do. They don't look beyond their noses when they make decisions about what to offer the customer and how to present it.

There is also a kind of organizational arrogance that makes some business executives and managers automatically assume they know what customers want or what's best for them. They want to push their idea of the product on the customer rather than discern truth and implement it. This happens in many industries. The hotel industry, for example, is notorious for this.

Over the past decade, the major hotel chains have engaged in an ever escalating "amenities war." From TVs in the bathroom, special shampoos, lotions and shoe horns to bathrobes, health clubs, and in-room VCR—the battle rages on.

The problem is it's being fought with very little consideration for what customers actually want or expect from their lodging experience. A recent *Wall Street Journal* survey of over 40 frequent business travelers found that they placed little value on in-room bars/refrigerators, hotel health clubs, and televisions in bathrooms. They did, however, place high value on the simple pleasures such as a quiet, nonsmoking room, direct-dial phones, and free morning newspaper delivery.

This research suggests that the secret to success in service quality for hotels might be to do an extraordinary job on the basics. Many hotels instead appear to be committed to delivering the extras as the right path to the customer's heart. But we know for sure that the extras don't buy you anything if you don't do the basics well.

Hotels are not the only ones doing things that don't matter. Many organizations are obsessed with performing against standards that are not relevant to the customer. Several years ago, a large American insurance company embarked on a quality initiative. Rather than start with customer perceptions, however, the executives started with measurable standards for processing policies. They had set a "quality standard" that dictated a five-day turnaround for issuing new policies. They implemented rigorous procedures and spent several millions of dollars to get the organization to perform to that standard. They achieved great success in meeting the standard.

However, when we interviewed agents who sold the policies and people who bought them, we couldn't find a single person who cared whether the policy arrived in five days. They didn't care how long it took, because the agent's verbal commitment was binding and no one was in a hurry to get the bill. And besides, very few people understood the policies in any case. *The company was doing the wrong thing—very well.*

HOW POORLY WE LISTEN TO OUR CUSTOMERS

As mentioned earlier, during the course of a presentation recently to a group of about 150 fitness instructors from exercise centers all over the United States, I asked for a show of hands in answer to the question, "How many of you work at a center that regularly surveys its members to find out how they feel about working out there?" Out of the whole group, about five people raised their hands.

The center where I work out doesn't have any customer-sensing process either—and it should. In the exercise rooms and locker rooms I frequently hear other members complaining about the loud rock music from the sound system, the state of disrepair of many of the machines, the operating hours of the snack bar, and on and on.

I got about the same statistical response when I asked a group of about 100 company personnel directors how many surveyed their employees regularly to find out how they felt about working there. A half-dozen or so responded that they did.

Apparently, many people want to remain in a comfortable state of ignorance. "If I go around asking the customers how they feel about things," they seem to think, "they'll start complaining and I'll have to do something about it." That's exactly the point. The purpose of asking customers how they're experiencing your offering is to find out how you can improve it and keep their business or get more of it.

The chief executive of a major furniture retailing firm installed toll-free numbers for customers who wanted to give feedback about the products they bought or about their purchase experiences. He directed that the toll-free lines be widely publicized to the customers. In the first two weeks, the lines were completely jammed with thousands upon thousands of calls from irate customers. The senior executives were devastated to discover the levels of dissatisfaction expressed.

The lesson, of course, is that the dissatisfaction was there all the time. Asking the customers for feedback only brought it out into the open. Although psychologically traumatizing, this process must ultimately be healthy, because at least they can begin to respond to the concerns and focus their quality improvement efforts on worthwhile results.

Customer Feedback:

**On the whole,
knowing is better than not knowing.**

Ford Motor Company experienced a similar deluge of customer feedback years ago, when it announced its ill-fated and short-lived "No Unhappy Owners" campaign. Presented with great fanfare in Sunday-afternoon TV commercials, the campaign vowed that the company would make sure there were no unhappy owners of Ford products.

Monday morning, the dealers were inundated with unhappy owners. People took the commercials seriously and brought in their cars for attention. A latent problem had at least been brought to the surface, but unfortunately it was at the expense of considerable embarrassment to the company. What began as a marketing campaign accidentally became a customer research project.

The irrepressible Ed Koch, during his terms as Mayor of New York, made a habit of personally soliciting feedback from citizens about his performance as mayor. His "How'm I doin'?" shouted across the street to passersby who recognized him became his personal trademark. One has to have a great deal of fortitude to ask for feedback about the job of mayor in any city, and asking New Yorkers is tantamount to psychological self-abuse. Yet Koch believed it was important to hear from the people on the street.

HOW NOT TO DO MARKET RESEARCH

Unfortunately, traditional market research methods can conceal as much as they reveal about the customer. Most of the generally accepted market research methods have come from the consumer products industry, and are not well suited to discovering the invisible truth about the customer. They tend to focus on products rather than on customers. This makes it more difficult to get at subjective factors that may play a critical role in purchase decisions, beyond the realm of simple "product" characteristics.

For example, much of the market research dollar is still invested in studies to determine whether there is a general market need or demand for a particular type of product or service. This type of research usually entails collecting reams and reams of data on the demographics, consumption patterns, and competition within a given marketplace or segment and then trying to match customers with products.

And much of what passes for *qualitative* consumer research is little more than testing hypotheses about product characteristics. The limitation with this form of research is that it begins with the answer—the already defined product or service package—and then asks the questions. Typical questions include

- Which product would you choose: A, B, or C?

- Which package is most attractive to you?

- What color for the product is most appealing to you?

- Which of these advertising campaigns—X, Y, or Z—is most appealing to you?

By getting these answers, researchers can decide how to refine an existing package or to bring something to market. However, they get no information on what the customers would like to see in the package. The customer doesn't have a chance to say "I don't like A, B, or C; I'd like to have X." If you've got a product or service that has not been designed according to a valid customer preference in the first place, all the positioning studies in the world won't help to get you into the customer's pocket or purse.

Due to the increasing importance of service quality, more and more organizations are gathering customer satisfaction data. Methods for this range from customer comment cards in hotel rooms and restaurants to telephone surveys using structured questionnaires. These "customer report cards" commonly take the form of scaled questionnaires. Typical examples are hotel, restaurant or airline satisfaction surveys in which the customers rate levels of their satisfaction on factors such as courtesy of front desk personnel, cleanliness of room, temperature of food served, appearance of employees, speed of room service delivery, and the like.

Although this report card information can be useful, it is really a form of *measurement*; it is not customer research. It tells you how well you're doing, not what you should be doing or what's actually important to the customer. A remarkable number of these customer report cards are based on nothing more than a marketing person's best guess about what should be measured. Many of them have no valid basis in customer perception and no supporting evidence that the factors they measure have anything to do with capturing the customer's business or building repurchase preference.

Let's look at some better approaches to customer research and find out how they can lead us to that invisible truth. Let's see how a discovery-based approach helps to get beyond product characteristics and discern the subjective value to which we must appeal if we want to win and keep the customer's business.

THE CUSTOMER'S PERCEPTION
OF VALUE: WHERE IT ALL BEGINS

We've agreed that the critical goal of finding the invisible truth is to learn what factors the customer *values* most of all. What are the elements of value in his or her perception of doing business with you or your competitors? And the second goal is to discover, if possible, any unexploited opportunities to add value to the experience and thereby gain higher customer approval or competitive advantage.

To put those two goals into perspective, we can think of customer value as following a kind of hierarchy similar to psychologist Abraham Maslow's famous hierarchy of human needs. We have a *hierarchy of customer value* with four levels (as suggested in Figure 6-1).

Basic—the absolutely essential attributes of the experience, either tangible or intangible; without them, there is no point in trying to do business. The new car will be properly assembled, finished, and prepared for delivery. The food will be edible and the place will be clean. The hotel room will be clean and properly appointed. The product ordered through the mail will be as promised in the catalog.

Expected—the associated attributes of the experience that the customer has come to take for granted as part of general business practice. Someone will explain the features of the car. The restaurant will have a reasonable selection of menu items and reasonable prices. The hotel will have a coffee shop, reasonable bell service, and a reliable system for guest messages. The mail-order firm will accept returns if the customer is not fully satisfied with the product.

The Hierarchy of Customer Value

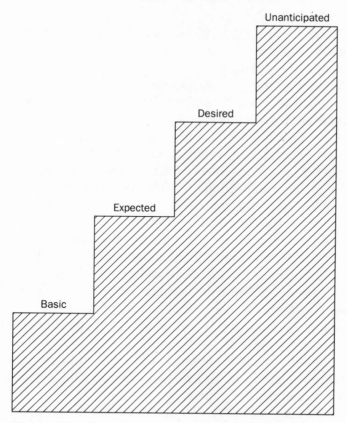

Figure 6–1   The Hierarchy of Customer Value.

Desired—attributes the customer doesn't necessarily expect, but knows about and appreciates if the experience includes them. Someone will give helpful suggestions about caring for the car. The servers will suggest special items or do special favors to make the meal more pleasant. The front desk people can provide information about local tourist activities or help with special problems. The mail-order firm pays the shipping cost for the customer to return the unwanted item.

Unanticipated—"surprise" attributes that add value for the customer beyond his or her typical desires or expectations. The car salesperson delivers the car to the customer's home or office. The restaurant manager passes through the dining room with fresh baked cookies, giving them out free to the customers. The hotel clerk offers the guest a glass of juice to enjoy while the clerk is taking care of the registration. Someone from the mail order firm phones the customer to ask how he or she liked the product.

This hierarchy conveys some obvious points about customer value. First, it tells you that you have to perform well on the basic and expected levels just to have the right to do business with the customer. A clean restaurant and good-quality food are not elements of competitive advantage: they are a minimum requirement to compete. The basic and expected attributes are merely your ticket to the game.

Differentiation from your competitors and competitive advantage set in only when you can do something better and the customer values the difference. If the competitor's hotel rooms are dirty, the TV sets don't work, and the elevators malfunction, then you have a competitive advantage if yours are satisfactory. But if the competitor does those things properly, then you have to look for advantage higher up the ladder of value.

If you only do the basics well, your customer will see you as poor, unless, of course, no competitor gets any higher on the hierarchy.

If you do the basics and the expected well, your customer will see you as mediocre, i.e., just about satisfactory but nothing special.

If you do the basics, the expected, and the desired well, the customer will begin to favor you—if you do them better than your competitors.

And if you surprise the customer with the unanticipated, you will have a special place in his or her heart. You have the opportunity for a breakaway competitive position.

However, keep in mind that the unanticipated, once familiar, becomes the anticipated. It's easy to fall from grace once you have the customer conditioned to a certain level of experience. And it's easy for your competitors to imitate many of the extras you can create. The chocolate-chip cookie on the pillow in the hotel room soon becomes an expected part of the experience. If it's missing, there's a problem.

Good customer research enables you to discern the responses and values of your customers that can help you function at the desired and unanticipated levels. Assuming you are already doing an outstanding job at the basic and expected levels, you can create an appeal that will cause the customer to prefer your organization. And if you can identify one or more attributes of value that your competitors can't readily provide, you can establish an element of sustainable competitive advantage.

MOMENTS OF TRUTH AND CYCLES OF SERVICE

We need to adopt a slightly different vocabulary to talk about customer value in service businesses. In the past we have learned to equate value with the *objective characteristics* of tangible products. The car has a number of desirable features; it has certain performance characteristics. The bone china is guaranteed not to chip. The garment will not shrink. The camera has automatic focus, a shutter speed of $\frac{1}{1000}$ second, and automatic exposure control. The coal has a certain sulfur content.

These are easily measurable, easily observable, and therefore easily quantifiable characteristics. The product–manufacturing tradition of Western management has led to a definition of quality as an objective, intrinsic characteristic of something tangible.

However, when the "product" is a "service," the element of quality changes profoundly. The quality is not in a tangible product, but rather in the *customer's reaction to an experience*. Even if the experience includes a physical "deliverable" of some sort, the essence of the total value delivered depends solely on the customer's mental and emotional state resulting from the experience. Ultimately, service is all about feelings.

> *Feelings:*
>
> **The end result
> of a service experience
> is a feeling.**

This difference has caused confusion for many executives and managers, who have been left grasping for tangible indicators they can measure and count. They tend to want something objective, something uncontaminated by the messy "human element." They'd like to be able to sit back and manage a service business based on good, hard, tangible measures they can count on, not a bunch of fuzzy feeling-data about customers.

We have to become much more comfortable with the idea of *subjective value* in business, and we have to learn to measure it. That isn't really such a difficult thing once you begin to think about it carefully—and differently.

To get at this issue of subjective value, we need a way to describe, analyze, and assess the quality of the customer's experience. We need to identify the basic elements of customer experience and then find quality indicators that tell us how well we're delivering that experience.

We do have such a basic element of service quality: the concept of the "moment of truth." This term, originally taken from bullfighting and made popular by Jan Carlzon, chief executive of Scandinavian Airlines, pinpoints the customer's fundamental experience: an event at which the customer perceives quality.

The Moment of Truth:

**Any episode
in which the customer
comes into contact with the organization
and gets an impression of its service.**

Actually, the term *moment of truth* was first used in this context by Swedish management consultant Richard Normann, who suggested it to Carlzon. Carlzon found the term highly useful in getting his quality message across to the SAS employees. According to Normann, "the business organization doesn't really exist in the mind of the customer the way it does in the minds of the executives or the people who work there. The customer doesn't go around all day thinking about your organization. You only exist for the customer when he has some sort of contact with you, either directly or indirectly.

"When the customer comes into contact with an employee of your organization, or calls on the telephone, or receives something in the post, or walks into your building, or whatever, it's a moment of truth. He knows nothing of your departments and systems, your computers, your hard-working people or your harried executives. He only knows what you do for him at that moment of truth. And that's the only thing he has to go on to grade the quality of your product."

Once you start thinking in terms of moments of truth, you can begin to reorient your thinking about quality—away from the work processes and outward toward those many episodes that comprise your customers' experience with your organization. By defining the moments of truth and by focusing particularly on the ones most critical to the customer's perception of quality, you can see things as the customer sees them. The moment of truth must be your focus for defining, delivering, and measuring quality.

The old slogan " TLC," which used to mean "tender loving care," now has a new meaning as well. It means:

T.L.C. = THINK LIKE A CUSTOMER.

Everybody in the organization, from the highest executive to the front-line employee, needs to have the skill of "other-worldliness," i.e., the orientation to understand and really appreciate how things look and feel to the customer.

After doing a job for a very long time, a person can no longer have a naive view of that job in terms of how it affects the customer. Airline ticket agents know the ins and outs of the airline system but their customers don't. Agents tend to take many things for granted. They don't get upset over things that upset customers. They don't apply the same priorities that customers do. To really appreciate the customer's experience, they need to try to set aside their knowledge and expertise and ask themselves "If I were the customer, how would I feel about this?" "Would that explanation satisfy my needs?" "Does this procedure make sense to me?" and "Do I understand what's going to happen to me?"

The same applies to most skilled service people. Medical people need to stop and think like customers now and then. So do bankers, insurance people, computer sales people, hotel operators, and everybody else.

One of the finest dentists I ever had treat me was an Army dentist, during my term as an Army officer. He said, "I think every dentist should have his teeth worked on two or three times a year by another dentist, just to be reminded what it's like."

An even more customer-valid definition of the service experience is the *cycle of service*. Customers don't see themselves as buying individual moments of truth, but rather getting needs met by going through a whole process from beginning to end (see Figure 6-2). A cycle of service is:

The Cycle of Service:

**The complete sequence of moments of truth
a customer experiences
in getting some need met.**

A very commonplace cycle of service would be going to the theater to see a movie. The cycle begins at some identifiable point of customer experience, such as seeing an advertisement for the film or talking to a friend who recommends it. Arriving at the theater, trying to find a parking place, standing in line to buy tickets, and waiting in line to enter the theater are all moments of truth.

As you trace the other moments of truth such as visiting the rest room, standing in line for refreshments, and searching for a seat, you begin to realize that the experience includes much more than just sitting in a seat watching a movie.

The key point to recognize is that *all* of these moments of truth contribute to the customer's *total perception* of quality, so far as the theater is concerned. If the movie itself is very enjoyable but the place is dirty, parking is a problem, the theater is located in a dangerous neighborhood, or noisy teenagers interfere with the enjoyment of the other customers, the theater has quality problems.

The cycle of service diagram gives us an obvious way to start looking at subjective quality: event by event in the cycle. For each moment of truth we can identify the types of experience that customers con-

The Cycle of Service

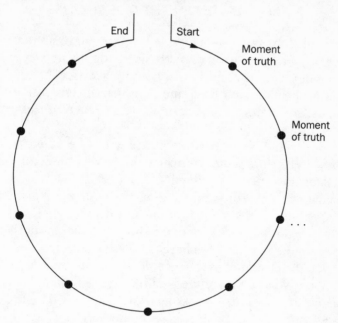

Figure 6–2   The Cycle of Service.

sider satisfactory, unsatisfactory, and superior. Then we can engineer that experience systematically to produce superior results. We can also analyze the cycle of service as a whole and identify overall characteristics we must manage in order to deliver a quality experience. A later chapter dwells more specifically on analyzing moments of truth and cycles of service.

The cycle of service diagram applies equally well to just about any kind of managed customer experience: a hospital stay, a hotel stay, a vacation cruise, having a pizza delivered, getting a haircut, ordering a product from a mail-order firm, going to the post office, having surgery, or any of thousands of other possibilities.

And, of course, it applies equally well to internal service. Every department within an organization has customers. Those who do not serve the external customers should be serving internal customers, who are the people and units depending on them to get their own jobs done. Those customers all experience moments of truth and cycles of service as well, and the same quality reasoning applies to them as applies to the external customers.

·CUSTOMER VALUE RESEARCH:
ASKING THE RIGHT QUESTIONS

We know that many investigators ask the wrong questions of their customers, and some ask the questions in the wrong way. So, what are the right questions, and how should we ask them?

Actually, there are four basic questions that discern customer value:

1. What attributes of the customer experience are of particular value?

2. How desirable is each attribute relative to the others?

3. How well do we score, compared to the relevant competitors, on those factors that are most valued?

4. What can we do to add value to the customer experience and thereby provide a differentiated or breakaway experience?

We must learn a new way of questioning if we are to succeed at this type of customer research. We have to set aside our preconceived ideas about what the customer experience *should be* and find out *what it really is*. We have to let go of the parameters, measurements, and normative questions and learn to ask new questions. We have to approach the investigation process with a sense of discovery, not a sense of filling in the answers to preconceived questions.

Sometimes we even have to ask the customers what questions we should be asking them. A significant part of customer value research is finding out about the customers themselves as people, and about the life context in which they experience the value package they get from us. For example, if we're trying to find out how small business owners value a particular business service, we first have to get some understanding of what it's like to be a small business owner. What are the issues, problems, and opportunities confronting such a person? What are his or her real priorities? What past experiences may have created biases in his or her mind about the subject? What drives that person? How does he or she interpret the reality of doing business with us or our competitors?

Once we understand the *context* of the experience, we can ask much more intelligent questions aimed at discerning the attributes that person values. If we're dealing with senior citizens, we need to understand their life context with respect to the service experience we offer. If we're dealing with teenagers, stockbrokers, homemakers, or pediatric cardiologists, we need to understand their contexts for being customers.

When Marriott Corporation's Host Division conducted customer research into the experiences of people who ate in their airport restaurants and cafeterias, they found that the personal context of the customer's experience dominated most of the other variables. According to CEO Ron Johnson, "At first, we got a lot of conflicting signals about the quality of the food. People also thought the prices were too high and that they were being gouged. In some ways, it seemed they were dissatisfied with everything. The research data didn't seem to tell a coherent story."

They asked me to participate in a special review session to study the data, looking for better ways to interpret the findings. When we analyzed the customer data looking for the invisible truth, i.e., the embedded number 8, so to speak, the message of the context came through loud and clear. This was not a dining experience in the conventional sense. People were not really coming into the restaurant voluntarily. They were captives; they had to be there, and they had to eat.

"It soon became clear," says CEO Johnson, "that we were dealing with a customer who was likely to be fatigued and stressed from traveling, away from home, out of his or her comfortable personal environment, and probably feeling somewhat abused by all of the experiences involved in a business trip. This stress and emotional discomfort were contaminating people's perceptions of the eating experience. We decided that our service package had to include a strategy for helping the customer feel more comfortable, secure, and at ease while dining with us. We went to work on that."

THE CUSTOMER FOCUS GROUP:
A GOLD MINE FOR DISCOVERY

It's remarkable how few organizations use the simple expedient of asking their customers for ideas about improving the value package they deliver. There are plenty of customers in all market sectors who have strong views, undiscovered needs and preferences, good ideas, and a desire to see things improved, but no one ever asks them.

One of the easiest ways to ask customers for help and one that usually turns up very valuable information is the *focus group interview*. It's a simple research method that any reasonably capable person can use to discover important customer perceptions and get new perspectives on customer value. In addition, most people enjoy participating in focus group sessions and typically try very hard to give useful input.

Virtually all organizations can benefit from holding focus group interviews with customers or potential customers. Not only commercial enterprises but government agencies, nonprofit groups, and even military organizations can understand their customers better through these meetings.

A focus-group interview, in its simplest form, is just a get-together with about seven to ten people who are typical of the kinds of customers you seek to understand better. A skillful moderator hosts the meeting, guides the discussion, asks questions to explore the participants' views about the aspect of service being investigated, and helps them express themselves comfortably.

The means for analyzing the findings can vary from simple note taking and later discussion to more sophisticated methods like audio or video recording, analysis of transcripts, theme analysis, and even observation through one-way windows.

You don't necessarily need market research experts to run focus-group meetings. Any capable moderator who understands the objective of the research can usually do a good job. The real trick is in thinking through the findings, interpreting what the group participants have told you, and relating it to the quality of your customer value package.

Focus groups work well for just about any type of customer, such as internal customers of organizational units, the general public as customers of a government agency, and even other military organizations as customers of a military agency. Once you start thinking about customers in the broadest possible terms, it becomes obvious that you need to find out what they've got on their minds.

At The Queen's Medical Center in Honolulu, Hawaii, internal department managers relied heavily on focus group results to formulate their unit missions, service strategies, and customer report cards. According to Angie Twarynski, Director of Organization Development for the hospital, "Several of our department managers wanted to understand their customers better, so we helped them conduct more than 20 focus-group interviews involving other employees and managers.

"The research covered areas such as food service, housekeeping, linen services, surgical supply, transportation, purchasing, print shop, and biomedical equipment services. Every one of the sessions produced useful results that had a huge influence on the thinking of the managers of the departments involved."

According to Bill Kennett, director of the Materiel Services Division, that includes most of the functions identified above; "We were surprised at how willing people were to talk to us and give us feedback. We got a little bit of bashing from some areas, but we also got a lot of appreciation and helpful input."

Dennis Burns, Director of Biomedical Engineering Services, said, "We found that people really appreciated being asked for their views. They felt we were taking our mission seriously, and that we really wanted to improve the quality of our service."

In this instance, the various department heads themselves served as moderators for their own focus groups. After we introduced them to the basic questioning strategies and ground rules for focus-group interviews, and demonstrated the methods a few times, they felt quite comfortable in doing their own research.

After the focus-group meetings, we met again to go over the results and begin to shape the findings into customer report cards and quality models for the groups. They also developed mission statements based on their concepts of the needs of their internal customers.

It often happens that an organization will get bogged down in its quality program and struggle with a sense of lost purpose. In many cases the missing ingredient is the customer. They just haven't taken the step of going to their customers with innocent questions and an attitude of discovery. For that reason, they're trying to develop a quality approach that's introverted and not anchored to any important element of customer need.

When companies form the habit of customer research and customer sensing, they often get a renewed sense of clarity and purpose that can guide them through the implementation.

For example, the San Francisco Symphony Orchestra recently conducted focus-group interviews with its major donors to find out what they could do to further cement the orchestra's relation to them. Prior to the focus-group research, the orchestra's leadership thought that these individuals might be interested in a sense of exclusivity, the chance to be part of an elite club. What they found out instead was that these donors wanted to know more about the orchestra and have a chance to interact with members of the orchestra on a regular basis as part of an extended orchestra "family."

For a much more thorough discussion of focus group methods and other useful customer research techniques, see *The Service Advantage: How to Identify and Fulfill Customer Needs*, by Karl Albrecht and Larry Bradford.[1] It tells you all you need to know to conduct basic customer research, and when to call for help from experts with more sophisticated methods.

THE CUSTOMER VALUE MODEL: THE INVISIBLE SCORECARD

The owners of a travel agency got together with a group of their customers in a focus-group session to identify the quality factors the customers considered critical in dealing with an agency. After the session, the owners waded through all the notes and findings, and extracted a *Customer Value Model*. This was a list of critical quality factors—eight of them, in this case—which they felt represented value in the minds of their customers.

Then they used the customer value model to create a customer scorecard, merely by making a questionnaire out of it. They gave each employee of the agency a copy of the scorecard and said, "This is how our customers are grading us on the service we provide. We want to do everything necessary to earn the highest possible marks on this scorecard." They made the customer value model and the scorecard the driving idea behind their entire approach to operating the agency.

What does a customer value model actually look like? In the case of the travel agency, it was a simple list of the eight factors they extracted from the customer research:

1. *Price confidence*—knowing the agent has secured the best available price on an airline ticket, hotel room, rental car, cruise vacation, or similar "product" and that some other agency could not have somehow secured a lower price.
2. *"Can-do" attitude*—willingness to tackle complicated or difficult travel problems with a spirit of helpfulness; patience with the customer's special needs; not treating the customer like a nuisance when he or she changes plans several times or has trouble arriving at a decision.
3. *Personalized and individualized treatment*—knowing enough about the customer to fit the solution to his or her special needs; having an up-to-date computer record on the customer's airline preferences, seating preference, special meal requirements, hotel preferences, health concerns, and so on; making each person feel like a VIP.

4. *Error-free "mechanics"*—doing all the basic things properly, such as getting the itinerary exactly right, having the travel documents accurate, getting the documents to the customer on time, and making all the special provisions properly.

5. *Agent continuity*—being able to deal with one particular agent on a long-term basis, so that he or she understands the customer's needs and problems in depth; not having one's arrangements passed from agent to agent and fearing that one of them may drop the ball by not having all the needed information.

6. *Information support*—taking the initiative to advise the customer of important matters he or she might not know about; voluntarily suggesting options or approaches that add value for the customer; providing whatever depth of information the customer needs in a particular situation, such as brochures, information about weather, health concerns, travel advisories, and local activities.

7. *Proactive safeguarding of the customer's interests*—alerting the customer if something about the travel arrangements changes, e.g., a chance for a better fare, special discounts that become available, warnings about changing conditions in a foreign country, taking action for the customer if a tour operator goes out of business, etc.

8. *Recovery when things go wrong*—taking action quickly and skillfully to help the customer deal with problems that arise or to correct mistakes made by the agency; making amends for inconvenience imposed on the customer through the agency's malfunctions.

Note that the element of price shows up in a slightly different form for the travel agency than it might for an airline or tour company. The customer realizes the agency doesn't control the price, so "low price" is not a value factor in dealing with the agency. However, the customer expects the agency to get the lowest possible price for a particular travel product. This shows up in the element of price confidence.

Those eight factors can easily become a simple customer questionnaire or become the basis for occasional customer interviews that gather feedback on the agency's performance. It is a simple matter to create a five-point rating scale for each of the eight elements and get customer scores on each. If the agency can get enough responses from customers, it can use a simple software program such as *Custometrics* to process the numerical scores and print reports for all staff members to review and analyze.[2]

Every organization can and should identify its customer value model, just as the owners of the travel agency mentioned above did. Of course, each customer value model will have its own unique factors, not the eight discovered by the travel agency. A retail store would probably find critical factors such as merchandise selection, price range, helpful staff, flexibility on returns and refunds, and the like. A restaurant would certainly see factors such as the overall ambience—the look and feel of the place, menu selection, flavorful preparation and presentation, and friendly staff. In each case there would be other factors to discover, unique to the individual business.

The exact same approach to the customer value model works for internal service departments. By interviewing its customers, a department can identify the critical factors on their value model, and then put those to use in measuring the quality of its overall customer value package, i.e., the total experience it offers to the customer.

In later chapters we'll see how the customer value model becomes the basic driving idea behind the business strategy, the mission, the design of the customer value package, and the whole process of transforming the organization so that it delivers superior value.

7

Quality and Business Strategy: Creating New Rules for the Game

Some men see things that are and ask "Why?"
I see things that never were and ask "Why not?"

Robert Kennedy

Be something special to someone in particular. This is the heart of customer-centered Strategy Formulation, the second key component of the TQS process, and the secret to creating a sustainable or renewable competitive advantage.

Making a quality initiative succeed requires FOCUS. It should be the strategic imperative of the whole organization. It should link up with the business planning process and in fact should subsume it. Quality should not be a "program," or a thing unto itself. It should be the driving idea behind the very existence of the organization. This is a key characteristic of fifth-dimension organizations: they have this focus.

And this is why the TQS model has a component for strategy. Many executives embark on customer-focus initiatives and many of them stop short when they realize that the basic business direction isn't clear enough to give meaning to the effort. Many of them find it necessary and productive to rethink the whole question of what they want the organization to be and where they want it to go.

Service management is an idea that "comes for lunch and stays for dinner." It seems simple at the outset, and appealing in its promise, but it starts to affect life in the organization to a much greater extent than anyone ever anticipated. It takes you places you never knew you wanted to go. It tends to call into question many things people have always taken for granted, and it eventually causes leaders to question and reexamine the very basis for the success of the organization. Sooner or later, it even attacks the bastions of executive thinking about strategy, mission, direction, and even organizational values.

THE CUSTOMER VALUE PACKAGE: THE HEART OF YOUR STRATEGY

Recall that the customer value *model*, or CVM, (as explained in Chapter 6), identifies the critical factors that drive the customers' desires and preferences—what they seek to get out of the total service experience with an organization. The customer value *package*, or CVP, is the total *offering*, both tangibles and intangibles, that the organization provides in response to those desires.

If an organization's leaders want its customer value package to be outstanding, they must ensure that each area that affects customer perceptions is well conceived and that the entire package is delivered at a price point that is favorably perceived. While the specific design of the customer value package varies greatly among industries and organizations, our research has identified seven critical components for a "generic" customer value package. These seven components become a natural framework for evaluating the appropriateness of the design of any customer value package:

1. *Environmental*—the physical setting in which the customer experiences the product. It could be a hospital room, a bank lobby, an airplane cabin, a barber chair, a department store, the sidewalk in front of an automatic teller machine, a fitness center, or any of a limitless number of possibilities. In the case of service at a distance, the environment may be the customer's own premises, augmented by the telephone through which he or she has contact with the business.

2. *Aesthetic*—the direct sensory experience, if any, that the customer encounters. It can include sights, sounds, flavors, physical sensations, discomfort, feelings, aesthetic features of an item of merchandise, and the visual or psychological ambience of the business environment.

3. *Interpersonal*—the interactions the customer has with employees or, in some cases, with other customers, as part of the total experience. This dimension includes friendliness, courtesy, helpfulness, physical appearance, and apparent competence at handling certain tasks.

4. *Procedural*—the procedures you ask the customer to go through in doing business with you. They may include waiting, explaining his or her needs, filling out forms, providing information, going to various locations, and being subjected to physical manipulations or treatments.

5. *Informational*—the aspects of the customer experience that involve getting the information needed to function as a customer. This includes simple things like whether the signage in a facility enables the customer to figure out where to go, whether the customer can decipher the invoice or account statement, and whether he or she can understand the insurance policy. It can include critical factors like whether anyone has adequately explained the use of some item of equipment or whether the customer knows what to expect after a critical medical procedure.

6. *Deliverable*—anything the customer physically takes custody of during the service experience, even if only temporarily. It would certainly include an item of merchandise purchased, but it could also include the tray of food served on the airline. It may not always be a "product" in the conventional commercial sense, but the customer receives it nevertheless. Other examples are checkbooks, rented video tapes, menus, travel documents, and life jackets.

7. *Financial*—what and how the customer pays for the total experience. In many cases this is obvious: it's the price. In others, it may be less obvious. For example, one internal service department might charge others for its services; no cash might change hands, but funds will go from one budget to another. An insurance company may pay the medical expenses, but the customer is still aware of the price.

Figure 7–1 illustrates the generic customer value package graphically. Having described your customer value package using this framework, the next step is to evaluate how well it delivers the value elements defined in the customer value *model*.

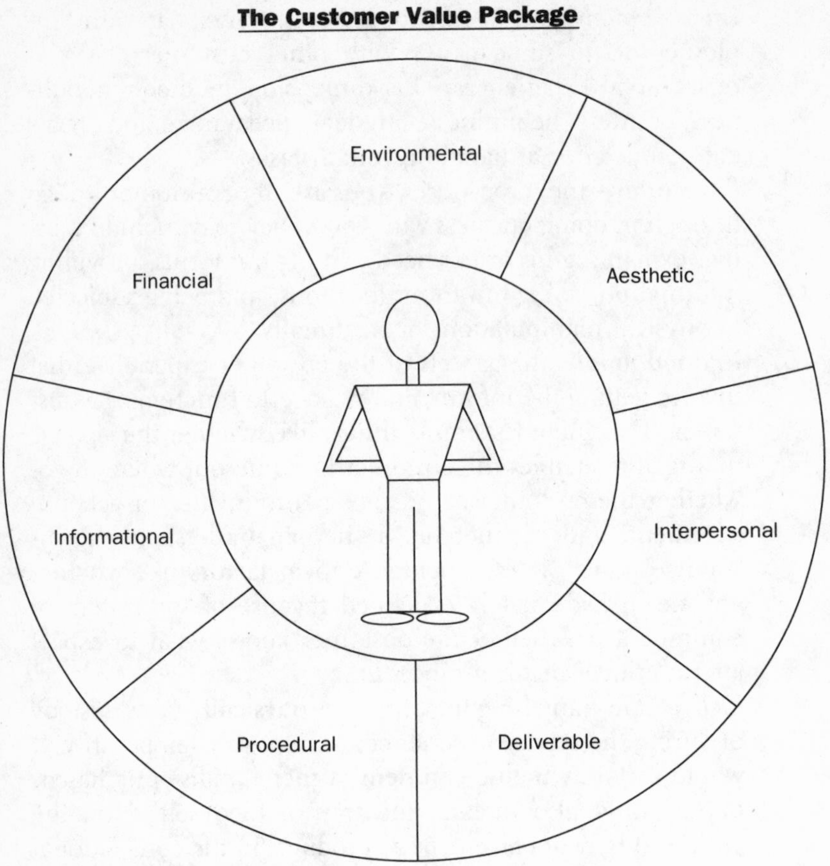

The Customer Value Package

Figure 7–1 The Customer Value Package.

Here is an example of how this framework might apply. In a hospital one of the critical components of the customer value model is usually trust, i.e., the customer's right to feel he can trust the individuals, the teams, and the system not to do horrible things to him or her.

We must design the customer value package—the total experience of the in-patient stay, for example, to "deliver" the trust element of the customer value model as well as the other elements. Even though there is no one part of the CVP called *trust*, collectively the elements of it should engender a feeling of trust if it is to meet that part of the CVM, as disclosed by the customer research.

For example, how well does the *Environmental*, or physical, component communicate trustworthiness? What can we do to increase trustworthiness in that component? How does the *Procedural* component reflect trustworthiness? What can we do to build trustworthiness there? In every one of the seven components, what features might cause the customer to doubt the trustworthiness?

The organization's overall *service strategy* should also match the customer value model, e.g., the trust element. In other words, everything should answer to the customer value model—vision, mission, core values, service strategy, and the design of the CVP.

In fact, the simplest way to look at the strategy formulation process is as a way of defining and designing a customer value package. It provides a means for delivering value that will win and keep the customer's business. The customer value package is the offering itself. The service strategy is the special concept or approach for delivering it, which you choose for your way of doing business.

THE SERVICE STRATEGY: DO YOU HAVE ONE?

As defined in *Service America!*, a service strategy is:

> ### Service Strategy:
> ... a distinctive formula for delivering service;
> such a strategy is keyed to a well-chosen benefit premise
> that is valuable to the customer and
> that establishes an effective competitive position. [1]

What are the requirements for a breakaway service strategy? *At America's Service* sets out the following criteria for an effective service strategy:

1. It is nontrivial; it has weight. It must be more than simply a "motherhood" statement or slogan. It must be reasonably concrete and action-oriented.
2. It must convey a concept or a mission that people in the organization can understand, relate to, and somehow put into action.

3. It must offer or relate to a critical benefit premise that is important to the customer. It must focus on something the customer is willing to pay for.
4. It must differentiate the organization in some meaningful way from its competitors in the eyes of the customer.
5. If at all possible, it should be simple, unified, easy to put into words, and easy to explain to the customer.[2]

A breakaway strategy should answer the question why a customer should do business with your organization as opposed to someone else's. Just as importantly, your strategy should identify the unique "personality" of your customer value package.

In his insightful book *The Reckoning*, David Halberstam explains in detail how Detroit automakers ignored all the early warning signals of the impending Japanese automobile invasion. They adopted an "it can't happen here" attitude and were caught with their pants down. The results have perhaps been as disastrous and tragic from an economic standpoint for the American automobile industry as the bombing of Pearl Harbor was in human terms for the American nation in general.[3]

Unfortunately, it seems that the real reckoning for the U.S. automakers did not occur until the first quarter of 1991, when the Big Three—General Motors, Ford Motor Company, and Chrysler Corporation—lost a combined total of $2.33 billion, breaking the record of $2.1 billion, which they lost in the fourth quarter of 1990. There are multiple reasons for those losses. However, a central issue has been the historical inability or unwillingness of the Detroit automakers to adopt a strong customer focus and to restructure themselves to produce a customer value package that is enduring, responsive to customer expectations, and experience-based.

While Detroit has been playing catch-up and trying to create quality products that are defect-free, a number of Japan's automobile manufacturers have gone to the next stage to focus on creating a quality experience for the automobile purchaser and owner.

Reliable cars are only the starting place for the Japanese—the ante for getting into the poker game. As Mazda Chairman, Kenichi Yamamoto puts it, quoted in *Business Week*, "Any manufacturer can produce according to statistics. In Japan that's called *atarimae hinshitsu*—quality that is taken for granted." His firm, according to Yamamoto, intends to compete on the basis of total customer value, in all its dimensions.

The Japanese don't stop with the car, either. They have paid as much attention to improving the selling and servicing environment. Their luxury franchises—Acura, Lexus, and Infiniti—have changed the industry's standards in these areas. Infiniti requires each dealership's owner and all of its key employees to attend an eight-day training school at a model dealership in Scottsdale, Arizona.

Lexus has established rigorous and expensive customer-focused requirements for the design of the dealership, including customer-friendly showrooms, service bays, and customer reception areas. Finally, in Japan, the auto dealers have gone one step further toward creating customer value. They expect to keep customers for life. Therefore, it is not unusual for them to maintain elaborate data bases on buyers' product preferences, to mail out birthday cards to the auto owner and family members, and to repair vehicles free to ensure customer loyalty.

As a result of this virtual obsession with the customers and a dedication to creating the "perfect" customer value package, Japanese automotive products in general score high in terms of perceived quality with the American public. In contrast, most American cars still get low marks.

The situation for American manufacturers became so desperate that in 1990, General Motors launched a $40 million advertising campaign admitting that for years its products had fallen short of customer expectations, apologizing, and then asking the public to believe that GM quality had improved and that it was committed to closing the gap between what customers wanted and the cars the company offered.

Columnist and commentator George Will wrote a scathing article at about the same time, titled "The Boast of U.S. Car Makers: We're Number Five!" He chastised GM for its ads showing that its Buick ranked fifth, behind Japanese and German cars, in having fewer owner-reported problems during the first 90 days after purchase. "So it's come to this," the article says, "an American corporation's boast that it has been beaten by only four foreign competitors." [4]

In an unprecedented television appearance on the show "Nightline," the leaders of America's Big Three automakers—Harold Poling of Ford, Robert Stempel of General Motors, and Lee Iacocca of Chrysler asserted that American cars had become the equal of Japanese, but that the American public just didn't realize it.

As these examples illustrate, some great ideas work and some don't. Every competitive strategy is a gamble. And every candidate for a service strategy must be carefully evaluated to see whether it can really be the one that makes a difference.

To further illuminate the concept of the service strategy, let's look at a legendary example of clarity and effective execution: Disneyland. While there are many examples of effective service strategies, Disney is one that serves especially well to illustrate the thinking process involved.

When you compare a Disneyland park to an ordinary amusement park, you can see the difference in the product offering. It's a wholly different thought process of doing business. A typical theme park has many of the same components as Disneyland: rides, attractions, performers, food, things to buy, and activities for children. Yet Disney has put it all together into a unifying concept of superior customer value.

We might describe the service strategy underlying the design of a Disney park as "delivering a total experience of fun and fantasy in a show business setting." Fun and fantasy are not unusual, but the show business setting is what gives it a unique focus. It's also an element that can be thoroughly exploited in Disney's special case. Two generations of Americans have grown up with the Disney characters—Mickey Mouse, Donald Duck, Pluto, and all the rest. So too have many people in other countries.

For that reason the Disney "brand recognition" factor is extremely high. Mickey Mouse may be the most widely recognized personality in the world, on a par with the Pope, national leaders, and famous movie stars. Mickey Mouse has even won elections as a write-in candidate. Disney has chosen to exploit the existing awareness and acceptance of its image and products, and to deliver the fun experience in a show business setting where it can capitalize on those factors.

The Disney service strategy has a powerful sense of *unity* about it. Nothing happens to contradict it. From the moment you walk into the park until you walk out again, everything is designed to trigger your childhood associations with fun and fantasy. The visual design, the signage, the design of the attractions, the sound effects, and the costumes of the employees all combine to reinforce the desired customer perception. This unity and focus, along with very skillful execution, have put Disneyland almost in a class by itself as an entertainment phenomenon. Few people would visit southern California or the Orlando region of Florida for the first time and pass up a visit to the Disney park. The same is true for the parks in Japan and France.

This is the essential value of a well-chosen service strategy, i.e., a way of presenting the customer experience that wins acceptance, approval, and customer preference. And the essence of the strategy-formulation component of TQS is identifying that special approach that can win.

THE POWER OF A BREAKAWAY STRATEGY

There are only two basic ways to establish competitive advantage: do things better than others or do things differently. In an established industry where all the players more or less imitate one another, you usually have to do things better than the others if you want to gain an unnatural share of the business.

However, some industries and some organizations are ripe for new thinking, new concepts, and new strategies for service. And some organizations have achieved breakaway strategies or positions even within well-established fields. This is the ideal possibility that deserves careful thought. Although some industries are well established in terms of the competitive orientations of a few dominant leaders, many others are still wide open for new thinking about customer value.

And even those industries considered "mature" may still see innovative moves made by new thinkers. It's dangerous to assume that the way an industry works today is the way it will work tomorrow.

The idea of a breakaway strategy for service has a great deal of appeal and deserves thoughtful consideration in the strategy formulation process. A breakaway strategy is a concept for winning and keeping the customer's business that can set your organization apart from the other competitive choices in the customer's mind. If you can create one, it can give you a strong focus for moving the organization toward better performance in its environment.

To accomplish this, you must focus on things as they could be, come up with a breakaway idea about service and customer value, and then design, develop, and deliver the customer value package in such a way that it can make a preemptive and quantum leap ahead of its competition.

BREAKAWAY LEADERSHIP: VISION, MISSION, AND VALUES

Breakaway leadership demands creativity, big-picture thinking, a receptivity to new ideas, the ability to go beyond parochial interests and work on teams, the courage to tinker with what's not broken and the capacity to reinvent and reengineer the entire corporation if that's required. The central role of the breakaway leader is to establish the framework for future success in response to the customer value equation. This framework sets out the organization's vision, mission, values, business direction, and strategic quality-improvement goals.

Those companies that wish to emulate these service leaders must begin by formulating a strategy that charts a clear course for satisfying the customer. That strategy must provide for:

- a clear corporate vision, mission, and values based on a valid concept of customer value.

- a well-defined customer value package designed to promote total quality as perceived by the customer.

- a system for managing the delivery of the customer value package to ensure a high-value experience for the customer.

- a statement of goals and benchmark targets that can drive the quality initiative.

Who is responsible for creating the breakaway strategy? The buck starts and stops with the executive management team.

Bob Galvin, the visionary ex-CEO of Motorola, emphasized this responsibility of the leadership group. In an *Industry Week* article he asserted that "the real test of quality in the early part of the next century is going to be what I call the quality of leadership."

He goes on to say that to achieve quality in their leadership roles, American leaders must become "better anticipators and better committers," opining that American management has been found wanting in both of these areas. Galvin suggests establishing "anticipation and commitment registries" at Motorola to track the performance of its leaders, believing that the "next generation of leaders" will be measured on the dynamics of "anticipations factoring."[5]

If the customer is at the center of the quality-improvement process, the business plan and program strategy are the centerpiece for the entire service-improvement initiative. A comprehensive strategic plan makes the quality-improvement initiative something more than a one-time project or program with a set starting and ending point and elevates it above operational and tactical concerns. The plan also provides the means for coordinating all quality-related activities and making all decisions related to the customer and quality.

The quality concept should be virtually inseparable from the whole strategy setting and planning process, even down to the operational levels. The "strategy package" (Figure 7–2) presents the quality focus by tying the customer value model and customer value package to the other elements of the planning hierarchy:

The Vision Statement—an image of what the leaders want the organization to be or become. It is the desired future state for the business, particularly as it relates to customer value and service quality.

The Mission Statement—a simple, compelling statement of how the organization expects to do business, in terms of customers and customer value.

The Core Values Statement—the critical few values to which the people in the organization must commit their energies. The core values are those essential to the accomplishment of the mission and the fulfillment of the vision.

The Operating Environment—the surrounding reality in which the organization must operate, including the sub-environments identified as customer, competitive, economic, technological, legal, political, social, and physical.

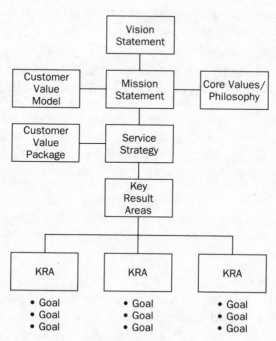

Figure 7–2 The Strategy Package.

The Business Strategy—the definition of the organization's "next move" to capitalize on the opportunities and respond to the challenges in its environment.

The Key Result Areas—the critical few areas of action that people can keep in their minds as they carry out the mission for the upcoming planning period. Each key result area should bridge across the whole organization, giving guidance and alignment for all units in making their contributions to the overall mission. Organizational unit plans should respond to the key result areas.

The Strategic Goals—a few clearly stated outcomes under each key result area, expressed in measurable terms of what the company intends to accomplish.

Relatively few organizations have vision statements or mission statements that offer unique or compelling concepts of how they do business. Many have no such statements at all. Many others have statements that are vague, fluffy, meaningless, or poorly expressed. Still others have reasonable statements that they have not communicated effectively to the employees.

Thinking through the vision, mission, and values, as well as transforming them into a workable strategy package, is one of the critical contributions of the senior leaders. It is an essential element of achieving an effective competitive position.

STRATEGIC QUALITY OBJECTIVES: TURBO-GOALS AND BEST BENCHMARKS

In 1960, president John Kennedy launched the space race with a very simple declaration. The Russians had recently put the first *Sputnik* satellite into Earth orbit, beating the Americans to the punch in a highly symbolic achievement. In one of his key speeches, Kennedy declared:

> I believe this nation should commit itself to the objective of landing
> a man on the moon and bringing him back safely to Earth within
> this decade.

That's what I call a *turbo-goal*. It was simple, compelling, challenging, and eminently worthwhile in the minds of many who heard Kennedy speak. It had impact. It had drama. And it focused people's attention as never before. It kicked off the Apollo program, a $23 billion effort that achieved the goal. Astronaut Neil Armstrong climbed down the ladder of the lunar landing craft and stepped out onto the surface of the moon in July 1969. And the world was forever changed.

Sometimes a single motivational symbol or rallying point such as a turbo-goal can help people achieve the unity of focus and action required to break away from the way things have been done in the past. Not all business goals can be as dramatic or as compelling as the space program. But I've seen some very interesting cases in which executives declared outrageous goals for their organizations and the people accepted the challenge and achieved them.

Sometimes a good candidate for a turbo-goal is a "best bench-mark," which is a world class performance target established by determining who does something best in a particular area or function and then determining to beat them. Benchmarking is a useful technique in quality improvement of any kind. By studying others who are doing what you do, you can get an accurate picture of what's possible. It may even be possible to go beyond the best benchmark, but at least you can prove that someone has achieved it.

In another case, the best turbo-goal may be something that's never been done by any counterpart or competitor, but that might be feasible with the right attack. It might be a possibility that, if achieved, could revolutionize the business and create such a significant advantage that it is worth the investment to learn how to do it.

Before Fred Smith launched the Federal Express Corporation, the accepted standard for package delivery was typically several days, even locally, to say nothing of across the North American continent. By focusing on overnight delivery as a turbo-goal, he forced a complete rethinking of how things could be done.

Twenty years ago, probably no American professor of in-dustrial engineering would have bought the idea that a large factory could operate without any storage space allocated to raw materials. But the Japanese created the just-in-time system by re-integrating the production system at a higher level and incorpo-rating the material suppliers as part of the overall system concept. Now it's normal practice in some factories for the steel that rolls up on a flatbed truck in the morning to go out the gate as part of a finished product in the afternoon. Some factories have virtually eliminated the holding of raw material in inventory and have driven down the costs of manufacturing as a result.

And in some cases a turbo-goal can be a literal do-or-die challenge. It may be something the organization simply must do in order to survive.

In the early 1980s, Corning Glass virtually owned the U.S. market for automobile catalytic converters. They had very little serious competition. Virtually overnight, a Japanese company introduced a competing product that not only worked better and showed fewer failures, but it sold for a lower price. The major American car manufacturers had no choice but to put Corning on notice that they couldn't continue buying its product unless it was at least as cost-effective as the Japanese product.

Says Corning Senior Vice-President David Luther, "That's what's known in the trade as a wake-up call. It scared the bejeebers out of us and really got us to move."

Out of sheer necessity, Corning launched a massive, wall-to-wall program to get the quality up and the price down. According to Luther, "it was the biggest thing that ever hit this organization. We knew that for this thing to succeed it had to personally affect every single human being at Corning."

Corning did manage to come up with a vastly superior product, at a competitive price. Had they not responded with a level of commitment bordering on total panic, it's quite likely that part of the company would have been out of the business.

Question: if the Corning people could do it then, why didn't they do it before? Presumably the changes they made could have been made at any time. The new ideas, the improvements, the refinements, and the rethinking of the processes were all possible before the wake-up call. Going back to Robert Galvin's point, the answer is that their consciousness didn't include that level of expectation as part of their view of how to do things. There is a profound lesson here about expectations, beliefs, and motivation.

Walt Disney used to tell a revealing story about his career as a producer and an idea person.

> During the development of Fantasia, all the people in the studio were working flat out, at a feverish pace. It was the biggest attempt at commercial animation ever undertaken and certainly bigger than anything I'd ever done up until then.
>
> I was walking around the studios one day, kind of watching people and getting a sense of the pace of things, when it suddenly dawned

on me: nobody here seems to have a shadow of a doubt in his or her mind that we can pull this thing off. I was having my own doubts, but they were whistling and working and having a great time; the cost had already gone over $7 million, and it would have to be our biggest-grossing product ever, just to break even. I got the strangest feeling when I realized they all thought I knew what I was doing!

Fantasia did succeed spectacularly well, not only financially but artistically. And something about the energy and commitment given by the people working on it made it something special. It was a case of the "Apollo effect," mentioned in Chapter 5. People got caught up in something meaningful, something bigger than themselves, something they believed in and were willing to go for. That is what turbo-goals can do for an organization and for the people working there.

DEFINING AND DESIGNING THE CUSTOMER VALUE PACKAGE

The customer value model sometimes tells such a compelling story that it leads to a substantial change in the organization's customer value package. This is especially necessary if quality has been defined historically using purely product-related or internal measures such as zero defects, conformance to requirements, and meeting standards. The customer value model forces us to look at quality comprehensively.

Midwest Express airline has built a sterling reputation because of its understanding of the clear connection between the customer value model and its customer value package. The motto of this breakaway organization (a subsidiary of K.C. Aviation, which is owned by Kimberly Clark Corporation) is "the best care in the air." The fact that the company was named "the best U.S. airline overall" for transportation value by the *Consumer Reports* Travel Letter suggests that it is more than just a slogan.

Midwest Express, with its hub in Milwaukee, is a niche carrier providing travel service to selected major cities. The company is committed to providing all of its passengers with luxury service at coach fares or less. In the words of its President, Tim Hoeksema, "We have a successful basic formula and stick to it. People want good service and good value."

The way Midwest delivers against these expectations is to have only two extra-wide leather seats on each side of the aisle on its planes, with extra space and legroom between rows. In-flight service includes gourmet meals served on china, with complimentary wine or champagne. The flight attendants frequently prepare fresh-baked chocolate chip cookies. Midwest delivers all of this at a price that matches or beats the standard coach fare of its major competitors.

Midwest recognizes that total quality and the perception of customer value is shaped by more than what happens in the air. All ground operations, support operations, and internal service departments are expected to operate in support of the basic customer value package the company offers.

At some point in the strategy-formulation process it may even be appropriate to approach the design of the customer value package directly and from scratch. It will certainly be necessary, at least, to evaluate it carefully and consider refining it to meet the demands of the customer value model.

The general strategy formulation process and the means for aligning the service strategy with the design of the customer value package and the customer value model are as follows:

1. Identify the customer value model.
2. Create the service strategy.
3. Evaluate the current customer value package against the demands of the customer value model.
4. Either refine and improve the design of the customer value package, or rethink it altogether and redesign it from scratch.

This approach to strategy formulation has the virtue of keeping the minds of the organization's leaders focused firmly on customer value as the guiding principle in all of their deliberations. It sets the stage for an implementation approach that can put the organization on the road to total quality service and keep it there. It makes quality the number-one driving force for the operation of the business, and it leads to the alignment of the strategy, the people, and the systems around the needs of the customers.

8

Empowering People with Knowledge: Winning the Hearts, Minds, and Hands

An individual without information cannot take responsibility; an individual who is given information cannot help but take responsibility.

Jan Carlzon
CEO, Scandinavian Airlines

W hen Scandinavian Airlines System launched its now famous service-quality drive in the early 1980s, it used a
universal-training approach to carry the message of quality and customer focus to every person in the organization. *Over 20,000 employees* went through an introductory two-day training session on service
thinking during a period of several months.

According to CEO Jan Carlzon, "we had to make the turnaround
very quickly. We were in red ink and we had to mobilize every person
in the organization. So I took my message to the front line, in the
form of seminars, meetings, and discussions all over the system. The
result was a great deal of alignment, at all levels of the organization,
toward the objective of customer value."

Of course, SAS did many other things along with the training
program, but the lesson to be learned by other businesses has to do
with the *sheer scale* on which Carlzon approached the process of communicating the quality message to the organization. To the best of my

knowledge, the SAS program was the first major application of training in a wall-to-wall effort to reach 100 percent of the people in the organization. In the past, industrial organizations had not considered the expense of training every person to be justified. Carlzon's view was that the *training was a way to communicate a message critical to the survival of the organization*, and several million dollars was not an unreasonable investment in his mind.

Since the SAS story became a legend in business circles, a number of other companies have adopted the universal-training approach as an element of change management. In fact, it is becoming more or less an accepted element of program implementation for organizations making a full commitment to service quality.

British Airways took a page from SAS's book when it trained over 30,000 employees worldwide in a two-day program called "Putting the Customer First." Many of the organizations I've observed and worked with have carried the service-quality message to frontline employees in much the same way.

To the best of my knowledge, the largest employee population involved in such an effort was in the U.K.'s National Westminster Bank, headquartered in London. NatWest's 55,000 employees went through a basic one-day introduction to service thinking over a period of less than six months. The company built four training centers to handle the large number of people and continues to train newcomers in the same way.

Although training certainly cannot accomplish the total mission of change management, the leaders of virtually all fifth-dimension organizations use it as an integral part of their strategies. They understand that *a quality initiative, in order to succeed, must touch the individual lives of everyone in the organization*, and the leaders are prepared to make the investment to ensure that it does.

All experience shows us that a quality initiative, no matter how well conceived, strategized, and planned, will fail without the active commitment and involvement of people throughout the organization. Although this sounds obvious, many executives seem to believe they can march merrily down the trail without giving much thought to the people who actually work with the customers. This lack of organizational commitment and unity of purpose explains why so many quality initiatives fizzle and end up relegated to the compost pile of fad ideas and management gimmicks.

The goal of twenty-first-century customer-centered organizations should be to make every employee a quality strategist, i.e., someone who can take ownership of customer problems or quality issues and has the capability and freedom of action to solve them. To do this, the employees must have the knowledge, attitudes, and skills to meet the needs and expectations of their customers.

As NatWest's Paul Goodstadt notes, disgruntled employees are *quality terrorists* — they can destroy the quality of service at the grass roots. Unwittingly, many organizations turn their employees into quality terrorists by the way they treat them. Too many executives treat employees like Neanderthals to be sprayed and deloused or as pagans to be converted, rather than as people and stakeholders in the success of the enterprise.

Executives have traditionally approached the problem of organizational change in a top-down manner. They want to tell people what to do and how to do it rather than engage them as owners of the process. Many don't want or care about the ideas and opinions of people in the organization. They expect to win allegiance to the change through command, control, and persistence.

Breakaway leaders view organizational change in a more subtle and complex way: as a top-down, bottom-up, managed-in-the-middle process. They involve everyone in organizational change and thereby multiply the results of their efforts. They win support through understanding, involvement, and commitment, not by trying to use control or superior staying power.

The way to win the hearts, minds and hands of people in the organization is not to tell them what to do, but to release them from the chains of traditional organizational thinking. The message from leadership must be, "We see you as assets, as people, and as participants, whose opinions and ideas are valuable to the success of the organization."

Some of the hardest employees to win over are those suffering from terminal cases of burnout. This may be the result of downsizing, reorganizations, buyouts, mergers, or the unique pressures of the industry itself. And yet, even these people can usually find their way back to working with energy and commitment if their leaders understand their needs and know how to empower them.

The Education, Training, and Communication component of the TQS model has this empowerment as its primary objective. It enables the employees to become partners in the change rather than victims of it, by helping them understand the customer, the organizational vision and mission, and their parts in delivering an outstanding customer experience.

Fifth-dimension organizations use formal training, informal learning processes, formal and informal communication processes, and a continual process of communicating the facts and values of customer focus to everyone involved. They are masters of the art of winning hearts, minds, and hands through the sharing of ideas and information, not through command and control.

EVERYTHING YOU DO COMMUNICATES

In his book *Moments of Truth*, Jan Carlzon describes an incident that occurred shortly after he became president of Linjeflyg, a regional airline carrier in Scandinavia. To become familiar with the airline's system, personnel, and service quality, he visited each airport the airline served. At one airport, the staff seemed somewhat uneasy, but he couldn't figure out why. Finally, one employee told him they were waiting for him to board the plane. "Is it ready?" he asked. "I didn't hear any announcement."

The staff person replied, "No, sir, but if you get on now and decide where you want to sit, we can board the passengers."[1]

Carlzon offered the view that if your actions indicate that you appear superior even to your customers, then you can hardly call yourself customer-oriented. He waited until everyone else was on board and then took an available empty seat. This is just one of many examples of Carlzon's habit of "walking the talk."

Another step Carlzon took was to eliminate the executive dining room. The opportunity presented itself when one of his managers spoke of the need for managers to be in better touch with the employees. "Excellent," he responded. "Let's start by eating lunch with everybody else. We'll do away with the executive dining room!" Eliminating that executive perk was an unmistakable sign. It told the employees "Everyone is here to work together." This action communicated a loud-and-clear signal that something new and different was happening inside the organization.

J. Willard "Bill" Marriott, Jr., second-generation chairman of the Marriott Corporation, holds much the same view. "We don't have executive dining rooms or private elevators. I don't believe in that stuff. If the executives expect people to live by the values of service, we have to live by those same values. We have to model what we believe is important, so the employees see it every day."

And far beyond the level of executive behavior, *everything you do communicates*. The look and feel of the operation, the pace of things, the way employees are treated by their bosses, the way bosses treat the customers they deal with, the importance attached to delivering the value package with style and quality—all of these are messages. Some of them are overt, conscious messages and some are unconscious messages. Every organization has an implicit level of communication that either reinforces or counteracts the message of quality and customer value.

A critical part of moving an organization to the fifth dimension of service as an art form is in unifying all of these types of communication around the message of quality and customer value and making sure they all speak the same truth.

ELIMINATING CONTRADICTIONS

The executives of a large public utility in the eastern United States launched a service-quality program with great energy. They announced the program, brought in consultants to help launch it, and conducted a series of employee group meetings to get their views on quality issues. I was asked to present a series of executive seminars on service management in conjunction with the effort. So far, so good.

But a few weeks into the program, the chief executive announced that there was going to be a 10 percent reduction in staff across the organization. All of the executives and middle managers immediately switched their attention to the impending reduction, and the quality initiative went to the bottom of their credibility lists. They perceived the reduction and particularly the way it was communicated as a fundamental contradiction to the service-quality message, and there was little hope of changing their minds.

In large organizations, and often in small ones as well, it can be incredibly difficult to get a single, unitary message about quality into the minds of the employees, in the face of other compelling messages that contradict it. Contradictions seem to be everywhere. Executives sometimes contradict themselves when their actions don't square with their exhortations.

Systems and priorities often contradict the quality message. When the focus is on cost first and quality second, the employees pay attention accordingly. When a budget crunch comes along and they see their executives slashing resources with no apparent consideration of quality priorities, they get the message: quality is something we all talk about, but it doesn't actually affect real life.

When the strategic plan comes down from the executive suite and there is no mention of a service focus, and no apparent concentration on customer quality, the message is: business as usual. Or when the plan has seven key result areas, one of which is "customer service," the message is: service-quality is just one of the things we put into the plan; it's not the overriding fact of life in our organization.

When the systems the employees rely on to deliver service to the customers and to one another as internal customers are out of kilter, and they see management paying no attention to their frustrations, the message is: we like service-quality, but we're not going to change anything important; just get along the best way you can.

When employees go to the training seminars and hear all about customer value and the spirit of service, and then return to their units to work with supervisors who never even refer to any of the things they learned, they get the message: service is nice, but we've got work to do around here. When their performance evaluations make no mention of their customer commitment or their contributions to quality, they know it's not something anybody really has to worry about.

One of the first things we must do in any organization, before launching a serious quality effort, is to make an honest appraisal of the contradictory messages the employees are getting and can expect to get. We need to see and hear things from their unique point of view. We need to understand the sum total of all the messages they're hearing from the point of view of quality and customer value. And we need to go to work on the sources of the contradictions.

We can learn a great deal from companies that are good at aligning their cultures toward service and eliminating the contradictions. For example, the Swedish furniture firm IKEA does an outstanding job of keeping all heads pointed in the same direction. According to managing director Anders Møberg, "our product line is aimed at families and working-level people in the Scandinavian countries and others with similar values abroad. We sell unassembled furniture that is attractive, stylish, and economical. That's our market. We don't cater to the wealthy. So our corporate culture reflects the values and lifestyles of our customers."

What its founder, Ingvar Kamprad, called "the IKEA way" is a social and psychological orientation that affects just about everything IKEA people do. The executives dress quite casually—no suits or ties to set them apart from the employees. They eat lunch in the canteen with everyone else. Offices are simple and unpretentious. CEO Møberg says "the only time we executives put on suits is when we have to meet with our bankers. They wouldn't take us seriously otherwise."

Møberg is especially proud of the way IKEA executives travel. "We believe in frugality. It's good enough for our customers, so it's good enough for us. We plan our travel far in advance so we can get the lowest APEX fares. We don't mind riding in coach; we meet a lot of our customers there."

Naturally, the design of the IKEA retail stores reflects this same sense of unpretentious focus on value for money. The stores are clean, bright, colorful, and cheerful, but not "expensive" looking. Each department displays samples of its furniture in assembled form, in settings that show the customer how the end result might look at home. Sales people are always on hand for advice on interior design and product choices.

The thing that struck me most forcefully in visiting IKEA headquarters in Almhult, Sweden, and several of its retail stores, was the uncanny sense of *unity* about the conceptualization of the business, the leadership style of the executives, the design of the company operations, and the whole employee culture shared by its 12,000 employees. To use a bit of American slang, IKEA is one of the most "together" companies I've ever seen. In other words, everything communicates the same essential message.

The company's vision and mission statements, its advertising and customer communication, its internal communications, the posters and placards in the warehouses and offices, and the design of the retail selling environment all transmit the same message: simplicity, quality, basic life values, and value for money.

Many organizations could take a page from IKEA's book when it comes to communicating the message of customer value. You have to do it clearly and compellingly, congruently, and constantly. All of the message systems in the organization, whether formal or informal, explicit or implicit, conscious or unconscious, must say the same thing.

SHARING THE VISION: WINNING THE HEARTS

In order for people to truly participate in an organization-wide quality effort, they need to understand the big picture—the vision of what the organization is attempting to do. They need to know why changes in the way the organization does business are advantageous and necessary, what the changes will mean to them personally, and how the organization will be different.

They need to know the focus of the organization's quality initiative, and that it's not just a tactical intervention, but something that will strategically affect the way everyone does business. They need to know that management, too, has a responsibility to work under the program and not just fob it off on the front line employees.

When SAS was rolling out its program of organizational changes, top management distributed a red-cover book to all employees titled "Let's Get In There and Fight." It became a useful tool to present the company's overall vision and strategy, as well as what it expected from the employees. The "little red book," as it became popularly known, conveyed the vision of the company and sought to convince employees that they should take responsibility to carry out that vision.

Jan Carlzon believed that in a decentralized, customer-driven airline, a good leader should work constantly at sharing the vision. During his first year on the job as the leader of SAS, Carlzon spent over half of his working hours out in the field talking to SAS employees in Norway, Sweden, and Denmark. He believed that as the top executive he had to ensure that every employee truly understood and absorbed the message, so they could apply it to their own work situations.

IKEA does a similarly effective job of mass-communicating the vision, mission, and values of the company. The founder's original letter to employees in 1976 still stands as the guiding principles:

> Once and for all we have decided to side with the many. What is good for our customers is also good for us in the long run. This is an objective which entails responsibility.
>
> In all countries and social systems, Eastern as well as Western, a disproportionately large part of all resources is used to satisfy a small part of the population. In our line of business, for instance, too many new and beautifully designed products can be afforded by only a small group of better-off people. IKEA's aim is to change this situation.

This philosophy links with the company's statement of vision:

> We shall offer a wide range of home furnishing items of good design and function, at prices so low the majority of people can afford to buy them.

The company then follows up with this message of core values:

- Cost consciousness
- Modesty and determination
- Simplicity
- Leadership by good example
- Willingness to accept and delegate responsibility
- Striving to meet reality
- Daring to be different
- Constant desire for renewal
- The importance of constantly being "on the way," i.e., being more stimulated by the way to achieve the goal than by the goal itself
- Fellowship and enthusiasm

The Natural Gas Company in Sydney, Australia, has a similarly focused and unified approach to communicating the direction and values to all of its employees. They use the key phrase "Everything we do ..." to focus attention and energy toward customer value. The message the employees hear, constantly, consistently, and from all directions is "Everything we do must help people choose natural gas."

By putting the message into employee booklets, on wallet cards, on wall posters, into training programs, and into video messages used throughout the company, its leaders share the vision and reinforce it at every opportunity.

Many organizations these days have vision statements, mission statements, and statements of core values. Some even have effective ones. And some even use them effectively. Unfortunately, it seems that most organizations have not capitalized on the potential for mobilizing and focusing the energy of the employees through clear, simple, and compelling messages. For many of them, this seems to be a great lesson waiting to be learned and a great opportunity to win and keep employee commitment to the quality journey.

EDUCATING SERVICE LEADERS: WINNING THE MINDS

A well-communicated, strong, customer-focused vision and a commitment to service excellence at the very top of the organization increases the likelihood that the organization will operate in a customer-driven manner. Becoming a customer-driven organization is a difficult job that requires service leadership, long-term commitment, and effort. Once you implement a service-quality initiative, you must provide constant support, attention, and energy to it. It's not an overnight job nor is it for the faint of heart.

Many of the most well known case studies in service excellence—SAS, Federal Express, Nordstroms, Xerox, Walmart, Stew Leonard's, etc.—have focused upon charismatic leaders who had certain customer-focused visions and philosophies and who could energize organizations and people.

At the same time, many other organizations have succeeded in their service-quality efforts without charismatic chief executives. The good news is that much of what it takes to be a service leader can be taught. Service leaders aren't always born. It just takes some education and training in the right steps.

This is not to say that training service leaders is an easy task. What you require first is a fundamental change in their orientation. *Managers need to think and act like service leaders—practical people who serve as role models to guide and support others in the organization—rather than as administrators who sit in offices and manipulate the organization's infrastructure to get things done.*

In traditional management, this is a totally foreign idea. Think for a moment about the academic degree awarded by our business schools—the Master of Business Administration (MBA). The traditional MBA program has always focused on finance, accounting, administration, policies and procedures, and systems. It views the manager's role as that of one who analyzes, decides, and presides. This usually produces managers who are structural and bureaucratic in their thinking and actions—what the Scandinavians call the "law and order" manager.

What we really need is a new management approach—proactive, entrepreneurial and broader in scope, and more focused on the customer than in years past. What we need is a radically different emphasis—perhaps a degree called Master of Service Leadership. Organizations of all types, not just typical "service businesses," are desperately in need of more and better leadership from top and middle management.

EMPLOYEE TRAINING: WINNING THE HANDS

Employee skills training is really product development, in a sense. One of the fundamental differences between service businesses and manufacturing businesses is that with service businesses, the product is produced on the spot by people, while manufactured products are produced and stored for later sale. Indeed, at the customer interface, or moment of truth, the employee in a service business *is* the product, or at least a key ingredient in the product.

No two moments of truth are exactly the same, because no two customers are the same. At these moments of truth, the customer's perception of service-quality depends far more on individual excellence than in a manufacturing organization.

Since individual excellence is so important, the development of people becomes critical. We need a new training paradigm. We should think of skills training as product development. Few manufacturing businesses could remain profitable and competitive for very long without investing sufficiently in product development—R & D. Yet in most service businesses, frontline employees are commonly put in a position of having to manage the moments of truth without adequate preparation.

The fact is that people don't always instinctively know how to treat customers. Additionally, managers don't always have what it takes to manage their own moments of truth and support and lead their people at the front line. If an organization is truly committed to service excellence, skills training becomes very important and very necessary.

In the previously cited survey of executive opinions about service, the Management Centre Europe identified a gap between the perceived need for customer commitment and the action required to make it happen. In a survey of 3,375 American, European, and Japanese executives, almost 80 percent of the executives regarded improving quality and service to customers as "the key to competitive success." Yet only 49 percent of European executives, 38 percent of American executives and 37 percent of Japanese executives responded yes to the question "Have most of the managers in your company attended a learning/training activity that focused on customer service?"

When asked "Have most of the nonmanagement personnel in your company attended a learning/training activity focused on customer service?" only 28 percent of American and European executives and 40 percent of Japanese executives responded affirmatively.[2]

You need only to look at those organizations known as service leaders to see how they view skills training as an important part of product development. For many years one of the best examples has been IBM Corporation. Etched in stone at the entrance to IBM's education center in Endicott, New York, are the words "There Is No Saturation Point in Education." IBM believes that the quality of its service depends on its training and educational capabilities and probably commits proportionately more financial resources to those areas than any other company in the world.

IBM's founder, Tom Watson, Sr., believed that the company's annual investment in education, training, and internal communication should increase at a rate greater than the company's rate of growth. The company currently invests more than $1 billion a year in education and training. On any given day, more than 20,000 IBM employees are attending formal training sessions.

Every year, IBM managers receive at least 40 hours of training, and that commitment extends all the way down through the organization. Because of the constant flow of new information and new products, even a veteran IBM marketing representative spends 15 days every year in classrooms, attending special industry schools, and at conferences. IBM invites customers to their training sessions, in order to create a real-world atmosphere and to discuss specific problems affecting their businesses.

At IBM, service-quality training programs are required for all employees at all levels. They require both initial and periodic training to help employees improve their technical and personal skills.

As the IBM example illustrates, the content and substance of service-quality training varies for each employee in the organization. Fundamentally, however, each training session must be designed to both improve the customer value delivered and help the individual grow as a person. Employees who feel better and more confident about themselves as people are better able to work with their external and internal customers.

At the upper-management level, service-quality training should have a strategic focus. It should concentrate on the importance of a customer orientation, communicate a vision of what the organization should look like, show how it should function (including the redefined roles of management), and marshal the assets and resources of the organization to support the service-quality efforts of everyone involved. In short, top-management training should offer a blueprint for service leadership.

At the middle-management and supervisory levels, training should focus on the mission of each department and unit in the service-quality effort, the redefinition of the role of middle manager or supervisor as supporter and coach, the definition of service leadership, service-quality improvement tools, and service-quality improvement planning.

At the frontline level, service-quality training should be more tactical in focus, concentrating on teaching each employee how to manage the moments of truth; how to use process improvement tools; better customer contact skills, i.e., active listening, problem solving, complaint handling, and stress management; and personal improvement planning and goal setting.

Most importantly, service-quality training for employees needs to go beyond traditional "smile training" or "customer relations" training. Although service with a smile and personal warmth are certainly necessary components of quality service, they don't provide a sufficient basis for long-term results. Results come from proactive training in real, practical knowledge that teaches skills and tools each employee can apply to increase his or her own satisfaction as well as please the customers.

Most adult employees resent being told "how to be nice." Many see it as an insult to their intelligence and therefore go into the training sessions with a negative attitude. Even when they do accept this kind of training as legitimate, they may fail to change their behavior on those dimensions of service quality that are really important to customers. Much of the fault with that result lies with the trainers and their programs, which tend to focus on teaching people to say "hello" and "thank you," on good phone manners, or on the importance of dress codes, name tag ribbons, and catchy closing phrases.

It's not that customers don't want or expect those things from employees, but they are only a part of what customers take into account when they evaluate a company's service performance. Unfortunately, executives who are naive about the realities of organizational change believe that by rounding up employees and running them through motivational courses and training workshops they can get their people to deliver better service. It's like throwing buckets of water on an oil-well fire; it's interesting and looks like it might work, but it doesn't get to the heart of the matter.

Training-only approaches for improved customer satisfaction seem to run rampant in some industries. During the 1970s and 1980s, "guest relations" training became the hottest quick-fix for an increasingly competitive health care marketplace. At that time, treating patients and their families like "guests" was a new concept supposed to enhance patient loyalty and increase hospital census figures at a time when many of them were closing their doors. Many hospital executives believed that by teaching their employees how to be nice to their "guests," they could improve "guest satisfaction," keep the patient census high, and keep the hospital in the black.

That sounded like a good idea, but many of them discovered that the real problems lay outside the scope of employee behavior. Many hospitals were fundamentally antagonistic to positive customer perceptions because of the way they were designed, constructed, and operated. Hospital employees can be nice to patients, but if the patient waits two hours in the hallway of the X-ray lab, all the smiling in the world isn't going to make any difference.

As the quality movement within health care organizations has begun to focus more and more on a customer-value point of view, more and more executives have begun to realize they need a total organizational approach, not merely a guest relations "be-nice" approach.

Smile training, guest relations, and other motivational training programs may temporarily raise the energy levels and the enthusiasm of the frontline people on the job. However, training employees to deliver customer value can really be effective when:

1. *The employees first learn what is truly important to their customers.* Next, they must learn how well the organization as a whole and the various departments individually perform against those expectations. Only when they're armed with that information can they discover new ways to deliver customer value. Knowledge, in this case, is power.

2. *The course curriculum, class design, and learning objectives focus on factors that are important to the customers.* Otherwise the training sessions waste time with irrelevant topics, gimmicks, or emotional arousal for its own sake.
3. *The training teaches employees to think about the needs of the customer first,* and then to do their jobs in ways that put the customer first.
4. *The employees are enabled, empowered, and supported by management in their efforts to improve customer value.* This fourth item is the key to any training program, regardless of size and scope. If management fails to support the training, it will have little long-term value. Every employee must see a commitment of top-down support.

Ultimately, the organization's whole approach to training and development must reflect the focus on customer value and the need to align all energies toward the vision and mission. All of the systems and processes related to human development, from the new employee's first orientation session to the content of technical skills training to the specific "service" training programs, should reflect this focus.

And all of the organization's collateral communication processes, both formal and informal, must carry the same message of customer value. Returning to the five action components of the TQS model, we can see that clarity of focus and unity of execution of the business mission is extremely critical to the success of a quality effort. When we understand clearly what the customer's true needs and value factors are and we have incorporated that reality into the design of our customer value package and built it into our entire organizational strategy, we must keep faith with that essential truth by teaching and preaching it to all the inhabitants of the land. This focus and alignment is one of the hallmarks of the fifth-dimension organization, and something all organizations should strive to achieve and sustain.

9

Process Improvement: Doing Better with Less

The biggest problem in the world could have been solved when it was small.

Lao-tzu

MAKING PROCESS IMPROVEMENT CUSTOMER DRIVEN

The Process Improvement component of the TQS model is where the action really begins. While it's important to understand the customer, clarify the strategy, and get people thinking about customer value, the proof of the pudding is in the way things get done on a day-to-day basis.

The purpose of process improvement is to make the reality match the dream — *to align all organizational systems and processes toward the ultimate purpose of delivering customer value.*

Too many organizations have invested hugely in training employees and task forces to use quality methods like statistical process control (SPC) and then thrown them out on the battlefield without any guidance about what they should be trying to improve.

In many cases this has caused people to go around looking for things they can measure and count so they could use their SPC yardsticks on them. No matter that the processes under attack make little or no contribution to customer-perceived value. It seems to be a matter of "it's measurable, so let's measure it." All process improvement efforts should have a sense of focus, priority, and impact. They should make a significant difference.

> *Process Improvement:*
>
> **Value delivered to the customer must be the driving idea behind all process improvement.**

Customer-driven process improvement begins with tools and techniques that focus on the customer's experience with the organization, such as mapping the moments of truth and cycles of service, and service blueprinting. Each of these simple diagramming methods portrays the customer as a part of the process being investigated. This keeps us from falling into the measure-and-count syndrome. It gives us an aiming point for improvement. It supplies the "why" part of the approach.

How do you choose where to begin? By looking at pain, problems, and opportunities. Start with the customer's experience of the value package delivered:

- ◦ Are there significant complaints, dissatisfaction, or demands to do better?

- ◦ Are there customer problems your system is neglecting, or even aggravating?

- ◦ Are there opportunities to add value for the customer, especially with minimum additional cost?

Work backward from these, into the organization and its processes.

And once you have improved the key problem areas, go to work on areas of possible innovation. Work on getting beyond the "expected" level of the hierarchy of customer value to the "desired" and "unanticipated." This is where the real payoff is.

QUALITY-CRITICAL PROCESSES: THE "SPACE" FORMULA

With the customer value model as a guide, and keeping in mind the vision, mission, and core values of the organization, we can begin to make the *quality-critical processes* of the operation more customer-friendly.

What is a quality-critical process? It's any organizational process for delivering value, either to external customers or internal customers, that has a primary impact on the customer's perception of that value. These are the processes to go after first.

How we define a "process" depends on the level of the operation we're looking at. We can focus on quality-critical processes at three distinct levels of operation: individual employees, teams, and departments. Let's look at each of them in turn.

For example, to the *employee* a process is usually a *task*, i.e., whatever he or she does on the job. The various tasks he or she performs produce results that represent his or her contribution to a team effort and ultimately to the department's contribution. Quality at the task level, whether the employee is dealing with a customer, a coworker, or an individual activity, depends on the nature of the outcome expected.

At the level of the *work team*, a process is likely to be an operational *procedure*: an interacting combination of tasks that produces results that become part of the department's contribution. Quality at the procedure level depends heavily on cooperation, coordination, and often on the proper hand-off of information.

And at the level of the *department*, a process is usually a *system*: a coordinated collection of procedures that create the department's ultimate contribution. It may be a *local system*, i.e., one existing completely within the department, or a *global system*, which threads through two or more departments. Quality in global systems requires close compatibility between the tasks, systems, and procedures in one department and those in another.

Quality-committed organizations extend the concept of process improvement to all aspects of the operation that may affect customer-perceived quality, including to their suppliers. They expect the companies who supply them with raw materials, components, subsystems, or services to make the same commitment to continuous quality improvement they have. They won't tolerate any weak link in the chain of quality, and they don't accept the notion that suppliers can't be influenced because their leaders aren't part of the organization. Virtually every process improvement concept or technique mentioned in this book applies to supplier quality or partner quality, which involves close coordination with other companies in delivering superior customer value.

An easy way to help people focus on quality is to designate a few key tasks, procedures, or systems as quality-critical ones, and work with the employees to set *quality priorities* for them. Quality priorities can fall into the five categories shown here.

> *Speed*—how time-critical is this?
>
> *Personal Touch*—how important is it to manage the customer's state of mind?
>
> *Accuracy*—how important is precision, conformance to specifications, safety, security, information clarity, and error prevention?
>
> *Cooperation*—how important is it to dovetail with another person's task or with what the customer is doing?
>
> *Economy*—how important is it to minimize the resource cost involved?

Although these five factors (which spell SPACE, in case you like acronyms) may not account for every single element of quality, they do go a long way toward helping the people decide how to focus their energies.

For example, if a disgruntled customer comes into a retail establishment for a refund, the employee and his or her supervisor might have already agreed that the sequence of priorities for the task will be Personal Touch first, then Accuracy, then Speed (to avoid wasting the customer's time), then Cooperation with the customer, and Economy last. It's not that Economy is unimportant, but that it takes its place in the priority list, which is keyed to keeping the customer's good will.

Of course, if the customer has damaged the item and a refund is not warranted, then the element of Economy will come more into play. But it will still be important to maintain the Personal Touch. All five of the SPACE priorities are important, but agreeing to a sequence for them gives the employee a better focus for quality and an avenue for improvement.

Other tasks under other circumstances besides the one mentioned as an example would require other sequences of the five quality priority factors. In a health care situation, a pharmacist explaining medications to a patient might want to concentrate on Accuracy as the first priority. Administering an injection might deserve to have Personal Touch as the first priority.

How would you arrange the quality priorities for examples such as:

○ entering a computer record for a payroll change?

○ handling a serious injury in a hospital emergency room?

∘ deciding how many copies of a large report to distribute?

∘ talking a customer through a computer software problem over the phone?

Note that the same five priorities being discussed here apply equally well to the *task* level where the employee works, to the *procedure* level where employees interact, and to the *system* level where procedures interact. The same SPACE factors—Speed, Personal touch, Accuracy, Cooperation, and Economy—are useful in evaluating a procedure or a system and for setting priorities on the way it operates.

For example, the Speed factor in a procedure or a system usually deals with the turnaround time, or "cycle time," as it's sometimes called. The Personal Touch deals with consistency of human contact and expressed concern for the customer throughout the procedure and in all aspects of the system. Accuracy applies to procedures and systems just as well as to individual tasks.

Cooperation, at the level of procedures and systems, involves effectiveness of interaction, smooth handoffs between teams or between elements of the system, and a sense of continuity and linkage from one part of the process to the next. And Economy is just as valid at the level of procedures and systems as it is at the individual task level.

We can use the SPACE formula for quality in two ways. First, we can set quality priorities for a quality-critical task, procedure, or system, based on valid information about customer value. And second, we can evaluate the performance of the task, procedure, or system using the five priority areas as evaluation factors.

Process improvement needs to go on in all areas of the organization, continuously, all the time. All of the quality-critical tasks, procedures, systems, policies, business practices, facilities, equipment, communication channels, work methods, and all the rest of the processes involved in delivering value to customers must be on probation all the time. We must be constantly looking for ways to make them work better.

There are three ways to improve a quality-critical process.

1. *Do it better*—eliminate mistakes, malfunctions, miscommunications, and duplications. Do things better, faster, more easily, and with less wasted time or resources. Make the process work as well as it possibly can.

2. *Do it differently*—redesign the process: rearrange the steps, eliminate steps, have fewer people involved, or do some things in parallel rather than sequentially. Reduce the cycle time, reduce the number of people the customer must deal with, and get the information to flow better.

3. *Do without it*—find a way to achieve the objective without going through the process at all. Are we putting the customer through unnecessary procedures? Are we generating information nobody needs? Can we use other existing processes to eliminate the time, effort, and demands on the customer associated with this process?

In order to improve any service process, we first have to understand it thoroughly. The tools for process analysis (described in detail later) can help you create a shared picture of what's going on that everyone can understand and begin to discuss. Once you have an accurate picture, you can begin to rethink the design of the process and look for ways to simplify it, streamline it, speed it up, and reduce its cost.

Process improvement very often involves getting several people together into a temporary action team and having them attack a very specific process or part of a process that causes problems or offers opportunities to do things better. This team can consist of executives, managers, process specialists, or employees who have been properly prepared for their collective challenge. The magnitude, complexity, and resource impact of the process involved will usually dictate who is actually involved and the degree of latitude they should have in developing innovative solutions.

Process improvement works best when it has a focus, rather than when people chase all over the organization trying to measure and improve everything at once. It's usually much better to start with a few areas of significant quality impact and opportunity, and to use success in those key areas to generate support and enthusiasm for process improvement.

Quality expert Joseph M. Juran has frequently commented on this need for focus. In his view, "quality improvement should happen at a project level. Don't try to do everything at once. Pick out a few key improvement projects, set goals for the improvement, and get people to work making it happen. When you get those accomplished, start on the next ones. Keep that up—forever."

MAKING THE SYSTEMS CUSTOMER-FRIENDLY

The definition of organizational "systems" is quite broad. It includes all of the elements involved in the delivery of service. These include equipment and facilities, policies and procedures, methods, communication processes—all of the things the organization's employees can use to guide or influence the delivery of value.

Making systems customer-friendly means designing or modifying them so they suit the needs of the customer, rather than just the needs of the organization. This is not to say that a system that helps the customer should be inconvenient for the organization. We should strive to establish systems with the customer's perspective and experience as the primary design focus, and make sure we meet the needs of the organization as well.

A well-functioning system is often invisible to the customer. When it is visible, it should create a positive experience for the customer. The best systems say "I'm here for your convenience—to make this experience positive."

Creating customer-friendly systems goes hand in hand with making the whole organization customer-friendly. In the Service Triangle model (shown in Chapter 1), the systems need to be connected to the organization's strategy and its people. All of these elements focus on the customer and his or her experience. If it weren't for the customer, none of these components would exist. For that matter, without the customer the organization wouldn't exist.

We've all encountered systems that abuse customers and cause negative moments of truth. For example, when people are admitted to some hospitals, they practically have to present their qualifications for being a patient. They must fill out a pile of forms and to do so they need to know or have with them the "right" information, such as insurance policy numbers.

All too often, the hospital admitting employee offers little help in the admitting process. This adds to the already high level of stress for the new patient. Nobody wants to go to the hospital and this tedious process only makes it worse.

Even after this step is complete, the patient-customer often has to wait for a room. Once in the room, the customer may undergo interrogation further by representatives of nursing, the lab, social services, dietary, etc. The customer may have to answer the same questions over and over for different hospital staffers. Each individual unit needs much of the same information, yet there may be no system for sharing the information among the various departments. In these cases, the system for gathering information clearly isn't designed for the convenience of the customer.

A large investment firm in the eastern United States created a system that was neither customer friendly nor organization friendly. After a great deal of investment and effort, they could provide a monthly customer statement that was a technological marvel. The firm's design department was very proud of this document, especially since they believed it to be unique in the industry. But although the statement was good for the industry, the customers couldn't figure it out. The designers had not interviewed customers about what they actually wanted or needed in their monthly statements.

The account executives found themselves spending a great deal of their time explaining and answering complaints about the statement. Ultimately, the company got rid of the design and started over. Unfortunately, they wasted a lot of money and created many negative moments of truth during this discovery process.

A colleague recently encountered a formidable policy, which, if enforced, could have been not only unfriendly, but life threatening. She rented a car from one of the companies at a large eastern airport. As she was being "processed" by the agent, another car rental employee ran into the glass enclosed rental trailer shouting, "There's a man with a gun shooting up the parking lot!"

Realizing she was in full view and a possible target, she asked the agent if she could get behind the counter with her. The agent replied, "I'm sorry ma'am, our policy is that only employees are allowed on this side of the counter." Needless to say, she ignored the policy and jumped over the counter until the incident was over.

Phil Wexler, a hospitality industry marketing consultant, went into his hotel restaurant one evening. Because he was on a tight schedule, he decided that all he wanted for dinner was the lobster bisque, a specialty of the restaurant. When he gave the waiter his order, he was told that he couldn't order lobster bisque separately but only as part of a full dinner. Since he didn't have time for a full dinner, he again repeated his desire to have lobster bisque. This time the waiter was even more insistent, saying, "Our policy manual says I can't serve lobster bisque other than with a full dinner order." Wexler replied, "Well, my policy manual says you can, and since I'm paying the check, let's go by my policy manual."

On the other hand, customer-friendly systems can impress us, even when they don't involve high technology. Good ones can result in competitive differentiation for the organization. Many organizations, ranging from limousine services to fast-food delivery shops, have come a long way in the last few years.

The Mandarin Oriental Hotel in Hong Kong has a computer system that enables the people handling guest reservations to know whether a particular person has stayed at the hotel before, and if so how many times before and the date of the most recent stay. They use this knowledge, plus an inventory of preference items, to enable the housekeeping department to set up the room exactly the way the guest wants it, before he or she even checks in.

USAA, one of the top-performing insurance companies in America, uses systems and technology to create an especially customer friendly interface. By feeding all customer letters and related documents into scanners that capture them as graphic images, USAA people can use their computer display terminals to create the effect of individualized personal-account representatives. Any claims employee can bring up an image of any document in the file, and have the very latest status when talking to the customer who calls.

The point is simply that systems, policies, and procedures should be a framework for serving the customer, not ends in themselves. They should be empowering, not imprisoning. They should be developed in cooperation with those who have to use and experience them. Policies should help people to improve the customer's experience, not detract from it. They shouldn't exist in an inflexible "vacuum." And, where necessary, employees should be empowered to bend or even break the rules to serve the customer.

Systems should never be created by managers without the input of those who use them—the employees or those who ultimately experience them—the customers. It only makes good sense to capitalize on the knowledge of the people whose lives they affect.

There is a special variation of the unfriendly system syndrome, which amounts to extreme "system craziness." This is the kind of system or policy that is so weird, so unhelpful, and so apparently unexplainable that the customer gets the impression somebody in the organization has lost his mind.

Another colleague encountered one of the more bizarre examples of system craziness one Christmas Eve. In making a last-minute gift purchase, he presented a well-known brand of credit card for payment. After a few minutes, the salesclerk sheepishly told him that the credit card people had denied authorization for his card. He paid with another credit card but was concerned because his card had been honored only a few minutes earlier at another store.

A few days later he called the credit card company regarding the credit denial. The clerk told him that because of the large number of requests for card authorizations the organization couldn't keep up with all the telephone calls. To speed processing of the calls, the company had decided to randomly deny credit rather than look up every account number. In this manner, they avoided a messy backlog of calls. While this policy helped them, it only inconvenienced and embarrassed the customers it affected.

You'll find system craziness whenever there's a disparity between what the customer has a reasonable right to expect and what he or she actually experiences. This occurs when the systems aren't compatible with the customer's experience, or when the systems are operationally driven, rather than customer-driven.

One of the biggest roadblocks to quality improvement comes from the administrative underbrush—the creeping bureaucracy and red tape that people in the organization have to deal with on a daily basis. In many organizations, administrative requirements, including reports, meetings, forms, policies, and procedures, have taken on a life of their own. They strangle the ability of the organization to respond and focus on the needs of its customers. A major part of process improvement should involve pruning the administrative underbrush.

Recently, a customer phoned a well-known consumer products company regarding the recall of a defective coffee maker, which had a nasty habit of causing fires (300 or so, to date). The customer relations department referred him to a special toll-free telephone number established specifically to handle the recalls.

In a period of 24 hours (day and night) on approximately 20 separate occasions, he dialed the number and each time heard the same recorded message: "Thank you for calling. Due to the tremendous response, we are unable to process your call. We are open 24 hours. Please call back at your convenience." Finally, just before hanging up after hearing the full recorded message for the zillionth time, he was startled to hear a person answer the phone. When he mentioned the recorded instruction to call back and indicated his surprise that the call was answered, the operator told him that on the previous day, during a five-hour period, 8000 calls were handled, but 110,000 hang-ups occurred.

He offered that a reasonable explanation for the high number of hang-ups was because the recorded message was telling people to call back. The very courteous, well-trained operator said that she thought the recorded message was misleading and should be redone, but that it was unlikely her input would result in any changes. From her perspective, based on the numbers, there would always be another caller at the end of the line anyway.

How often have you heard a frontline employee respond in a similar manner? "I didn't invent the system. I have to use what they give me." "I didn't write the policy—there's nothing I can do. They don't listen to me when I complain about it."

We need to incite a level of intolerance for system craziness and unfriendliness on the part of everyone in the organization. It shouldn't be necessary for the customers to hound us into building better systems. If we do it right, everyone gets a payoff. The customer gets better value, the employees get to work more sanely, and the organization usually wastes fewer resources getting the work done.

EARLY WINS: GIVING PEOPLE THE TASTE OF SUCCESS

A quality-improvement effort can sometimes take quite a long time to bear fruit. During the early stages, there is usually a certain amount of doubt, skepticism, and sometimes downright opposition to making the investment. Not everybody believes in it. During this crucial period, it is very helpful to show some early results—positive impacts that tell people things are beginning to happen. This is the "early wins" element of the TQS action menu and it can be a very important one.

In most organizations, there are usually some easily identifiable areas for improvement that don't require extensive analysis and that can create highly visible impacts. The early wins approach enables us to pick this low-hanging fruit at the outset, so people can begin to associate a feeling of value and success with the quality effort.

Sometimes it's just a matter of a leadership directive that says "That system has been a mess for years. Fix it—*now*." There is often a big temptation to appoint a committee and have them try to do the job properly. But this is not necessarily the best approach for early wins. Sometimes any noticeable improvement at all will make a hit with people. You can always do it even better later.

At a Los Angeles hospital, for example, the TQS task force had identified signage as a factor desperately needing attention. When anyone walked into the lobby, he or she saw a mish-mash of confusing directional signs, all done in different sizes and styles. This forest of signs almost defied the visitor to figure out where to go.

After some debate about a project to take care of the signs properly, including the option of bringing in a "signage consultant," the group finally decided that the signs needed changing right away. They commissioned three people to sit down and work out a new set of signs for the lobby and around the main bank of elevators. Then they went to a local sign shop and had them made and installed. The whole process took about two weeks instead of the three months it could have taken if done "properly."

The value in choosing an early win item like signage is that it affects almost everyone right away. It's something everyone can see and begin to associate with a new attitude about quality. The same task force identified and implemented some immediate changes in the hospital lobby, including removing the dead and dying plants, replacing the waiting-area furniture with pieces that matched, and getting magazines that were less than three years old.

You can find early win opportunities in a number of areas. Some places to start looking are

1. Areas of extreme customer dissatisfaction
2. Processes that cause high employee frustration
3. Obvious system craziness that needs curing
4. Ways to increase employee discretion and empowerment with little risk or debate about appropriateness
5. Changes that are visually noticeable by all or most customers and all or most employees

It is important that the changes you make in the name of early wins be valid and worthwhile improvements. They don't have to be momentous in their impact, but be careful not to fall into making cosmetic changes just to get attention. It is important to manage the "box office" effect, but not at the expense of real improvement.

SEVEN HANDY TOOLS FOR PROCESS IMPROVEMENT

Process improvement is not the sole province of experts or highly trained problem solvers. Frontline workers can make huge contributions to quality improvement if they know how to use a few simple pencil-and-paper diagramming tools to analyze their processes. The TQS approach uses seven basic diagramming tools. Each has its particular area of applicability and all are easy to learn and use.

These seven process-improvement tools are defined briefly here and discussed more thoroughly in the book's Resource Section.

Process Improvements Tools:

1. *The Customer Bug List*—a simple list of things that "bug" your customers about your service.
2. *The Moment of Truth Chart*—a simple chart with three columns that deals with one selected moment of truth. The center column lists the customer's *standard expectations* of that moment of truth, as verified by the research. The left column lists *minus factors*, i.e., things that can happen or fail to happen that make the moment of truth unsatisfactory. And the right column lists *plus factors* that can add value in the customer's eyes.
3. *The Cycle of Service Chart*—a circular "clock-face" chart showing the sequence of moments of truth encountered by the customer in any complete service delivery experience.
4. *The Service Blueprint*—a flow diagram depicting the customer's experience in the cycle of service, side by side with the respective actions of the various departments involved in delivering the service.
5. *The Why-Why Diagram*—a branching "tree" diagram that helps you identify the root causes of a quality problem by asking the question "why" several times in succession and diagramming the various "becauses" for each why.
6. *The How-How Diagram*—a diagram that helps you identify the various actions that could help to solve a quality problem by reversing the sequence of the why-why Diagram.
7. *The Tracking Chart*—a simple graph used to keep track of the number of times various errors, malfunctions, customer complaints, or problems occur.

Please refer to the Resource Section for a more complete explanation of these seven tools.

By training employees to identify areas in need of improvement, and by teaching them to use these seven simple diagramming tools appropriately, you can create a team of expert service problem solvers. Quality Service Action Teams, for example, can use these tools very effectively.

All of these tools work best when you have facts. It's one thing to sit around and speculate about why things go wrong and what you should do about it. But when you invest the effort to gather some solid facts about the problem, you can target your energies much more effectively. How often does each type of malfunction occur? Under what circumstances is it most likely to occur? What is the impact, both on the customer and on our operation, when it does occur? All of these facts help to keep your quality-improvement effort grounded in reality. And they make the use of the process-improvement tools much more productive.

UNDERSTANDING THE COST OF QUALITY

Many organizations do not pay enough attention to analyzing the costs of their operations. While on the one hand manufacturing businesses tend to look at costs very carefully, and the sophisticated ones can identify in detail the cost elements involved in making and distributing their products, most service businesses only look at costs in the most general way.

It is vitally important to isolate the costs involved in a particular service process as part of a quality analysis. A high-cost process justifies careful attention, not only from the standpoint of customer value, but from the standpoint of cost savings as well.

Quality experts W. Edwards Deming, Joseph M. Juran, and Philip B. Crosby all contend that most organizations give insufficient attention to the issue of "cost of quality." Definitions of cost of quality vary, but in the TQS framework it is the total cost of making, doing, or delivering something, including the cost of doing it wrong. In other words, the real cost of delivering customer value includes:

1. *Performance Cost*—the basic cost of doing it one time, assuming it happens perfectly, without errors or problems.

2. *Failure Cost*—the prorated cost of having to correct it, redo it, or make up for it when it's done wrong; this can include the cost of making amends to the customer if necessary.
3. *Prevention and Detection Cost*—the prorated cost of safeguards and processes that exist for the sole purpose of minimizing failure costs; these include inspection, double-checking, special accuracy procedures, and extra processes that act as safeguards for proper performance.

For example, the real cost to a travel agency of selling an airline ticket to a customer is the one-time cost of booking the reservation, printing and processing the ticket, and the associated labor and materials costs all along the way, plus an allocated cost that reflects the number of times it goes wrong, plus an allocated share of the direct cost of the safeguards installed to ensure good performance.

If 10 percent of the tickets involve things going wrong, then the agency must prorate the failure costs of those 10 percent across all the tickets processed. If the procedure involves another person double-checking the accuracy of the computer record and verifying the assembled ticket, then those costs figure into the cost of quality for that operation.

Quality cost analysis can be fairly simple, or you can make it quite elaborate if you want to analyze a process in great detail. It's important to associate all of the relevant costs with the process you want to understand. For example, in the travel agency case, the cost of a bounced customer check or a rejected credit card is part of the cost of quality. Even though the causes may be beyond the full control of the agency, it is important to know the actual costs of doing business. These quality costs are often surprising.

The Service Blueprint tool described in the Resource Section is ideally suited for quality cost analysis. It enables us to answer the question "How much does it actually cost to perform this particular cycle of service one time for one customer?"

It is possible to associate a cost with each box on the service blueprint chart. The cost will usually involve direct labor, materials or supplies of some sort, or both. By adding up all of these individual item costs, you can arrive at a total one-shot cost for the cycle of service.

It also makes sense sometimes to analyze the customer's cost of doing business with us, over and above whatever charge we make for the service. This is an aspect of customer value almost universally ignored by service businesses. Most companies pay no attention to the cost inflicted on the customer, including costs incurred through no fault of his or her own when the organization does things wrong.

Suppose, for example, a commercial medical lab loses a tissue specimen sent by a doctor's office for tests. What is the cost to the physician and to his customer of a retake? The patient may have to take time away from work, which might involve lost pay, travel costs, parking, etc. The physician loses billable time having to repeat the procedure. There is the extra staff time and administrative cost of dealing with the lab and the courier service. And, of course, there is the unmeasurable cost of having lost the patient's good will and trust.

Service cost analysis can do a great deal to place quality and customer value in perspective. When employees take on the task of blueprinting service processes and calculating out their costs, they become much more aware of the need to do things right the first time.

Using the simple quality tools moves the traditional focus of management attention from cost reduction to quality improvement, while retaining the opportunities to reduce cost along the way. *While very few cost-cutting programs ever have the side-effect of improving customer value or quality, the reverse is often true.* In other words, an attack on quality may very well bring cost reductions along with it. The reason:

The Quality Axiom:

**Doing things well
usually costs less
than doing them poorly.**

At a large metropolitan hospital, nurses were having a hard time getting clean linen for their patients. The linen department had focused its energies on controlling linen use in order to reduce costs. Unfortunately this resulted in an unexpected linen shortage and forced the nurses to waste time looking for linen. Often, nurses hoarded it, even disposing of clean linen they didn't use. The result was greater linen consumption for the hospital and less time spent actually caring for patients. Paradoxically, the attempt to reduce linen costs actually caused those costs to increase.

The linen shortage problem first showed up through an internal customer survey. In the survey, the linen department asked nurses for feedback on service provided to them. Based on the input, the linen department and nursing personnel created a new process to get sufficient clean linen to the nurses and their patients. Linen services agreed with nursing to supply individual patient rooms with clean linen, rather than storing linen in a general supply area. Nurses, in turn, agreed to stop hoarding it.

As a result, the nurses could spend as much as 20 minutes more per day with their patients, because they weren't wasting time looking for linen. Linen consumption *decreased* by 25 percent in some areas because clean linen was no longer hoarded or tossed out. Working relationships between nurses and linen personnel improved dramatically, and patient satisfaction with nursing care also went up. Seeing a positive change in the experiences of their customers (nurses and patients), the linen department felt motivated to look at other areas to improve.

This is a curious effect of the customer-value focus in quality improvement:

> ### *Quality and Cost:*
>
> **You seldom improve quality
> by cutting costs,
> but you can often cut costs
> by improving quality.**

QUALITY SERVICE ACTION TEAMS: GRASS ROOTS INVOLVEMENT

Quality Service Action Team (QSATs)—small groups formed for the purpose of improving service processes—help to improve processes that directly involve the team. Typically, QSATs are formed at the department or work-team level and consist of five to ten members and a team leader who meet regularly to discuss and solve service-quality problems.

The major difference between QSATs and traditional quality circles is that QSATs begin with the customer's experience, focus on customer-impact issues, and use the service-quality improvement tools discussed previously—Moments of Truth, Cycles of Service, Service Blueprints, Why-Why Diagrams, How-How Diagrams, Customer Bug List, and the Tracking Chart.

Many organizations are beginning to use QSATs or similar team problem-solving approaches for quality improvement. One of the largest of such efforts is at the National Westminster Bank, in the U.K. According to Paul Goodstadt, "We launched a large number of QSATs immediately after people started coming out of the introductory training sessions on service. The employees at the various branches took to the idea very enthusiastically. With over 3000 branches around the U.K., we've had about 5000 QSAT projects to date, ranging from very small problem areas to some very extensive ones."

Riverside Methodist Hospital launched a number of QSATs as part of its service-quality effort. According to Chief Operating Officer Nancy Schlicting, "QSATs are a very important part of our approach to service quality. We believe they're an effective way to get good solutions to quality problems and build employee commitment and enthusiasm at the same time." The hospital has had as many as 100 QSATs operating at one time, each going after a self-selected service-quality problem.

INVITING THE CUSTOMER TO JOIN YOUR IMPROVEMENT TEAM

When an Australian commercial real estate firm faced the prospect of disgruntled tenants during a long-term, major refurbishment of one of its high-rise office buildings in downtown Sydney, it made sense to ask the customers to help define the proper quality focus. We convened a management meeting to examine the issues and invited representatives from several of their largest tenant organizations, both retailers and office tenants.

According to Bruce Bland, manager of Lend Lease Corporation's MLC Centre in Sydney, "We wanted to find out firsthand what they considered quality to be. We had our own ideas, but we quickly found out the tenants had certain points of view we hadn't considered. The discussions really opened our eyes and gave us a better focus on the value factors that were critical in keeping them happy during the extended period of the refurbishment."

Another Australian firm, Australian Airlines, used a similar approach (as mentioned in the first chapter). James Strong, then CEO of that country's major government-owned domestic air carrier, decided to ask the customers to define value. He also asked the employees to be the market researchers.

In a series of luncheon meetings all across the country, volunteer employees met with an equal number of customers to discuss the experience of flying with the airline. The employees turned out to be skillful investigators and the customers were very forthcoming with their views. They literally designed the ideal flying experience and identified critical value factors from the customer's perspective.

Asking customers and employees to participate in orchestrating process improvement not only uncovers creative solutions, it also has the bonus effect of getting the employees turned on. According to James Strong, "At first, we weren't sure enough employees would volunteer to make it feasible, but we were amazed at the response. It turned out to be one of the wisest things we ever did. The employees did a great job of interviewing the customers, we got great information, and they loved it."

More and more organizations are bringing the voice of the customers into the center of their businesses. They are even going beyond customer focus-group research, and asking customers to participate on quality committees, customer panels, and even employee action teams. According to Dr. David Gaffney, chief executive of ICI Australia, a maker of a wide range of chemical products, "We regularly ask our cutomers to help us improve the quality of all aspects of our products and our service. We consider it critical to know how they feel about the value we deliver, and to get their best ideas about how we can do it better."

10

Keeping Score, Scoring Points, & Pointing the Way

Not everything that counts can be counted;
and not everything that can be counted counts.

Albert Einstein

HOW NOT TO MEASURE QUALITY

The leaders of one of the largest worldwide hotel chains learned a hard lesson about measuring quality when they launched a company-wide effort a few years ago, aimed at increasing guest satisfaction. They went through all aspects of the operation—front desk, housekeeping, food and beverage, accounting, maintenance, and all other departments— and set quality measurements and standards. There were measures and standards galore, but some of them backfired.

As one part of the quality program, they specified a "courtesy standard" for front-desk employees. A big part of this courtesy orientation was the requirement that the employee address the guest by name at least twice during the check-in procedure. Training programs emphasized and repeated the rule. Supervisors monitored employee behavior and reminded them about it. Little signs under the counter touted it.

After more than a year of hammering away at the "name rule," they saw the rate of compliance level off at about 50 percent. The employees almost unanimously hated the rule. Many of them felt that it insulted their intelligence and demeaned their skills as ambassadors of service. The supervisors were frustrated with it. Worst of all, the customer research showed it had no detectable effect on customer perception of service quality or on repurchase intention. Some customers actually found it artificial and annoying.

The company finally abandoned the rule, along with a number of other equally ineffective quality standards. This retreat came as part of a widespread disillusionment with the whole quality effort and a feeling at all levels that the hotel was not approaching the problem intelligently.

When they reexamined the quality issue through the framework of the TQS approach, their intuitive sense of failure became clear intellectually: they were applying the wrong quality measures and standards in view of the objectives they wanted to achieve. They sought a very subjective outcome: customers feeling they were welcome at the hotel and feeling that the staff would go out of their way to meet their needs. But they were trying to legislate "courtesy behavior" rather than empower the employees with customer-pleasing ideas and strategies and expect them to use their own minds.

Many quality efforts get confused on this point: the way you measure or assess quality must vary according to how *objective* or *subjective* your desired quality outcome is. And the amount of discretion you give the employees to achieve the outcomes must vary accordingly.

There is no one "correct" way to measure all aspects of quality. You need a range of measurement strategies depending on how the customer defines each aspect. And there is no one way of telling employees how to achieve every aspect of quality. You need a whole range of levels of discretion, again depending on how subjectively the customer's experience of quality is defined.

Our research has shown that there is not just one quality strategy, there are four. Each one is a combination of a particular type of *quality objective*, a matching level of *employee discretion* for achieving that objective, and a matching way of *measuring success* in achieving it.

Figure 10–1 illustrates these four approaches. Each varies according to the type of quality objective shown on the horizontal axis, ranging from the very specific and objective to the very subjective. (Please refer to Figure 10–1 as you read the following explanation.)

Let's look first at quality objectives, then at the corresponding levels of employee discretion, and finally at the corresponding ways of measuring their achievement. There are four main kinds of quality

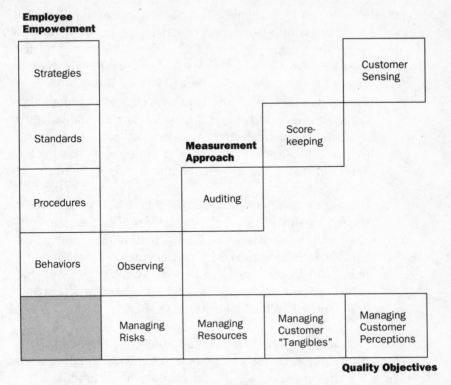

Employee Empowerment

Strategies				Customer Sensing
Standards		**Measurement Approach**	Score-keeping	
Procedures		Auditing		
Behaviors	Observing			
	Managing Risks	Managing Resources	Managing Customer "Tangibles"	Managing Customer Perceptions

Quality Objectives

Figure 10–1   Quality measurment should empower employees.

objective, if you classify them according to the type of thing you're trying to accomplish:

1. *Managing risks*—this is the most tightly controlled kind of quality outcome. With this type of quality objective, you want to make sure something important doesn't go wrong. You want to minimize the risk of human injury, high-cost accidents, legal liabilities, and the like. This is basically a *defensive* quality objective, and one that is internally focused. How you accomplish it and how you measure its accomplishment reflect that focus.
2. *Managing resources*—if you didn't care how much it cost to provide a high-quality experience to the customer, you wouldn't need this type of objective. But in most cases you do care, and you want to deliver high value at the lowest appropriate cost to the organization. This is also an internally

focused quality objective. You do it because you want the organization to perform cost-effectively.

3. *Managing customer "tangibles"*—this is an externally focused quality objective. You know that a certain tangible experience for the customer is critical to your success. An item of merchandise must function perfectly, something must happen at the right time, some customer information must be absolutely correct, and so forth. You set this objective because you want the customer to approve of the tangible aspects of his or her experience and decide to continue to be your customer.

4. *Managing customer perceptions*—this is also an externally focused quality objective. You have identified a certain feeling reaction, or state of mind, or perception of subjective value that the customer seeks in a particular aspect of doing business with your organization. You want to enhance that subjective perception as a way to build a bond of acceptance and approval in the mind of the customer.

Once you identify a particular quality objective as one of the four options just mentioned, you can figure out the corresponding amount of discretion the employee should have in accomplishing it.

Clearly, it's not appropriate to give employees unlimited discretion. That would produce utter chaos. It isn't what leadership is all about. However, most employees in most organizations can handle considerably more discretion than their bosses have allowed them to have.

Western management theory has for many decades worked on the principle of *minimal* employee discretion rather than *optimal* discretion. A sacred precept of management has been that, if a person has no formal supervisory responsibility, he or she needs to be told specifically what to do. Only supervisors and managers have authority to act independently.

But we know from a wealth of experience that certain aspects of quality are very difficult, if not impossible, to prescribe in unambiguous terms. This is especially true when the quality objective deals with customer perception. When the employee must handle a critical moment of truth with the customer, it makes no sense to try to define detailed procedures or behaviors. We are asking the employee to do something that is essentially an art—for example, pacifying an angry customer who has been treated inhumanely—by following some standard procedure. It doesn't work well.

This, above all, has been the failing of the measure-and-control school of thought in regard to service quality. It's a confusion of means and ends. The degree of discretion the employee should have in any area should depend on the quality objective we're asking him or her to accomplish.

For each of the four types of quality objective previously identified, there's a corresponding level of employee discretion, or empowerment to act, that's appropriate. Again referring to Figure 10–1, we see that they are:

1. *Behaviors*—the lowest possible level of discretion and sometimes the most misused in service-quality programs. You're asking the employee to say or do a certain very specific thing or set of things, without deviation from the prescription and without exercising any personal judgment about its appropriateness. Behavior control is usually the most effective approach for achieving the quality objective of *Managing Risks*.

2. *Procedures*—a higher level of discretion, but still a fairly well controlled one. Think of a procedure as a predesigned set of steps that makes sure one person's contribution to the ultimate result is compatible with another's. A procedure allows a degree of discretion in doing the individual tasks but little discretion in the overall sequence and timing of events. This is generally an effective approach when the quality objective is *Managing Resources*.

3. *Standards*—the next highest level of discretion, allowing variations in procedures so long as the results meet a defined condition. Think of a standard as a target measurement that a tangible outcome should match. The measurement could prescribe physical characteristics, turnaround time, arrival of an item at a location, accuracy of information, or any of an unlimited number of other possibilities. You're asking people to work together to achieve an outcome that meets the standard. This is generally an effective approach when your quality objective is *Managing Customer Tangibles*.

4. *Strategies*—the highest level of discretion, allowing the employee considerable latitude for action in achieving the

desired customer response. Because you can't measure the customer's response objectively, i.e., it's internal to the customer and subjective, you can't predefine specific behaviors, procedures, or standards to achieve it. You must depend on a well-informed, well-oriented, well-trained employee to use his or her best judgment in the situation. This is virtually the only sensible approach when your quality objective is *Managing Customer Perceptions.*

Now the quality-measurement approach begins to make more sense. *You measure quality by using the means appropriate to the combination of the quality objective and the level of employee discretion you're dealing with.* In other words, each combination of quality objective and level of discretion implies one preferable means of measurement.

Many organizations have created nightmarish measurement systems without any clear concept of what they were trying to accomplish in the first place. To paraphrase an old expression, if you don't know what you're trying to accomplish, then it doesn't matter how you try to measure effectiveness.

Measuring quality simply means finding out how well we are achieving the quality objectives we set. If we have no quality objectives, it's pointless to measure.

Referring again to Figure 10–1, we see that the four corresponding quality-measurement methods, shown in the diagonal boxes, are

1. *Observing behavior*—the only way you can verify that an employee behaves in a certain way is to have someone observe him or her behaving. It isn't necessary to have as many observers as workers, but if the behavior is critical, somebody has to observe it and verify it.

2. *Auditing*—just as an accounting audit is a review that makes sure people are following accepted accounting practices, so a quality audit makes sure people are using accepted quality practices. An audit starts with the assumption that the quality procedures are appropriate (which is not always a safe assumption) and simply determines the extent to which people are following them.

3. *Scorekeeping*—this is where the measure-and-count approach is appropriate. When your quality objective is *Man-*

aging Customer Tangibles and you have properly defined objective standards for those tangibles, then you simply keep score. You measure the number of customer incidents that meet the standard and you express the results numerically.

4. *Customer sensing*—this is a very different kind of measurement method from the previous three—the measurement has to come from the customer. There is no way you can accurately gauge the mental, emotional, or subjective reactions of customers over a period of time without asking them to express themselves to you. Customer sensing is one of the most misunderstood and misapplied of all forms of quality measurement. When you put it into perspective as part of one particular approach, it makes much more sense.

As Figure 10–1 shows, these various options match up with one another in a very specific way. We can think of a *quality strategy* as a particular combination of one quality objective, shown on the horizontal line, a corresponding level of employee discretion for achieving it, shown on the vertical line, and a corresponding method of measuring it, shown on the diagonal line.

Figure 10–1 suggests four basic quality strategies, which we can designate as QS-1 through QS-4:

QS-1. Managing Risks + Behavior Control + Observation
QS-2. Managing Resources + Procedures + Auditing
QS-3. Managing Customer Tangibles + Standards + Score-keeping
QS-4. Managing Customer Perceptions + Strategies + Customer Sensing

Figure 10–1 also shows that there isn't one single way to specify and measure quality; there are four to choose from. Getting specific about quality improvement becomes largely a matter of selecting one of these four quality strategies and putting it into effect. Let's look at some examples.

American police officers in most cities and states are required to formally advise an arrested person of his or her legal rights before questioning. Let's see how that works from the point of view of the quality strategies shown in Figure 10–1.

The quality objective at hand is Managing Risks. What is the risk for the police? It is the risk of having the arrest declared invalid and having the prosecution fail as a result of a "technicality." Many criminals have gone free simply because their attorneys argued successfully that they confessed without knowing that the law did not require them to speak to the police.

The allowed level of discretion for the arresting peace officer—on this particular quality aspect, but not on others—is virtually zero. Quality here is at the level of behavior. In fact, many police organizations require their officers to read the arrestee's rights verbatim from a small wallet card. They may not summarize, paraphrase, or extemporize; they read the statement word for word and then ask the arrestee to affirm that he or she understands the rights involved before asking any questions.

The third piece to the quality strategy in this case is observation, which corresponds to the behavior level of discretion. Police officers observe one another and give feedback to ensure they're all complying with the behavior. Supervisors check occasionally to verify the practice. Refresher training reinforces the need to follow the practice exactly. In many police organizations, "reading the rights" has become almost completely instinctive as part of the arrest process.

For this particular aspect of police work, the quality strategy is QS–1. In other aspects, such as controlling an accident scene, covering a given territory during the period of the officer's watch, or managing a domestic dispute among members of a family, higher quality strategies would apply.

Some situations involve multiple quality objectives, and consequently should involve mixed quality strategies. In a hospital, for example, a nurse or technician might be treating a patient with a procedure that involves some unavoidable discomfort. While the exact procedure may allow little or no discretion, i.e., QS–2, the worker needs to be a strategist when it comes to supporting the patient's mental state and winning his or her cooperative acceptance of the procedure, i.e., QS–4.

It's not necessary to measure all the microscopic elements of quality in a business. Most of them, in fact, are best left in the hands of competent and committed employees. This quality-strategy approach simply helps provide a focus on the *critical* quality areas. However, it does help in reviewing quality issues throughout the organization and in detecting inappropriate strategies.

An effective quality strategy spotlights a significant problem or opportunity, empowers the employees to attack it effectively, enables them to feel a sense of having contributed value, and measures results in a way that helps people see their accomplishments.

Returning to the case of the hotel's front desk courtesy standard, Figure 10–1 shows that they were trying to operate with QS–1 while the situation called for QS–4. After all, the desired outcome was presumably to have the customer consider the staff friendly, helpful, cordial, and courteous. The managers were trying to use the form of discretion and measurement appropriate to QS–1 to meet the quality objective of QS–4. They were reluctant to make the employees customer strategists. They wanted to treat them like robots instead.

People get turned on about their jobs when they feel a *sense of power* about what they do. They want to feel they're doing work worth doing. They want to feel their effort has impact and that it's appreciated. And they want to feel part of something they can respect and feel good about. All of this spells a desire for a feeling—something lately being referred to as a feeling of *empowerment*.

Power, ultimately, is all about *discretion*—the entitlement to act on one's own. It means being authorized to size up a situation, see what's needed, make a decision about how to handle it, and act on that decision without fear of being countermanded or vetoed by someone higher up.

Not surprisingly, the issue of how to measure quality ties in very closely with the issue of how to empower employees and help them feel they are doing something worthwhile.

Some organizations get so wrapped up in measurement that they measure destructively. One variety of this is the "speed trap," in which they seize upon any available time variable as a measure of quality. For example, in the early days after the break-up of AT&T, the executives decided that operator call-time performance had to improve.

They instituted a measurement program that focused on the number of seconds each operator took to get a caller off the line. And that's exactly what the operators began to do. Knowing they'd be punished if they took longer than the assigned standard number of seconds, they began to "slam-dunk" the callers as quickly as possible, whether they had really taken care of their needs or not. The operators became stressed and irritable, courtesy went down the tubes, and service went to hell. A company that had for years prided itself in looking after customers' needs had become a sweatshop, because its leaders no longer knew what business they were in.

Here's a working definition of empowerment:

> **Empowerment is responsible freedom.**

When we empower employees, we give them the freedom to act responsibly and effectively, not recklessly. We give them the information, knowledge, and skills they need to take responsibility, and to balance the interests of the customer with the interest of the organization.

INFORMATION: A POWERFUL WAY TO CHANGE BEHAVIOR

When Christian Sinding, marketing director of SAS's International Hotels Division, wanted the marketing staffs at their various hotel properties to focus more on their conference and meeting business, he needed a way to get them thinking about it. Early assessments showed that the salespeople felt they understood clearly what the customers, most of whom were experienced meeting planners, wanted. As Sinding describes,

> The customers wanted the lowest prices, according to the consensus of our salespeople. But somehow I doubted that conclusion. I wanted to find out from the customers themselves what they considered critical to a successful meeting experience. So we launched some basic research projects to figure out the customers' value model.
>
> We isolated seven value factors in our discussions with meeting planners; price, of course was one of the factors on the list. Then we asked the salespeople to predict what factors the customers would name, before we showed them the actual factors and the rankings.
>
> The results surprised them. While they put price first on the list of critical factors, the meeting planners put it in about fifth place. The first-place item for the meeting planners wasn't even on the staff's list: *no hassles.*

According to Sinding, the critical concern of the meeting planners was that everything happen when and how it was supposed to happen. They worried constantly that the hotel would foul up on some arrangement, that instructions wouldn't be followed, that audiovisual equipment would malfunction, and that Murphy's Law was just waiting to claim its next victim. Assurance of a "no screw-ups" commitment was the primary thing they wanted. Although price was important, it came into play *after* they assured themselves the hotel could handle the job without bungling it.

"The salespeople were a bit taken aback with the results," says Sinding. "They had to rethink the approach to making the sale. They were emphasizing something the customer wasn't ready to think about— the price, and ignoring the number-one factor on the customer's list— assurance that things wouldn't go wrong."

In this case, Sinding used information in a dramatic way to make people think differently and behave differently. He could have simply written a memo and emphasized the factors he considered important. However, he engaged the employees creatively in a dialogue. The element of suspense created by asking them to predict the customer priorities in advance heightened the impact of discovering the real priorities.

Whenever you can introduce a sense of discovery into the presentation of important information, you can amplify its impact on peoples' minds. The information takes on a new sense of significance. It becomes more compelling and it invites action.

I have used this method and seen it used many times, with similar results. People in organizations get deluged with information, to the extent that none of it seems to have any real impact. If you want something to really sink in, it's often a good idea to make it available in some provocative or novel way so that it hits with greater effect.

What you measure and share sends a message. It tells the people in your organization what you consider important and where to place their attention. People learn more through observation than through conversation. What gets measured says more than what gets talked about. This is why so many "cosmetic" quality programs don't get very far. The employees quickly detect the fact that it's just nice words, and they go on about their business.

Giving people useful information can empower them, to a much greater degree than simply preaching at them or telling them what to do. In the early stages of a quality effort, information can help people recognize the significance of customer value, understand what it means for their organization, and accept the commitment to quality. It can make the whole effort real for them on an individual, personal basis.

As the quality effort progresses, information can help them see progress, feel good about their contributions, and work with a sense of optimism and purpose. This is what the fifth component of the TQS model—assessment, measurement, and feedback—enables you to do.

MEASURING CUSTOMER VALUE: FROM "THERBLIGS" TO "MOTs"

A fundamental change in the quality focus takes place when people start thinking in terms of measuring customer value rather than just work activity. This shift from an activity focus to an outcome focus changes everything.

Traditional Western management has for several generations conceived of the basic measurement unit of value and quality as the "therblig," although many people don't know it by that peculiar name. Years ago, during the golden years of the profession of industrial engineering, "efficiency experts" measured and counted people's therbligs.

A therblig was the smallest observable human action, such as a reach, a grasp, a return, a joining of two parts, a twist, a wait, the press of a switch, or the action of drilling a hole. The term was actually a reversal of the letters in the last name of Frank Gilbreth, who was well known in the 1940s as the hero of the movie "Cheaper By The Dozen," a film about an efficiency expert who raised 12 children using the principles of time-and-motion analysis and efficiency engineering.

Gilbreth's wife, Lillian, was also one of the first industrial engineers. The two of them developed a procedure to measure work activity and redesign it to make it more efficient and less costly. Although their work had a great impact during the time when manufacturing processes were very labor-intensive, it applies less today with high technology involved. Even worse, many people are still trying to use therbligs today as a way to define and measure quality, even in personal contacts between employees and customers.

When you want to describe and understand service quality rather than the assembly of a manufactured item, you have to junk therbligs and change to "MOTs," or moments of truth. As defined previously, a moment of truth is any episode in which a customer comes into contact with some aspect of the organization and forms an impression of its service. Customer value is what the customer perceives as a result of the moments of truth that make up his or her experience of the value your organization tries to deliver. This applies to dealing with internal customers as well as external customers.

There can hardly be a more profound shift in one's thinking than the shift from therbligs to MOTs. It is a shift from a focus on activity to a focus on outcome. The challenge is not to prescribe the *activity*— the therblig, such as "address the customer by name twice during the transaction"—but to prescribe the *outcome* of the MOT—"the customer feels welcome here and confident that we care about the quality of his or her experience while with us."

Probably most of the quality crimes committed in trying to improve service quality over the last decade or so have been committed by people trying to apply therblig thinking to moments of truth. Good quality strategy only rarely calls for prescribing therbligs. More often, it calls for defining and managing moments of truth.

Many organizations are now making the shift from therbligs to MOTs. Toastmasters International, headquartered in Mission Viejo, California, for example, uses moments of truth in assessing the quality of the value provided by the headquarters organization to its 5000 Toastmasters clubs and 170,000 members worldwide.

According to executive director Terry McCann, "I've been personally conducting service management workshops with all headquarters employees, emphasizing the way we handle our moments of truth. We identify critical moments of truth, such as when a club president calls up needing information or materials. Then we work out quality criteria for making sure we handle those moments of truth as well as we can."

Apparently TI's focus on moments of truth is paying off. According to McCann: "We've always had a good reputation for serving the clubs. But since we adopted this focus over the last year or so, we've had more praise and compliments from the clubs than I've seen at any time during my 17 years as executive director."

McCann goes on to say, "I'm convinced that Total Quality Service, with its focus on customer value, is the most important business idea to come along in three decades."

AVOIDING "MEASUREMENT PARALYSIS"

In the classic story, *Gulliver's Travels*, Lemuel Gulliver visited a land where the most revered people were mathematicians and astronomers.

These learned men spent their time calculating, recording, and plotting the movements of the heavenly bodies. They had done it for so many generations that they eventually lost sight of the relationship between their measurements and the real thing. The learned ones had come to believe that, unless they performed their calculations and drew their charts every day, the heavenly bodies wouldn't move.

They had confused means and ends, and this is what many people do when they try to launch a quality initiative by starting with measurement rather than starting by defining customer value. Measurement should not be an end in itself, but rather a means to an end.

Why measure anything? Presumably, the reason for measuring something is to be able to do it better or differently as a result of the knowledge you get from the measurement. From the standpoint of quality improvement, this means you either want to identify an opportunity for improvement, establish a baseline for the improvement, or verify that you have accomplished the improvement.

Measurement paralysis sets in, as it did with Gulliver's astronomers, when people make measurement an end in itself, not a tool for targeted quality improvement. Their unstated belief is that somehow the measurements themselves will improve the processes being measured. While it is true that, used effectively, measurement information can help people change processes, it is by no means obvious that the mere existence of the data causes anything to change.

From this point of view, a reasonable philosophy of quality measurement would consider measurement a way to close the loop around any particular quality improvement effort, to lead and guide it rather than drive it. The measurements help everybody know how well they're accomplishing it.

The key factor in closing the loop is not the act of measurement, it is the information itself—in the hands of those who can best respond to it. There may be a subtle distinction here, but I believe it is an important one, and in some ways a rather profound one.

The idea of measuring people is deeply embedded in Western cultures, as a counterpart to judging people. Something in the deepest roots of Westernized, Judeo-Christian thinking demands that people be kept in line, that they be reminded that they're not perfect, and that they be shown the difference between what they are and what they should aspire to be. We're judged as schoolchildren, as workers, as wage-earners, and husbands or wives, girlfriends or boyfriends, neighbors, citizens, and on and on.

Unfortunately, when many executives and managers talk about measurement and about measuring quality, they're still talking from a mindset of judging and evaluating people, not one of empowering them. Some managers seem to have a vague notion that, if they can get the right set of measurements on the organization, they'll be able to direct and control it better. But in many cases, managers have too many measurements; too much information; and they still can't get the quality results they want. Why? Because they aren't the ones who need the information. Their workers need it.

What information get measured in an operation is less important than who gets it. In many organizations managers need less information than they get, and employees need much more than they get.

We've had a misplaced focus for many years in talking about quality measurement. We should be talking about *quality information* in the hands of those who need it. We should ask ourselves questions such as

- What information do employees need in order to know how well they're succeeding?

- What information do supervisors need to help them enable and support the workers?

- What information do middle managers need to help them support the supervisors and workers?

- What information do executives need to help them guide the organization in the direction of total quality service?

This point of view takes the emphasis off measurement and puts it on feedback.

ORGANIZATIONAL ASSESSMENT: WHERE ARE YOU STARTING FROM?

Before an organization has reached the point where it uses customer feedback effectively and makes good use of quality measurements, it needs at least some form of self-appraisal. People need an assessment of some kind to give them a sense of where they really are. They need to know the starting point from which they will proceed in improving the quality of their contribution.

A situational assessment can be one of the simplest and most effective ways to begin a quality-improvement program. Such an assessment can determine where the organization stands right now and pinpoint specific strengths, weaknesses, opportunities, and threats as they relate to the delivery of total quality service.

It can be done for the organization as a whole or for departments within it. The assessment findings can help improve those areas that will yield the biggest payoff in terms of customer preferences and perceptions.

Situational assessments vary substantially in their formats and levels of sophistication. The key to conducting an effective assessment is to start with a comprehensive perspective that produces valid and reliable information. Two basic techniques that can accomplish those objectives are a service-quality audit and a culture audit.

The Service-Quality Audit

A service-quality audit is like an operations review. It's an objective and detailed examination of the organization's service-delivery capabilities.

The purpose of the audit is to identify areas in which the organization's mode of operations may be out of sync or in conflict with customer value and to assess the degree to which resources need to be realigned in order to fulfill customer expectations. The audit typically includes interviews with executives and key department heads and managers, focus groups with representative employee populations, review of facilities and systems support; communications review, and organizational structure analysis.

The exact areas of focus and nature of the audit must be unique to the organization. However, at a minimum, it should be designed to cover the dimensions of the service triangle, shown in Chapter 1, in order to determine the following:

- adequacy of the service strategy
- customer-friendliness of systems and policies
- competence and customer focus of service people
- commitment/support provided by service leaders
- degree to which the culture is customer-centered
- extent of staff empowerment

Just conducting the service-quality audit, however, doesn't make anything happen. The important thing is to share the findings in a clear and compelling form so the action people in the organization can understand them and begin to respond to their implications. The service-quality audit report can be one of the first "official" documents of a quality initiative.

The Culture Audit

Employees, especially those at the front line, probably know more than anyone else in the organization about what customers expect, what customers experience in their moments of truth, and what the company does right or wrong in terms of service quality. Employees also know how they feel about working for the organization, what makes life difficult for them, and what gives them satisfaction. A culture audit taps into these critical factors.

A culture audit gives you a glimpse of the collective state of mind and heart of the employees of the organization. It also tells you, at least by inference, how employees are likely to respond to a quality initiative. If you have an angry, cynical, disgruntled, burned-out population, you have one particular set of implementation issues on your hands. If you have a workforce that is generally psychologically comfortable, enthusiastic about working for the organization, and optimistic about its possibilities, the implementation challenge will be quite different.

Too many executives have regretted launching quality programs without the benefit of a culture audit. Some have encountered remarkable levels of employee cynicism and even distrust of senior management. Others have discovered that basic psychological "hygiene" factors have distracted the employees' attention from the quality focus. Others have misread the effects of stress and job burnout, and have tried to appeal to people to make psychological commitments they weren't in a position to make.

Although it should go without saying that any effective leadership team should have an accurate picture of the state of the culture at all times, the reality is that most don't. For this reason, the early stages of any quality initiative should include a realistic culture audit if the picture is not clear.

As part of its initial service assessment of its operating subsidiaries, Bausch & Lomb's International Division conducted employee surveys designed to capture baseline data regarding perceptions of the subsidiaries' service cultures and their impact on customers. The Division is currently in the process of conducting a second round of surveys designed to measure changes in employee perception and relate them to other measures of customer perception and organizational performance.

The most widely accepted method for a culture audit is a well-designed questionnaire that provides a reasonable statistical profile of employee views related to the quality initiative and any other major topics related to it. Some of the areas to cover in a culture audit are the employees' perceptions of

- value delivered to the customer
- the internal effectiveness of the organization, and areas in need of improvement
- quality of work life, because that affects the quality of their work
- the need for a quality initiative such as the one being considered
- the chances for the quality initiative succeeding in the organization
- top management's commitment and capability for making the effort succeed

It makes sense to conduct a culture audit fairly early in a quality effort and to make use of the information it provides in developing the program strategy. With so much depending on winning the hearts and minds of the employees, it would be foolish to try to make a sale to them without knowing what they're prepared to buy.

USING THE CUSTOMER SCORECARD

The customer scorecard tells you how your customer value package performs against the critical factors in the customer value model. If the hospital patients say a key element of value is trust and freedom from fear, how does our hospital score with our patients on trust and freedom from fear?

If the mail-order customers say they value accurate portrayal of the merchandise in the catalog copy and photographs, how do we score on that dimension?

If the retailers say they value absolute reliability of our deliveries — when and where needed — how do we score with them on reliability?

At this point in the progress of the quality revolution, it still seems that relatively few businesses are using valid customer scorecards to evaluate their customer value packages. Many of the firms that do use scorecards at all have merely thought up some reasonable-sounding questions and put them into a questionnaire or feedback card. The questions they've thought up may or may not correspond to the real elements of value in customers' minds and hearts.

If the leaders of the organization have failed to perceive the "invisible truth" about the customer's desires for value, the scorecard will be a guess-card.

For example, a chain of retail pharmacies in Australia learned from customer research that customers valued "easy access to a pharmacist" as one aspect of the experience of buying medications and health products. According to consultant Kevin Austin, who conducted the customer research, "that factor was nowhere to be found in the company's original working definition of customer quality. They weren't measuring it because they didn't even know it existed."

When they began to grasp the significance of that factor, they realized their pharmacies were designed to *minimize* public contact with the pharmacist, not to make it easy. The pharmacist stood behind a secondary counter, located well behind the first one. A customer would have to make a special effort or a special request to get the pharmacist's attention. This led to a redesign of the store layout and a reorientation of the pharmacist's job.

The customer scorecard is simply a feedback device that includes each of the critical value factors identified by the research and asks the customer to rate each one, typically on a simple five-point scale.

Assuming you have a valid customer value model and a correspondingly appropriate customer scorecard, the next step is to set up an information-gathering system that creates a flow of customer feedback to the workers, managers, and other action people, whose efforts affect the scores. Creating that flow of information can sometimes be more of a challenge than it may appear.

For example, many hotels put customer scorecards in the rooms, assuming their customers will fill them out. Unfortunately, the industry norm for responses on hotel cards is about 1–5 percent, which is seldom sufficient to make a statistically valid estimate of customer approval. With concerted efforts, some have raised the response rate as high as 20 or 25 percent. It's usually necessary to supplement feedback cards with other ways of getting the customer to respond.

Another method is to interview a selected number of customers, with the interviewer going over the questions one at a time and asking for responses. That can be fairly costly in view of the labor involved, but it may be worthwhile in terms of the unexpected information it can discover.

A less-formal method, but one that has its value, is to have employees ask customers from time to time for feedback on specific elements of quality. This only works if the employees are really oriented to work at getting the results. When the cashier at the restaurant says breezily, "How was your dinner?" while turning away from the customer to operate the credit card machine, not many customers will tell how they really feel.

It often requires a combination of methods to get the information you need, simply because most people won't voluntarily fill out questionnaires. Most seem to believe they'd be wasting their time, and that nobody will do anything about their complaints anyhow. And they're probably right. And as for compliments, most people aren't in the habit of complimenting service people unless they're truly outstanding.

One novel survey technique is the "synthetic survey." Say, for example, that the customer scorecard has ten questions about different aspects of perceived value. Instead of trying to get all customers to fill it out, you can have each contact employee ask, say, one assigned question of every customer he or she deals with. This will present very little inconvenience to the customer, because most people are willing to answer one specific question.

With each employee asking a different question, you can merge the results. This gives you a "synthetic" response, as if all customers answered all questions. It's usually a sufficiently reliable technique to track quality perceptions if you get a good number of customers to reply.

The scorecard should also show how well an organization performs on different components of service quality in comparison to its competitors. It might not be possible to get competitive information by the same means used to get customer scores on your own operation. It might be necessary to conduct a separate investigation using anonymous surveys or other research techniques.

Every year the Granite Rock Company of Watsonville, California, asks its customers to complete an opinion survey in which they grade their top three suppliers in terms of the total service relationship. "We have a strong belief that if something is worth doing, it's probably worth measuring," says Dave Franceschi of the 100-year-old family-owned building supply company's quality planning and management department. "This is a way for us to sound an alarm if something's not right."

Once you have a valid, reliable, and economical process for getting feedback on the customer scorecard, you can begin to build a history of the scores. You can establish a baseline measurement that shows where you are at the beginning. Then as time goes on and you implement various quality improvements, you can look for the impact to show up on the scorecard.

And, of course, it's important to share the scorecard results on a regular basis with the employees as well as their leaders. The more people know about their quality scores, the more they can commit their energies to improving them. Make the feedback, review, and discussion of customer scores a regular part of the information-sharing process in the organization.

APPRECIATION: THE BASIC NOURISHMENT OF HUMAN MOTIVATION

According to psychologist William James,

> **The deepest need in every human being is the desire to be appreciated.**

We've known this for centuries, and yet we still don't capitalize on it. One psychological study after another confirms that most managers don't fully grasp the significance of recognition and appreciation to workers and that most workers feel they don't get adequate recognition for the contributions they make.

At Santa Monica Hospital, a nurse returns to her desk to find a small vase of flowers has appeared there. It has a note: "Just wanted to let you know we hear a lot from the doctors and patients about what a wonderful job you're doing. Thanks—we're proud of you." It's signed by a member of the service-quality task force.

A lobby security guard gets a note from hospital president Len La-Bella: "You're the best ambassador we could have. I hear over and over about how you make the patients and family members feel welcome when they come in the front door. Thanks for your contribution."

A San Diego city police officer gets a note from Chief of Police Bob Burgreen: "I received a note from a lady you stopped recently for a traffic violation. She wanted to let me know how courteous you were and how professionally you handled the incident. Thanks for representing us so well."

Note the presence of a key phrase in all of these messages: "thank you." That one expression, coming from someone in authority, can have enormous impact. When was the last time you thanked one of your staff for his or her contribution? When did you last thank all the employees for playing on the team? Most companies make an effort to thank their biggest customers for their business. They even thank their key suppliers for supporting them. Do they thank their employees adequately and sincerely?

A question often asked in executive seminars on total quality service is "What kind of system should we set up for employee recognition?" My answer is usually "None." Don't set up a system. A system cannot appreciate someone. A system cannot thank someone. A system cannot make someone feel special, or proud, or cared about.

That's part of the old way of thinking: turn everything over to a system. Do the employees need to be rewarded? We'll set up a reward system. They need to feel appreciated? We'll set up an appreciation system. *Appreciation is a part of leadership, not a part of management.*

The system approach to appreciation makes everything into a procedure; it takes the heart out of something that fundamentally touches the human heart. If you do good, you get a jelly bean. Five jelly beans and you get a key chain. Five key chains and you get an ice chest. Then you're eligible for employee of the month. It's all done by a system. It could all be done by the computer, in between printing the financial reports and the paychecks.

No, *appreciation is something leaders do*. They have to decide that people count, that they really care about how people feel, and that they want people to know they've made a valuable contribution. There are zillions of ways, material and nonmaterial, for showing people they're special and that they're appreciated. Use your imagination and use yourself.

MEASURING MANAGERS: CRITICAL LEADERSHIP BEHAVIORS

When the executives of the State Bank of South Australia began to examine their roles in the company's quality initiative, they didn't like the image they'd earned as leaders in the eyes of the employees. The workers, supervisors, and middle managers saw them as just a bunch of bank executives, not as real service leaders. They decided to earn a better reputation by becoming better leaders.

In one of our executive sessions, we drew on their organizational surveys to create a prescription for executive leadership behavior. We defined about a dozen critical behaviors that represented the kind of committed service leadership that would be necessary to move the organization forward.

Then we established a process for tracking the executives' progress as they evolved toward this new style. The process included regular sensing of managerial and employee perceptions, by means of a questionnaire supplemented by group interviews and discussion sessions. This was a case in which the executives saw clearly that their own behavior was a critical element of customer focus and that they needed to have feedback for their own benefit.

As executives get further into a total quality initiative, they often begin to see more clearly the need for assessing and developing leadership skills at all levels, including their own.

> **Measuring leadership is a part of measuring quality.**

How does the measurement of leadership in customer-centered organizations differ from that in traditional companies? First of all, most performance-appraisal or evaluation systems currently in place focus on the "managerial" aspects of roles rather than their leadership elements. Secondly, they rely almost exclusively on top-down evaluation and feedback from the boss rather than the bottom-up feedback from the employees. If service quality means inverting the traditional management pyramid and teaching managers new behaviors, then our measurement systems need to keep pace with those changes as well.

In the traditional "command and control" environment, managers concentrate on planning, organizing, staffing, controlling, and monitoring activities. These are the areas in which performance goals are established and progress against those goals measured. Management by objectives (MBO) systems are a common example of this type of approach.

In customer-centered organizations, the emphasis needs to be on service leadership. *An effective service leader is one who contributes six critical skills to the organization:*

1. Vision and Values
2. Direction
3. Persuasion
4. Support
5. Development
6. Appreciation

Vision and Values—the ability to define and articulate a clear business concept and mission around the organizational unit's customers and contributions. It means keeping abreast of the environment by staying in touch with customers and changes in the marketplace. It also means spotting critical issues before they become problems, and being proactive rather than reactive.

The effective leader is a good problem solver, one who can state a problem clearly and concisely, then marshal the necessary facts and information to formulate an answer or the approach to getting an answer. It means making decisions and acting boldly when action is necessary. Lastly, the true service leader "walks the talk." He or she is an everyday role model of the values being espoused.

Direction—setting goals effectively by establishing targets that give people a sense of ownership and something to shoot for. It means aligning unit goals with the higher goals of the rest of the organization. It means delegating effectively in order to involve those closest to the work in decision-making, thereby assisting in their development and freeing yourself up to do things that truly demand your attention.

An effective service leader sets clear policies and standards, ones that are easily understood and communicated, while also setting and enforcing the priorities that help keep people focused on what's really important to the unit.

Persuasion—projecting self-confidence in yourself as a leader and as someone who can be trusted. Using authority skillfully, without always relying on "clout" is another important trait, as is communicating the big picture so that people understand and stay focused on their individual and collective goals. Strong service leaders can also deal effectively one-on-one with a variety of people in order to get their ideas and message across, listening as well as persuading. Lastly, follow-through is critical to ensure that actions are carried out once decisions are made and that people know that you mean what you say.

Support—staying in touch and informed about the ongoing activities and critical projects of the unit. You don't have to know the details, but you need to have the latest news. It means planning well and using resources wisely in order to accomplish as much as possible. Building, using, and maintaining effective organizational systems helps people work productively. An effective service leader is also a valuable member of the team who contributes creative ideas, solves problems, makes good decisions, and manages his or her own time well.

Development—expecting high performance from the team, insisting that each person give his or her best. It means helping people develop by making the work environment a learning environment. The good service leader is a good teacher and coach, one who can show people how to do something when necessary and who addresses performance problems by dealing with them directly in a supportive manner.

Building a unit that has true team spirit is critical to the ultimate success of the service mission, as is developing a culture that values innovation and creativity. Lastly, since working in groups or teams is fundamental to most service organizations, the ability to run effective meetings that get the most out of the time and effort of all involved is a vital part of service leadership.

Appreciation—giving the proper rewards, both tangible and intangible, in a fair and equitable manner. Praising people and giving them the "positive strokes" we all need is an essential part of this behavior, as is providing the frequent feedback necessary for high service performance in a caring way. It means demonstrating respect for the ideas, values, and opinions of others in the organization.

Keeping your staff informed about both positive and negative events is important to the spirit and cooperation of the unit, as is sticking up for your people and defending their interests appropriately in the face of other competing demands on organization resources. Effective leaders also understand the use of symbolic communication, the rituals, celebration, and ceremony that are central in keeping the spirit alive.

More and more organizations are now moving toward *multi-level leadership feedback*. This involves asking a unit leader to assess his or her own skills on a standardized model such as "Leadex," then asking the employees who work for that person to give their anonymous assessments, and having the boss give his or her assessment. By using a standard multiple-choice scale, it is possible to give each leader a computerized comparison of his or her own assessment with those of the boss and the employees.[1]

Just as with other forms of information, this kind of feedback can empower. It can enable individual leaders to understand their strengths and identify the areas in which they may need to develop.

And ultimately, the quality of the leadership available to an organization has a huge impact on the quality of the experience it provides to its customers.

11

Your Change Management Strategy: Getting It Right This Time

There is a tide in the affairs of men
Which, taken at the flood, leads on to fortune;
Omitted, all the voyage of their life
Is bound in shallows and in miseries.
On such a full sea are we now afloat,
And we must take the current when it serves,
Or lose our ventures.

Brutus,
Julius Caesar, Act IV, Scene 3

I f you like to use analogies, consider an outstanding service organization as something like a symphony orchestra. And think of a mediocre organization as a mob of people with instruments in their hands. What's the critical difference? What makes the orchestra different from the mob?

The difference between the orchestra and the mob is mostly invisible, but it's crucial and it's worth a lot of money. It also costs the people in the orchestra a lot of money, time, human effort, and commitment to achieve this critical difference. The results are obvious, but the underlying difference is mostly intangible. It's the skills, feelings, attitudes, collective know-how, and ability to cooperate that makes the difference.

And it's the same with outstanding organizations. The difference between the first-dimension organization, i.e., the one going out of business, and the fifth-dimension organization that makes quality into an art form, is in this *collective capability*.

Just as a great orchestra has a skilled conductor who knows the music and knows how to help the musicians deliver an outstanding performance, the great organization has a skilled leader who knows where the organization must go and knows how to help people deliver on the challenge of customer value.

Just as the great orchestra plays great music, the great organization carries out a great mission: the mission of delivering value to its customers and meeting the needs of all its stakeholders.

Just as each member of the great orchestra has acquired the individual knowledge, attitudes, skills, and habits of performing needed to play his or her part effectively, so each member of the great organization has acquired the capabilities needed to make his or her best contribution.

And just as the members of the great orchestra have a kind of magical sense of being in tune with one another, cooperating skillfully and adapting subtly to one another, interpreting the music brilliantly, and carrying out the conductor's masterful direction, so the members of the great organization work together cooperatively and skillfully to fulfill the vision and mission of their organization.

The big challenge to the leaders of any organization who want to build a culture based on service, quality, and customer value is to turn the mob into an orchestra. Think of an organizational quality program as an adventure of transformation. It is an adventure of learning, growing, and discovery. It is a revolution in their way of life. It requires helping people arrive at a state of collective knowledge, attitudes, beliefs, self-expectations, spirit, motivation, and operational competence that makes the organization a winner in the eyes of its customers.

The revolution is first and foremost a psychological revolution. If we want to be a fifth-dimension organization, we have to start thinking like one. We have to raise our expectations of who we are, how we should operate, and what we should contribute.

Making this transformation happen requires great skill in itself. The leaders and change agents in the organization must have a *strategy* for change. They must approach the people of the organization with ideas that make sense, a way of going about the transformation that makes sense, and valid reason for doing it all. The change must be energized at the human level if it is going to succeed.

Make no mistake—it takes an enormous investment of energy, time, money, and intelligent action to move an organization to the fifth-dimension way of life. And there is no guarantee it will stay there. Quality is like physical fitness: if you stop doing the things that made you fit, you get out of shape again. This is why the change leaders must think very carefully about where they want the organization to go and about the change-management strategies needed to take it there.

According to management consultant Peter Schiffrin, one of the founders of The TQS Group, Inc., "You need at least four things to bring about a profound change in an organization's way of thinking and operating: vision, energy, power, and plan."

Change:
Change = Vision + Energy + Power + Plan

According to Shiffrin, "lots of people have vision, and some of them have lots of energy. But without the power, or a way to get access to the power, they're going nowhere. And even with vision and power together, without a plan they won't accomplish much in the way of significant change."

Your *program implementation strategy* must have all four of these elements in good measure and in good balance if you are to have any hope of moving an organization to the fifth-dimension of service, quality, and customer value.

Developing an effective program strategy involves a certain amount of creative skill, but it also involves some sound logical thinking. You need to take a close look at your organization's business reality, its culture, its leadership, its traditions, and its reflex reactions to change. Each organization's implementation strategy for a quality initiative must be unique to that organization and its situation.

FIZZLE PHENOMENA: HOW NOT TO SHOOT YOURSELF IN THE FOOT

There are more ways to muck up a quality program than there are ways to do it well. It only makes sense to learn from the mistakes of others and avoid the ones they've made. Let's at least be sure we don't fall into the most obvious holes in the road.

Some of the failure phenomena we've observed that prevent quality programs from going far or even getting off the ground include:

○ *Executive apathy*; authorizing lower-level people to go ahead with the program but offering no meaningful support or encouragement; setting it adrift and letting it fade into oblivion.

○ *Splintered executive commitment*; some executives are for it, some are against it, and some don't care. As a result the employees are confused.

○ *Putting the wrong person in charge of a task force or quality initiative*; an incompetent person, or one who has a hidden agenda, private ambitions, lack of credibility, or any of a number of other political handicaps can doom the program right from the start.

○ *Bureaucratizing the effort* with steering groups, committees, review boards, and splinter groups; too many "scientists" and not enough "hunchbacks"; taking forever to get organized and get things underway; degenerating into a *rigor mortis* condition of overmeasuring and imposing standards without employee participation.

○ *Letting the program become a political football in the organization*; middle managers may use it to "game" top management in a passive-aggressive struggle against top-down domination; it may become the focus of a pushing contest between headquarters and the field or become a casualty of other ancient political feuds.

○ *The "I don't want to play" syndrome*; the head of a major department doesn't want any part of the program and decides his or her mob is big enough to passively resist the thing and wait until it goes away.

○ *Methodology battles among factions*; different groups advocating their favorite approaches, theories, or consultants.

○ *Trivializing the objective* with a bunch of empty motivational messages and meaningless slogans; trying to "rev up" the employees without having a real quality message to share; smile training, cosmetic fixes, and advertising campaigns that try to hoodwink the customers and employees into thinking something has changed.

- *Jumping off too soon without a clear sense of timing, sequence, and momentum;* getting people fired up and then allowing the energy to fade for lack of effective follow-through.

- *Contradicting the whole meaning of the effort with opposing messages;* such as imposing massive budget cuts and layoffs right after launching a service initiative, or shaking up the organization for no good reason right after preaching about participative management, shared vision, and all the rest.

- *Axing the whole thing the first time the organization runs into rough sailing;* abandoning the business vision and direction for the reflexive "slash and thrash" budget-cutting mayhem; an attitude of "we can't afford that now" telegraphs the fact that senior executives never expected much good to come of it in any case.

I hope this catalog of fizzle options doesn't cast a pessimistic pall over the undertaking, but it is important to be realistic about the challenges that will present themselves. There will be enough surprises, obstacles, twists and turns in the road, and honest mistakes in store for any organization to make the journey anything but boring. So why victimize ourselves with the same old failure modes? Why not at least make some original blunders of our own?

Let's look at the key implementation issues, and see how to cope with them.

FIVE CRITICAL SUCCESS ISSUES

The most critical issues or questions facing the leaders of a quality revolution in an organization are:

1. *How big an investment are we prepared to make?* Will this be a token effort, a cosmetic fix, or a marketing gesture? Or will it be a major commitment of money, time, talent, and energy? How high on the ladder of quality achievement do we really intend to climb? Do we aspire to be a fifth-dimension organization, one capable of making service to our customers an art form? If so, do we really understand what it will take to get there?

The organization's executives must make the decision about the magnitude of the venture, if not consciously then at least unconsciously. The resource commitment they are prepared to make will be the dominant reality as the effort proceeds.

2. *How do we gain and sustain executive commitment?* When executives take a passive, disinterested posture toward a quality initiative, it has less chance of producing excellent results than if they lead it themselves. How should they lead it? What should they actually do?

3. *How do we activate the middle managers and leverage the initiative through their energy and commitment?* One of the surest ways to sink a quality program is to ignore, go around, go over, or otherwise leave out the middle managers. How should we view their roles, and how can we help them take charge of the objectives and lead their organizations in the quality revolution?

4. *How do we avoid employee cynicism and earn acceptance and credibility in the minds of those who have to make it all happen?* How do we engage the employees in quality thinking at the outset and enable them to contribute their best ideas? How do we arrange things so they are truly a part of the venture, not just passengers on a train being driven by somebody else?

5. *How do we sustain the momentum of the quality initiative when things get difficult?* A large number of programs simply grind to a halt. The leaders get busy, distracted by other pressing problems, and impatient with the rate of progress. How do we create a process or a mechanism that keeps feeding energy into the initiative and keeps it going over the long run?

The first of the five questions just posed must be answered by the executives. There is little more we can say about it here. The other four issues, however, do deserve a bit more consideration.

GAINING AND SUSTAINING EXECUTIVE COMMITMENT

One of the best ways to get executives interested in and committed to quality is to "inoculate" them with evidence from the business environment, showing that quality works. Len Bleasel, chief executive of Australia's Natural Gas Company, decided to take his executives out of their habitat and see what quality looked like in other countries and companies.

Bleasel, Grant King, and several other executives had recently traveled through the United States on a study mission to examine the best practices of American service businesses. Bleasel commissioned a Sydney-based company called Management Frontiers, who had organized and conducted the study tour, to create a study tour exclusively for the senior executives of his firm. They traveled across the United States for two weeks, visiting some of the top American firms and questioning their executives about their ideas for managing service.

According to Tony Randall, the tour organizer for Management Frontiers, "after visiting some of the top American firms, the executives were amazed at the levels of commitment and service performance those companies took for granted as their way of operating. Watching Federal Express employees working through the wee hours to move packages to their destinations, talking to sales clerks in a Nordstrom department store, seeing how McDonald's trains thousands of restaurant managers to a level of quality commitment seldom matched anywhere in Australia—these were mind-blowing experiences.

"They came back to Australia changed people. They had a whole different concept of what could be done, and a different level of expectations for what their organization was capable of."

Bleasel commented on the experience: "It forever changed the way we think about our business and our company. We're now clearer than ever about where we're going, and about how we're going to handle the challenges in getting there."

Another very effective way to build executive commitment is to make sure the executives get "hands on" experiences in the early part of the program. Have them attend special executive seminars on service management, to make sure they fully understand the TQS model and its implications for them.

Have them interview customers and sit in on focus-group sessions. Have them get personally involved with the customer research data and work closely with the researchers to find meaning in it. Have them conduct employee meetings to gather ideas and information that can lead to quality improvements. Encourage executives to conduct briefing sessions and workshops to share their vision, mission, and values with all managers and employees. Have them sit in on action-team meetings to see how employees look at quality issues. You can even have them teach employee seminars.

In short, *put them to work.*

One of the most important and valuable executive experiences that builds commitment is the very process of formulating the strategic quality direction. An effective way to do this is with an executive strategy retreat.

Creating and refining a breakaway strategy is a very demanding challenge for senior executives. In many operationally focused organizations, the leaders have been so busy getting the day's work done that they have gotten out of touch with the strategic issues. And they may have gotten "out of shape" for the strenuous thinking process required of them.

This demanding thinking process requires the proper setting, frame of mind, and cooperative effort if it is to produce something truly meaningful. This is why many executive teams choose to attack the problem in a retreat-type setting, away from the demands of everyday problems.

It is essential that the format for the strategy retreat maximize teamwork, spontaneity, synergy, and innovation on the part of the executives. Most successful retreats employ professional facilitation, either on the part of unbiased internal facilitators or consulting firms that specialize in these kinds of activities.

There are many group-process and meeting techniques that can create this type of environment. A specific approach we have developed to facilitate executive creativity in the strategy formulation process is one we call the breakaway service-strategy retreat.

The breakaway strategy retreat enables executives to start with a clean slate and a zero-based approach to strategy development. The retreat usually involves 2 to 3 days of intensive activity in a setting away from the office. It is intentionally structured to enable the organization's executives to "unfreeze" from the usual day-to-day problem-solving methods and to engage in big-picture thinking as they wrestle and struggle to define the service strategy and customer value package that will give them a competitive advantage into the foreseeable future.

Each retreat is unique, depending upon the particular circumstances and needs of the organization. However, a typical retreat consists of four parts:

- ° Visioning

- ° Valuing

- ° Missioning

- ° Planning

These stages promote a logical progression of thought over the course of the retreat's agenda from the more futuristic, conceptual, and abstract to the more immediate, tangible, and actionable.

In the *Visioning* segment of the agenda, the executives examine customer research data for their organization and virtually immerse themselves in it. They may pretend that they are the planning team for a new organization and that their assignment is to identify the customer value model within the customer data, and then to create the perfect customer value package and design the perfect organization to deliver that package. No idea is too radical. No reference is to be made to their existing organization.

Once the executives have come up with the customer value package and organization for the future, they compare that organization to their own and identify the gaps that exist. Then, they make the transition from the hypothetical to the actual by describing what their vision for their customers and business will be. Next they identify turbo-goals that will become the top priorities for the organization to enable it to close the gap and realize its vision.

Next comes the *Valuing* phase. In that process the executives pinpoint the core values of the organization that will support the delivery of superior customer value and meet the needs of all stakeholders—the customers, the owners, and the employees. Core values are not the usual "motherhood" statements like "commitment to quality," "ethical business dealings," or "concern for the individual." Core values are the *critical few values* that the organization must live by in order to achieve its business mission.

The third segment of the retreat, the *Missioning* phase, involves drafting a mission statement that builds upon and is consistent with the vision and values statements produced to this point. The mission frames and shapes the breakaway strategy. After they draft the mission, they critique it against agreed criteria for an effective mission statement, revise it, polish it, and finalize it.

The final segment of the retreat is *Planning*. This segment moves the agenda from the conceptual level to the operational. It identifies the key result areas for concentration to support those turbo-goals and broad strategies to be pursued in order to ensure the accomplishment of the vision and mission.

The retreat closes with the executive team reviewing all of the elements of the strategy package, as defined in Chapter 7, and making a group and individual commitment to implementing it. Frequently, this includes individual responsibility assignments and all of the members of the team signing the strategy statement.

After the retreat, a formal written report and strategy package are prepared. This statement becomes the Magna Carta and blueprint for framing and guiding the organization's ongoing quality improvement efforts, including the most critical—the refinement of the customer value package. It can be shared with employees at all levels. It can also be used to evaluate progress on behalf of the customer.

ACTIVATING MIDDLE MANAGEMENT LEADERSHIP

Service quality and customer focus are the responsibilities of line managers. When task forces, steering groups, quality committees, and consultants usurp this responsibility, you can't expect managers to live up to it. One of the most common complaints of quality people about why their programs didn't progress faster or more effectively has been the benign neglect of middle managers. But in many cases, quality programs have worked *against* middle management acceptance and participation, not for it.

One of the most damaging examples of bypassing middle managers happened, of all places, in Scandinavian Airlines, during Jan Carlzon's first major service-quality initiative. Although SAS became famous for its pioneering efforts, its original implementation strategy is definitely not the model of choice for today.

The approach SAS took then makes some sense in view of the fact that the company was in an emergency situation, and no one had really accomplished anything like this before. But Carlzon's approach to the middle managers of the organization caused a great deal of anger and resentment among them. It took quite some time to repair the damage and win their support. The negative side effects continued to haunt Carlzon for years, and in fact still exist in SAS to some extent today.

Carlzon felt so strongly that he needed to activate the employees that he bypassed all the middle management levels and took his message personally to the front line. He believed that, had he tried to move the quality message downward through the various management levels of the organization, it would never have reached most of the working people at all. While his appearances and the high-energy motivational seminars he implemented had a huge impact on employee acceptance, most of the middle managers took it as an insult. They felt pushed aside and disenfranchised as leaders.

While it is probably true that the message wouldn't filter down in any significant way through the hierarchy, nevertheless without the energies of the middle management group the program didn't progress as fast or as far as it might. This was a strategy dilemma in SAS' case, and a very difficult question to resolve.

Since the time of the early SAS program and other major organizational initiatives we've learned a great deal about the role middle managers must play in quality programs. *They must lead the effort.* They are the ones who must take the ball, accept the responsibility, and run the play.

The problem of middle management leadership is so significant that it justifies a major part of the thinking process behind the program implementation strategy. In the book *Service Within: Solving the Middle Management Leadership Crisis,* I presented a fairly complete prescription for putting the middle managers back into a leadership role. This involves an educational approach that helps them define their customers, their missions, and their service strategies, and then think through the customer value model and their customer value package, to make sure their units all deliver superior customer value.[1]

Many organizations have learned the middle management lesson the hard way, by trying to bypass them and then later making them scapegoats for failed quality programs. Many others are learning from those mistakes and making their middle managers essential to the implementation process. The results show clearly that changing middle managers into leaders pays off.

FIVE WAYS TO AVOID EMPLOYEE CYNICISM AND BUILD CREDIBILITY

Many executives are unduly anxious about employee acceptance of the quality message during the early stages of an initiative. They worry that the employees will tune out the message before they give it a chance. They worry that the whole thing will meet with a wall of cynicism that will keep it from ever taking flight.

This needn't happen. All you have to do to avoid cynicism and begin to build credibility is to remember one word: SHARE.

Share the enterprise with everyone in the organization. Make it their idea, their vision, their mission, their destiny, not that of top management. Make it something they can be a part of, not just participate in. Rather than sit a bunch of experts down in a back room somewhere and have them cook up a quality program, take the idea to the people right away. Begin sharing ownership right away. Be willing to give up control of all the details and let the enterprise take shape at the hands of many committed people. You'll get better results, and there will be fewer cynics.

According to John Stanek, chief executive of International Survey Research, Inc., "We've done statistical analyses of many culture-change efforts in organizations. One success factor seems to stand out clearly: *co-determination.* The most successful ones were those in which the employees played a significant role in actually defining and contributing to the changes. The least successful were those in which the executives defined the changes and tried to push them through the organization." *Here are five simple things you can do to build that kind of commitment.*

1. *Share the knowledge.* People need to know the rationale for undertaking a customer-centering initiative and why their personal involvement is both beneficial and even critical to the success of the effort. To the degree that customer-research data exist, people need to know what has been learned about the customers, their needs, expectations, and satisfaction with the current performance of the organization. They also need to know what's going to happen and how they can get involved.

2. *Ask for their help.* People in the organization, especially those at the front line, often know better than anyone else what's important to customers and what obstacles prohibit the delivery of high-quality service. Frequently, however, their opinions and ideas are either not sought or not genuinely considered. One method for collecting the opinions of employees is to use an opinion survey. It can assess employee views on important customer needs, the organizational performance in fulfilling those needs, and the organizational climate for service delivery.

3. *Give them more authority, responsibility, and discretion.* If people are truly going to become customer strategists, they need more authority, responsibility, and discretion to act on behalf of their customers. Their jobs need to be reengineered and enriched so that they can manage the experience of their customers.

4. *Capitalize on their native creativity.* Management has no monopoly on creative ideas for customer value. However, management does control the data and information people need to solve problems and remove obstacles that improve the customer's experience.

   Most of the best solutions to service-quality problems come from employees, *if* you can get access to their knowledge and ideas. Management needs to let employees apply their creative brainstorming and problem-solving skills to address problems and generate solutions that improve service quality.

5. *Give them the needed skills.* The ability to become a customer strategist requires both problem-solving (technical) and interaction-management (interpersonal) skills. *Training should be an ongoing investment, in good times and bad.* Leaders need to see the skills and knowledge of employees as critical factors in the quality war and continually work on making them better.

KEEPING THE TRAIN ON THE TRACK: THE TQS TASK FORCE

I admit to a personal bias with regard to launching a quality program and keeping it on track: it needs a full-time shepherd. In most cases, I like to see a strong, committed task force get behind the quality initiative and help everyone keep their attention focused on the objective. Not all executives like the task-force approach, fearing that the organization's managers might tend to push their responsibilities off on the task force, or that the task force might end up being the only advocate for change. But under the right circumstances a task force can play a significant role in moving the quality initiative along, and especially in keeping it moving when it tends to stall or stagnate.

A TQS task force can be a critical factor in the success of a quality initiative if

° It has a clear definition of its expected role.

° It has a clear mandate for action from senior management.

° It has a strong, competent leader who can help it function as an effective team.

° It has well-chosen members whose skills, knowledge, and organizational perspectives go together well.

° The members understand the limits of the task force's role and pay careful attention to supporting rather than undermining the leadership of the line managers.

° The members can maintain healthy political relationships with the various power people in the organization and engage them constructively in the change-management process.

Although it is possible to move a quality program along successfully by having executive management drive the process on an ongoing basis, a great deal of experience confirms the value of having skilled people constantly pushing it. The executives get distracted and overloaded with major issues, they travel constantly, and it's difficult for them to get together often enough. A strong task force can keep the energy up all the time and sustain the momentum. It cannot substitute for the commitment of the executives, but it definitely can augment and extend it. Task-force members provide the continuing impetus, creative thinking, flow of information, communication linkage, and source of expertise that others can draw on to make their own departmental efforts more effective.

READING THE "VITAL SIGNS" OF PROGRAM SUCCESS

Because a quality initiative of any kind, even in a fairly small organization, will usually take quite some time to show significant results, we need some road markers or success indicators that give evidence that the changes are beginning to "take." We need to assess certain key human and organizational responses, which we might think of as the "vital signs" of program success.

Some of these vital signs will be obvious; others may need special assessment. Here are some of the important ones to consider:

Executive support and involvement. Do the senior executives give clear evidence that they personally have the mental and emotional conviction that quality and customer value are the keys to the organization's success? Are they showing it by what they say and do on a regular basis?

Middle management acceptance of the quality idea. Do the heads of the various organizational departments walk and talk the values? How many of them have taken personal charge of the total quality mission in their groups? What are they doing to make it a reality?

Employee acceptance of the quality idea. To what extent do the employees hear, understand, and endorse the message? What's the current ratio of optimists to pessimists?

Momentum of change. Are there things going on all the time that keep inviting people's attention to the values of total quality? Or does the effort go in fits and starts, with long periods of nothing happening punctuated with the occasional meeting or pronouncement? Does the ball keep rolling?

Reinforcement and contradiction. What's reinforcing the quality message, and what's contradicting it? Do people at the front lines get a consistent message of customer commitment from what they see and hear going on around them, or is the real message one of "keep the costs down and to hell with the customer?" Are there powerful managers in the organization who are mean-mouthing the program or damning it with faint praise?

Resource impact. Are people actually putting their time, energy, and funds into the quality effort? Is it beginning to color their trade-offs and debates about budgets and plans? Are managers beginning to invest in training their people and in communicating the quality message to them? Are we seeing real cost savings, profit improvements, or sales growth due to the effort?

Customer impact. Are customers, either external or internal, beginning to notice and respond to what's happening? Are the changes beginning to affect the actual outcomes at the moments of truth? Are we winning and keeping customers better than before?

Measuring and responding to those vital signs is the difference between a program that works like a ballistic missile and one that works like a guided missile. The leaders of the movement must be prepared to "bob and weave" as things move along. They must be willing to rethink their approach from time to time and either make sure it's still a good one or be willing to redesign it. They must test the organization's responses to the quality effort constantly, and then use what they learn to keep fueling the energy that carries it along.

As mentioned previously, there is no one perfect, foolproof implementation strategy for all organizations. It is something you must design for yourself. When executives or task-force leaders express apprehension or uncertainty about committing to a program strategy and moving ahead with it, I usually advise them to think of a quality effort as similar to writing a novel, not building a house.

When you're trying to transform a whole organization, you don't have a blueprint to work from because nobody knows what the end result will look like two, three, or five years into the transformation. So quality leaders are more like novelists than architects.

When you write a novel, you don't have all the characters and scenes and actions laid out in advance. They come to you as you write. You must, of course, begin with a basic story idea, a general plot, and some key characters. These are equivalent to your quality program implementation strategy.

As you write the novel, the story comes to you. You create characters as you need them and then they come to life and develop almost as if they were real people. You construct branching stories off the main axis of the plot in order to give depth and reality to your story. And you introduce scenes that tell the story and make it real for the reader.

And that's the way you "do" quality. You build it as you go, learning from your mistakes and capitalizing on your wins. You have to know what story you're writing, but you won't know exactly how it comes out until you get to the last page.

The exception to the analogy of writing the book is that the quality journey has no last page. There is no "The End." It's something you keep thinking about and working on all the time. It's the way of life you have chosen for your organization.

If a quality initiative stalls for any appreciable length of time, it's as good as dead. It's a lot like keeping a fire burning at the beginning. It needs a lot of attention, nurturing, and a touch of optimism. As it grows and begins to flourish, it needs more fuel and careful development. This is why a strong visionary leadership is critical to creating a truly customer-centered enterprise.

Resource Section: Seven Tools for Customer-Centered Process Improvement

The seven process-improvement tools described briefly in Chapter 9 can work wonders in the hands of frontline employees who understand them, know when to apply them, and know how to get the best value from them. This Resource Section describes them in greater depth and gives examples of ways to use them.

The Customer Bug List—a simple list of things that "bug" your customers about your service. It gives you an immediate sense of where the problems and opportunities are. By prioritizing the items on the Bug List according to customer impact and contribution to customer value, you can decide which improvements to work on first.

This tool works best when you want to get people started thinking about customer value and help them see service quality in very concrete, specific terms.

Figure RS–1 shows a typical Customer Bug List, using the example of an internal purchasing department.

Organization: Purchasing Department

1. Long turnaround time on purchasing actions.
2. Phone goes unanswered when customer calls.
3. Lost purchase orders.
4. Customer not notified when items arrive.
5. Lack of flexibility; they only go by the book.
6. Too much paperwork involved in purchase request.
7. Won't take responsibility for mistakes.
8. Won't consider our vendor recommendations.
9. Refuse to speed up for urgent requests.
10. Things get lost in storeroom.

Figure RS–1. The Customer Bug List.

The Moment of Truth Chart—a simple chart with three columns, that deals with one selected moment of truth. The center column lists the customer's *standard expectations* of that moment of truth, as verified by the customer research. The left column lists *minus factors*, i.e., things that can happen or fail to happen and make the moment of truth unsatisfactory. And the right column lists *plus factors* that can add value in the customer's eyes.

This tool works best when you want to focus on a single, critical moment of truth in order to help people develop strategies for making it come out successfully.

Figure RS–2 shows a typical Moment of Truth Chart, using the example of a lost suitcase after an airplane flight.

Moment of Truth Chart

Moment of Truth: lost suitcase.

MINUS FACTORS	STANDARD EXPECTATIONS	PLUS FACTORS
Waiting in line	An apology	Flexible delivery procedures
Forms to fill out	Promise of fast action	Someone calls me about status of suitcase
Indifferent attitude of luggage clerk	Minimum "red tape"	Token of apology of some kind
Long delay in getting suitcase	Prompt delivery	
Suitcase arrives damaged		

Figure RS–2.   The Moment of Truth Chart.

The Cycle of Service Chart—a circular, "clock-face" chart showing the series of Moments of Truth experienced by the customer in any complete service-delivery interaction. Starting at the one o'clock position and continuing clockwise, each dot represents a moment of truth the customer actually experiences. Thus, the chart forces us to see things as the customer sees them, without contaminating our perceptions with our knowledge of what's supposed to happen behind the scenes.

This tool works best when you want to focus people's attention on the customer's chain of experience and how the succession of moments of truth builds to a complete perception of quality by the completion of the cycle. It helps them realize that the customer's perception of service quality is *cumulative*—each moment of truth adds or subtracts something to the perception of value depending on whether it goes well or poorly. In other words, the total perception of quality is the sum of the perceptions of the various moments of truth.

Further, the customer enters into the cycle with certain expectations, and how the actual experience compares to the expectations determines how the customer feels by the time the cycle is complete.

Figure RS–3 shows a typical Cycle of Service Chart for opening a new bank account.

Cycle of Service Chart

Cycle of Service: opening a bank account.

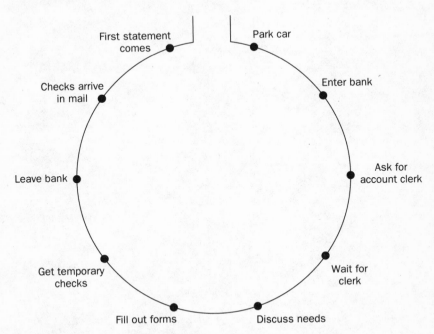

Figure RS–3.   The Cycle of Service Chart.

The Service Blueprint—a flow diagram that depicts the customer's experience in the Cycle of Service, side by side with the respective actions of the various departments that are involved in delivering the service. It shows the time line of the various actions taken by the customer and the contributing departments as well as how they feed into one another.

This tool applies best when you're dealing with quality issues involving several departments, all of whom must cooperate successfully to achieve a quality outcome. The exceptional value of the Service Blueprint is that it makes all of the "back room" processes customer focused and shows exactly how they intertwine to make the cycle of service come out the way it does.

Figure RS–4 shows a typical Service Blueprint, for a room-service order in a hotel. Note that the boxes under the "customer" column are the Moments of Truth the customer experiences, and that they make up a complete Cycle of Service.

The Service Blueprint

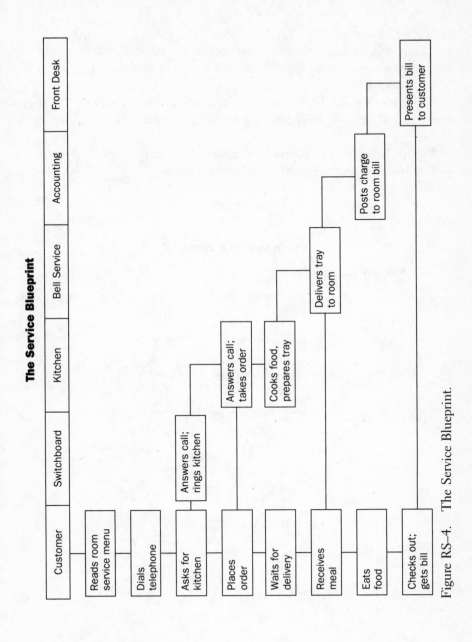

Figure RS–4. The Service Blueprint.

223

The Why-Why Diagram—a branching "tree" diagram that helps you identify the root cause of a quality problem by asking the question "why" several times in succession and diagramming the various "becauses" for each why. Each because breaks down to another why question followed by more specific becauses. At the bottom of the tree diagram you have specific factors you can evaluate as possible root causes of the problem.

This tool applies best when you're dealing with a specific quality malfunction but don't have everyone's agreement on the primary cause.

Figure RS–5 shows a typical Why-Why Diagram for a lost mail-order shipment that never reached the customer.

The Why-Why Diagram

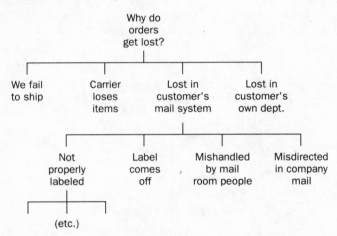

Problem: lost order shipments.

Why do orders get lost?

| We fail to ship | Carrier loses items | Lost in customer's mail system | Lost in customer's own dept. |

| Not properly labeled | Label comes off | Mishandled by mail room people | Misdirected in company mail |

(etc.)

Figure RS–5.   The Why-Why Diagram.

The How-How Diagram—a diagram that helps you identify the various actions that could solve a quality problem by reversing the procedure of the Why-Why Diagram. You start by asking How, e.g., "*How* can we prevent such-and-such from happening?" The "how" breaks down into a series of "by" actions, i.e., by doing this, by doing that, etc. For each by item, you ask how again, and break the "bys" down further to more specific actions. At the bottom of the tree diagram you have specific options you can choose from in solving the problem.

This tool applies best when you want to get some creative ideas for doing something specific, rather than just make sure something happens correctly.

Figure RS–6 shows a typical How-How Diagram, aimed at increasing customer referrals from existing customers.

The How-How Diagram

Objective: get more customer referrals.

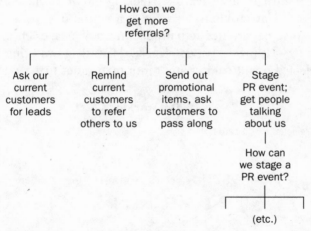

Figure RS–6.   The How-How Diagram.

The Tracking Chart—any simple numerical graph, chart, or work-sheet that shows how one or more quality variables change, usually during some period of time. It might simply be a plot of the number of times customers complained about a certain item within a six-month period, or the total value of refunds given during some period, or the number of employee grievances filed, and so on.

Whatever area you want to work on in terms of quality improvement deserves to be observed and measured if possible. Many quality experts call this "management by facts." The Tracking Chart gives you facts to go on. How often does a particular error or problem occur? Is it often enough to warrant a concerted quality-improvement attack? How much damage or inconvenience does it cause? How much attention does it deserve?

This tool applies best when you have isolated a very specific malfunction you want to correct and you need some facts about its occurrence. By keeping a log of all occurrences, and perhaps notes about the probable cause in each case, you can quickly build a factual picture of the source of the problem. Then you can make changes to improve the score. You can also use the Tracking Chart to show how many times a particular problem occurs over a period of time and how the frequency of its occurrence actually declines as you take action to cure it.

Figure RS–7 shows a typical Tracking Chart, monitoring the number of rejected credit card charges in a mail-order firm's operation.

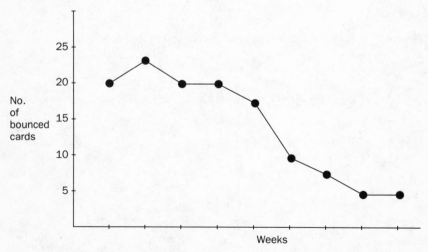

The Tracking Chart

Variable: rejected credit cards.

Figure RS–7. The Tracking Chart.

Figures RS–1 through RS–7 show how simple these diagramming tools are. Each has a certain particular value, depending on the nature and complexity of the quality problem you want to analyze. Together they form a useful tool kit for process improvement. They are all quite simple, easy for people to learn, and easy to apply.

Let's analyze a particular service problem and see how the various tools might apply, say, in a health-care business. We might start with the Customer Bug List. Interviews with physicians turn up an especially irritating bug, in this case a service malfunction. The Bug List will probably have quite a few bugs, but let's focus on one in particular.

Let's say a physician has sent a tissue sample across town to a commercial laboratory for testing to see whether his tentative diagnosis of his patient's condition is valid.

The sample hasn't returned, even though five days have elapsed and the expected turnaround time is two to three days. He instructs his assistant to call the lab and ask about the results. When the assistant calls, the person at the lab can't find the specimen. There is no paperwork and no record of it having arrived at the lab.

This is a fairly big moment of truth. If nobody can locate the specimen, the physician has problems. He will probably have to ask the patient to come to the office again for another test. This will cause credibility problems in the mind of the patient and add to the physician's cost of doing business. It will also introduce another delay in the diagnosis.

Clearly, the lab has a quality problem on its hands. Let's look at some ways of managing this problem, by studying its impact on the lab's customer, i.e., the physician. Let's also keep in mind that the customer has a customer, i.e., the patient. Bear in mind that the lab itself might not be at fault. It could be that the physician's office misdirected the specimen, or the courier service lost or misdelivered it. Nevertheless, the lab representative needs to manage the situation effectively. And in the future the lab needs to be able to prevent or minimize these occurrences.

First, let's use the Moment of Truth Chart. We begin to list the customer-physician's standard expectations in the center column.

Standard Expectations might be

- The lab takes immediate action and gives it a high priority.

- Someone at the lab looks into the matter quickly and calls the physician or assistant within a matter of hours.

○ The lab technician handling the matter expresses a sense of concern and urgency about the matter.

○ If the specimen turns up, it gets top priority for processing and return.

○ If it cannot be located, the lab notifies the physician's office immediately.

Minus Factors might be

○ The lab person tries to place the blame, either on the physician's office or the courier service, rather than focusing on solving the problem.

○ There are further delays in dealing with the problem.

○ The lab person communicates a sense of indifference about the impact of the problem on the physician's operation.

○ The lab person deals with the problem bureaucratically, invoking policies instead of giving the matter special consideration.

Plus Factors might be

○ The lab person takes full charge of the problem, offering to contact the courier service as well as recheck the specimens currently on hand to see if the lost one might actually be there.

○ The lab person offers to send someone over to personally pick up the new specimen when it's ready and bring the results back when they're complete.

○ The lab person offers to telephone or fax the results to the physician's office if he needs them more quickly.

Next, we might want to look at the entire cycle of service to see how the process might be made failure-proof. Because there are several players involved with the customer, it makes more sense to use the Service Blueprint, which incorporates the Cycle of Service.

We would plot the Service Blueprint with the physician (as the customer), the courier service, and the lab being the main players. If it is a large lab, it might be appropriate to plot several departments, such as receiving, storage and handling, testing, data processing, and billing. It might also be appropriate to include a column next to the physician's column showing the patient's moments of truth and cycle of service.

Then we could study the various steps in the process and identify the ones where things are most likely to go wrong. This could lead us to ideas for improving the turnaround time, accuracy, and reliability, as well as reducing the overall cost of the process.

Next, we could use the Why-Why Diagram to analyze the question "Why does a specimen get lost?" This could lead to an itemization of possibilities, such as: it never leaves the physician's office; the wrong courier service picks it up; the courier never picks it up; the courier loses it; the courier delivers it to the wrong lab; we lose it in-house; we address it to the wrong physician's office; the courier loses it on the way back, and so on. Once we have the main possibilities identified, we can attack each one.

This calls for the How-How Diagram. We might zero in on one specific root cause, for instance, the one our research shows to be the most frequent. If it's the courier losing the specimen either on the way to the lab or on the way from the lab, we might need to meet with the courier's people to begin working out methods for ensuring the safety of the specimen. Or the How-How Diagram might include options such as choosing another courier service.

To supplement the previous tools, you might also use the Tracking Chart to keep track of the number of lost specimens over a trial period, say, one month. Appoint someone to keep the chart current and have that person record any relevant information about possible causes in each case. At the end of the trial period, look at options for eliminating or reducing the number of lost specimens. Continue using the Tracking Chart to verify that the number of incidents is truly declining. Keep this up until you have the problem solved.

As mentioned in Chapter 9, all of these tools work best when you have facts. It's one thing to sit around and speculate about why things go wrong and what you should do about it. But when you invest the effort to gather some solid facts about the problem, you can target your energies much more effectively. How often does each type of malfunction occur? Under what circumstances is it most likely to occur? What is the impact, both on the customer and on our operation, when it does occur? All of these facts help to keep your quality-improvement effort grounded in reality. And they make the use of the process improvement tools much more productive.

Notes

CHAPTER 1   CUSTOMER CENTERING:
THE NEW QUALITY IMPERATIVE

1. Peters, Thomas and Waterman, Robert. *In Search of Excellence*. New York: Warner Books, 1982.
2. Albrecht, Karl and Zemke, Ron. *Service America!: Doing Business in the New Economy*. Homewood, IL: Dow Jones-Irwin, 1985.
3. American Management Association Europe study, "Service: The New Competitive Edge." Brussels: AMA, 1988. Contact: Management Centre Europe, Rue Caroly 15, 1040 Brussels, Belgium.

CHAPTER 2   MINDSETS AND MALFUNCTIONS:
MANUFACTURING THINKING AND DINOSAUR LOGIC

1. Albrecht, Karl. *At America's Service*. Homewood, IL: Dow Jones-Irwin, 1988, pp. 105–107.

CHAPTER 3   PARADIGM LOST, PARADIGM
FOUND: NEW THINKING ABOUT QUALITY

1. "Prizm," report published by Arthur D. Little. Spring 1991.
2. The Federal Quality Institute, P.O. Box 99, Washington, DC 20044-0099.

CHAPTER 5   THE SPIRIT OF SERVICE:
THE SOURCE OF "THE FORCE"

1. Garfield, Charles, *Peak Performers*. New York: Avon Books, 1986.
2. "Prizm," report published by Arthur D. Little, Spring 1991.

CHAPTER 6   THE PSYCHE OF YOUR CUSTOMER:
FINDING THE "INVISIBLE TRUTH"

1. Albrecht, Karl and Bradford, Lawrence. *The Service Advantage: How to Identify and Fulfill Customer Needs*. Homewood, IL: Dow Jones-Irwin, 1989.

2. *Custometrics: the Customer Satisfaction Survey System.* PC software system available from Shamrock Press (Div. of Karl Albrecht & Associates), 910 Grand Avenue, # 206, San Diego, CA 92109, USA. (619) 272-3880.

CHAPTER 7 QUALITY AND BUSINESS STRATEGY: CREATING NEW RULES FOR THE GAME

1. Albrecht, Karl and Ron Zemke. *Service America!: Doing Business in the New Economy.* Homewood, IL: Dow Jones-Irwin, 1985, p. 172.
2. Albrecht, Karl. *At America's Service: How Corporations Can Revolutionize the Way They Treat their Customers.* Homewood, IL: Dow Jones-Irwin, 1988, p. 64.
3. Halberstam, David. *The Reckoning.* New York: Avon, 1987.
4. Will, George. "The Boast of U.S. Carmakers," The *Washington Post* Writers Group, August 23, 1990.
5. McKenna, Joseph F. "Bob Galvin: Predicts Life After Perfection," *Industry Week,* January 21, 1991.
6. "Prizm," published by Arthur D. Little, Spring 1991.

CHAPTER 8 EMPOWERING PEOPLE WITH KNOWLEDGE: WINNING THE HEARTS, MINDS, AND HANDS

1. Carlzon, Jan. *Moments of Truth.* New York: Ballinger, 1987, p.15.
2. AMA Europe Survey

CHAPTER 10 KEEPING SCORE, SCORING POINTS, & POINTING THE WAY

1. "Leadex: Leadership Assessment System", feedback instrument and PC software systems published by Shamrock Press (Div. of Karl Albrecht & Associates), 910 Grand Avenue, # 206, San Diego, CA 92109, USA. (614) 272-3880.

CHAPTER 11 YOUR CHANGE MANAGEMENT STRATEGY

1. Albrecht, Karl. *Service Within: Solving the Middle Management Leadership Crisis.* Homewood, IL: Dow Jones-Irwin, 1990.

Index